Prizing Children's Literature

Children's book awards have mushroomed since the early twentieth century and especially since the 1960s, when literary prizing became a favored strategy for both commercial promotion and canon-making. There are over 300 awards for English-language titles alone, but despite the profound impact of children's book awards, scholars have paid relatively little attention to them. This book is the first scholarly volume devoted to the analysis of Anglophone children's book awards in historical and cultural context. With attention to both political and aesthetic concerns, the book offers original and diverse scholarship on prizing practices and their consequences in Australia, Canada, and especially the United States. Contributors offer both case studies of particular awards and analysis of broader trends in literary evaluation and elevation, drawing on theoretical work on canonization and cultural capital. Sections interrogate the complex and often unconscious ideological work of prizing, the ongoing tension between formalist awards and so-called identity-based awards—all the more urgent in light of the "We Need Diverse Books" campaign—the ever-morphing forms and parameters of prizing, and scholarly practices of prizing. Among the many awards discussed are the Pura Belpré Medal, the Inky Awards, the Canada Governor General Literary Award, the Printz Award, the Best Animated Feature Oscar, the Phoenix Award, and the John Newbery Medal, giving due attention to prizes for fiction as well as for non-fiction, poetry, and film. This volume will interest scholars in literary and cultural studies, social history, book history, sociology, education, library and information science, and anyone concerned with children's literature.

Kenneth B. Kidd is Professor of English at the University of Florida, U.S.A.

Joseph T. Thomas, Jr. is Professor of English and Comparative Literature at San Diego State University, U.S.A. where he also serves as Director of the National Center for the Study of Children's Literature.

Children's Literature and Culture

Jack Zipes, *Founding Series Editor*
Philip Nel, *Current Series Editor*

For a full list of titles in this series, please visit www.routledge.com.

Prizing Children's Literature
The Cultural Politics of Children's
Book Awards

**Edited by Kenneth B. Kidd
and Joseph T. Thomas, Jr.**

Routledge
Taylor & Francis Group

LONDON AND NEW YORK

First published 2017
by Routledge

2 Park Square, Milton Park, Abingdon, Oxfordshire OX14 4RN
52 Vanderbilt Avenue, New York, NY 10017

Routledge is an imprint of the Taylor & Francis Group, an informa business

First issued in paperback 2019

Library of Congress Cataloging-in-Publication Data
CIP data has been applied for.

ISBN: 978-1-138-65054-1 (hbk)
ISBN: 978-0-367-34656-0 (pbk)

Typeset in Sabon
by codeMantra

Contents

List of Tables

Series Editor's Foreword

The Children's Literature and Culture series is dedicated to promoting original research in children's literature, children's culture, and childhood studies. We use the term "children" in the broadest sense, spanning from earliest childhood up through adolescence. The already capacious term "culture" encompasses media (radio, film, television, video games, blogs, websites, social networking sites), material culture (toys, games, products), acculturation (processes of socialization), and of course literature, including all types of crossover works. Since children's literature is defined by its audience, this series seeks to foster scholarship on the full range of children's literature's many genres and subgenres: fairy tales, folk tales, comics, graphic novels, picture books, novels, poetry, didactic tales, nonsense, fantasy, realism, mystery, horror, fan fiction, and others.

Founded by Jack Zipes in 1994, Routledge's Children's Literature and Culture is the longest-running series devoted to the study of children's literature and culture from a national and international perspective. In 2011, expanding its focus to include childhood studies, the series also seeks to explore the legal, historical, and philosophical conditions of different childhoods. An advocate for scholarship from around the globe, the series recognizes innovation and encourages interdisciplinarity. In Zipes' words, "the goal of the Children's Literature and Culture series is to enhance research in this field and, at the same time, point to new directions that bring together the best scholarly work throughout the world."

Philip Nel

For June Cummins, dear friend and colleague

Acknowledgments

Kenneth: Thank you to all the wonderful contributors here, as well as my family, friends, and colleagues whose support made this undertaking possible and pleasurable. Special thanks go to Martin Brooks Smith III, Doris Kidd, Carolyn Smith, Kathryn and Lyn Benson, and the Provencher-Baumstark family: Allison, Jason, Dylan, Austin, Kasimir, and Addison. Much gratitude also to colleagues in the Children's Literature Association, especially those who so generously responded to my queries about the Phoenix Award. Deserving his very own and *most* special prize is Joseph, who brainstormed the project in a San Diego bookshop and worked tirelessly to see the dream realized. As we write in high school yearbooks: You are so sweet. Don't ever change.

Joseph: Thanks to my friends and colleagues here at San Diego State University, particularly the wonderful June Cummins, without whom I would have crashed and burned years ago. You've been more patient and loving than I deserve. Gratitude also to Kenneth Kidd: for years you've inspired me, and you continue to be a delight. The contributors to this volume, of course, deserve the greatest thanks; we'd have nothing without you. Michael Joseph deserves more thanks and love than words make possible: you're the best friend and most stimulating writing partner I've ever had the pleasure of playing with. Finally, love to Katie E. Strode, also an inspiration, and to Becky, Lauren Elizabeth, and Samantha.

A Prize-Losing Introduction

Kenneth B. Kidd and Joseph T. Thomas, Jr.

The prizing of children's books has a long history, especially if we mean something broad by "prizing": understanding, affirming, and promoting the value of books, whether aesthetic, moral, educational, economic, or some combination thereof. In that sense, prizing is core to children's literature. In her excellent chapter "Reading for Social Profit," Courtney Weikle-Mills notes how the publication of miscellanies and "premium books" in early America bespoke a preoccupation with a high quality children's literature in which we all should "invest" and with which children can earn "credit" and "capitalize" on their learning. The Sunday School movement in particular, she explains, "attempted to make the imaginary profits of reading literally exchangeable as currency" (143), in part by instituting "programs in which children could earn tickets and 'premium' certificates as payment for reading [...] Premium means a prize'" (144). We should note, "prize" once referred to a ship taken in naval combat, "to prize" was to take—from the Old French *prise*: to capture, as in booty, to turn the prized into chattel, a thing taken. The child reads; the child takes; she wins prizes (a kind of booty), yet these rewards of merit included not only tickets and certificates but also medals and books—beginning with the Bible (as rendered humorously in Twain's *The Adventures of Tom Sawyer*).[1] These books, then, were *prizes*, like captured ships, and yet they were also prized in terms of their value to the child's education. Weikle-Mills stresses that the children capitalized on their reading not only in terms of "the worth of the prize" (think: Tom Sawyer's coveted and expensive Doré Bible) but also in terms of the child's own "apprecia[tion] of value as a result of reading" (144): the child is bettered by the taking of this prized literature (in this case the literature is *taken* as one *takes* medicine). The giving of books as prizes helped lead to prizes and medals *for* books—children's books, specifically—which are, in turn, prizes for children or childhood.[2]

The professional and institutional prizing of children's literature began in the early twentieth century and in the United States. On June 21, 1921, publisher Frederic G. Melcher proposed to the American Library Association (ALA) that a medal be given for the most distinguished children's book of the year, suggesting that it be named in honor of the eighteenth-century English bookseller John Newbery. Newbery has been dubbed the "father of children's literature," and the Medal's founders wanted to trade on that reputation, creating legitimacy for the Medal and for an emergent public sphere of "quality" children's literature. The proposal was accepted in 1922 and announced during Children's Book Week, another relatively young institution (established three years earlier in 1919). The Newbery Medal was the first such award for children's literature in the world and the second literary prize on the American scene, after the Pulitzer Prizes in 1917. The Newbery strategy worked so well that in 1938, the ALA created an award for distinction in picture book illustration named for the English illustrator Randolph Caldecott. The Newbery and the Caldecott remain the dominant awards in American children's literature in terms of both prestige and sales. In her 1957 history of the Newbery and Caldecott prizes, Irene Smith emphasizes their aspirational, culture-building purpose:

> It would be gratifying to prove step by step that our two Medals have improved children's books. We believe this to be so, but their weight abides in the attitude they have built. Their influence is a generality, and there is no concrete way to pinpoint causes and effects. The award books show what can be done. They provide a regularly renewed, firm, accessible guide for measuring literary and artistic endeavor. Most of them are very good examples, in theory of course our best examples, of standards that critics uphold. They are ideals demonstrated.
>
> (103)

The Caldecott and Newbery awards are to American children's prizing what the Nobel Prizes are to adult prizing (and we don't mean here the prizing of "adult" materials—i.e. pornographic or erotic. That's another matter). Like the Nobel Prizes, these two children's awards have become points of origin, ongoing standards, and incitements to discourse.

The Newbery and the Caldecott soon had British counterparts, introduced by the British Library Association: the Carnegie Medal, established in 1935 and named after Scottish-born American philanthropist Andrew Carnegie, and the Kate Greenaway Medal, founded in 1956 and named in honor of the English illustrator. Other British awards commemorate authors, journalists, or publishers, and more recently various commercial interests have established high-profile awards (such as the Whitbread Prize) (Allen 7). A few international organizations also sponsor awards, such as the International Board on Books for Young People (IBBY). Children's book awards have mushroomed and diversified especially from the 1960s forward, as prizing more generally became a favored strategy for commodity promotion as well as cultural leveraging (again we think of the archaic, naval roots of *prize*: children's literary awards have become a kind of booty to be won, gold bullion in the form of a shiny foil medal). There are over 300 awards for English-language texts and authors alone, many of them nation- or genre-specific, most meant to recognize a single text but some dedicated to the author and/or a body of work, such as the Laura Ingalls Wilder Medal, recognizing "significant and lasting" contributions to children's literature. More recently established awards prioritize social vision, such as the Coretta Scott King Award, the National Book Award for Young People's Literature, the Pura Belpré Award, and the Jane Addams Book Award. Prizing is also genre-indexed. Mystery fiction has its major award, as does historical fiction, and there's a plethora of prizes for young adult (YA) fiction. Some awards are regional, even local in concern, while most are national. Just about every nation that claims a children's literature participates in prizing. Some prizes are ostensibly global or transnational (The *Lion and the Unicorn* Poetry Award, for instance, limits itself to North America), although they tend to promote the ideologies of nation, language, and culture. Americans have been particularly prize-crazy, or in the more charitable phrase of Ruth Allen, "award-led" (7).

Prizing has always had its discontents, of course. In 1935 Fred B. Millet complained that prizes "have a predictability for literature on about the level of crystal gazing or astrology. It is extremely doubtful," he continues, "whether the awarding of literary prizes furthers the cause of good literature" (269). The progressive social movements of the 1960s and 1970s ushered in a different though related concern, one still very resonant: that prizing is elitist. More particularly, critics worry that prizing affirms and secures social privilege, favoring white male authors over female minority authors, for instance. Prizing obviously works by exclusion, no matter how much it eschews the language of failure; for every winner there are countless losers. Prizing creates canons, and canons are tricky things. At the same time, the increasing ubiquity of prizing led some to the concern that prizing was failing its mission of evaluative discrimination or taste management. Because there are so many prizes, and so many opportunities for winning them, prizing becomes meaningless or pointless, some worry. As the Dodo declares after the absurd caucus-race in Carroll's first *Alice* book, "*everyone* has won, and *all* must have prizes!" On the one hand, cultural elitism; on the other hand, cultural inflation. According to its detractors, prizing either works too well or not well enough. Actually these aren't incompatible concerns: we might argue that prizing works too well (continues to have elitist functions and effects) *and* also not well enough (isn't so helpful in identifying excellence or distinction in useful/progressive ways). Most of the contributors to this book have mixed feelings if not strong doubts about prizing. They also develop intriguing lines of analysis that build on but also depart from these established concerns.

Whatever its problems, prizing has been a remarkably effective mechanism for publicity, sales, and scandal, if not also for the production of "literature," in the form of instant, modern classics. Prize-winning books claim to bypass the usual test of time, or rather, the prizing process simulates that test. But prizing has middlebrow as well as more highbrow features and effects. It encourages both the making and unmaking of canons, underwrites but also undercuts faith in popularity. So complex and ubiquitous is cultural prizing more broadly that James English, in his superb study *The Economy of Prestige: Prizes, Awards, and the Circulation of Cultural Value*, argues that the prize

> *is* cultural practice in its quintessential contemporary form. The primary function it can be seen to serve—that of facilitating cultural "market transactions," enabling the various individual and institutional agents of culture, with their different assets and interests and dispositions, to engage one another in a collective project of value production—is the project of cultural practice as such.[3]
>
> (26)

Rather than declare prizing good or bad, English focuses on how and why it works in our cultural economy. Prizes, English points out further, are neither purely economic nor aesthetic, neither simply sacred nor profane. Prizing does not, as we might expect, tend toward cultural saturation; quite the opposite. Prizing follows and generates what English calls a "logic of proliferation" within the relational field of culture. Each new prize makes possible another.[4] Perhaps the most striking thing about prizing is that there's seemingly no end to it. Not only that; its tempo has sped up. Writing in 2005, English informs us that a prize is born every six hours (20). The universe of prizing is ever expanding, and ever more quickly.

Moreover, while problematic, prizing is not a problem to be solved. Rather, it is a complex phenomenon with many facets and consequences. We may want to reform or improve prizing, and some contributors to this volume make recommendations to that end. Without undercutting their insights, as editors we want to stress our belief that neither a comprehensive analysis nor a total overhaul of literary prizing is possible. At best we can analyze the forms and functions of prizing and perhaps make modest changes or interventions.

We would point out further that the prizing of children's literature (which English does not consider at any length) doesn't simply mirror the prizing of adult literature. There are significant differences between such. At least in its first few decades, children's literature prizing in the United States and England was carefully orchestrated by a network of librarians, publishers, editors, and to a lesser extent teachers. As Rebekah Fitzsimmons notes in her dissertation *The Chronicles of Professionalization*, the professional management of children's literature in America was outsourced to librarians in the early twentieth century because critics and scholars had little stake in the field, a polite way of saying they didn't think much of it. The Newbery and Caldecott Medals were efforts in both public-making *and* taste-making; likewise, the awards were asserted against lowbrow reading materials and aligned with other middlebrow efforts with highbrow aspirations. The prizing apparatus didn't merely help justify excellent children's literature; it helped to create it. Melcher and other publishers assisted with this enterprise, but the ALA was vital to its long-term success. In turn, the rise and expansion of library professionals would have been much more difficult without prizing and related mechanisms like Children's Book Week (which celebrated its 97th anniversary in May 2016). The larger point here is that prizing isn't incidental but central to the creation of modern children's literature. Keith Barker makes this point in his essay "Prize-fighting," which surveys the scene of British prize-giving and children's publishing from World War II to the 1990s. "The area of awards," he writes, "is almost a microcosm of the history of children's publishing" (57). Despite other differences, prizing was vital to children's publishing on both sides of the Atlantic.

Adult literary prizing has its own links to librarianship, of course, but they are more tenuous. Moreover, as Fitzsimmons emphasizes, librarianship is rooted in ideals of public service, ideals at once genteel and progressive. The same is true of public school teaching, social work, and other altruistic professions long occupied primarily by women. Even though children's books are clearly commodities, and even though the Newbery and especially the Caldecott Medal help sell those commodities, prizing is ostensibly an altruistic business (the seemingly paradoxical coupling of "altruistic business" is intentional). This belief marks the adult prizing scene too, but it's particularly characteristic of children's literature prizing. Over the years, the librarianship ethos of altruism has collided (if also colluded) with a rapidly shifting commercial marketplace: the altruistic business of prizing often seems like just another marketing gimmick.

A related point concerns the character and tone of scandal. Scandal and "bad" publicity (or publicities of badness) are now central to prizing, especially with high-profile awards. English argues that scandal is not some sad distraction from or cheapening of the noble affair of prizing but rather an essential part of its public function and its logic of proliferation. Recipients of adult prizes now often denounce or otherwise disavow their prizes, even as some prize-givers or administrators express dissatisfaction with selections or process, while those on the sidelines criticize perceived nepotism and (as the poets behind the muckraking website *Foetry* put it) "the fraud, favor-trading, and corruption" so often associated with prize-granting institutions.[5] Such is the "new rhetoric of prize commentary," to quote English again: the "scandalous currency" and "strategies of condescension" is vital to the game of prizing. The better-known the prize, the more scandalous or scandalizing. Until recently, however, the prizing of children's literature seemed to generate a lot less scandal. Granted, the Newbery Medal process has rightly engendered criticism across the decades, most significantly a critique of the Medal's white privilege and heteronormativity.[6] Only grudgingly and with mixed results has the Medal responded to the pressures of pluralism and fair social representation. The year 2015 ushered in a Medal winner written by an African-American author, Kwame Alexander's *Crossover*—a novel in verse, no less—and with both Newbery

Honor Books dealing explicitly with issues of cultural diversity *and* in a less traditional form (for Newbery winners, anyway): Jacqueline Woodson's poetic memoir *Brown Girl Dreaming*, and Cece Bell's graphic memoir *El Deafo*. (These recent, culture-wide successes have been met, unfortunately, by an even more recent [if more narrow] backlash: the sci-fi- and fantasy-focused Hugo Awards were shanghaied in 2015 by a very vocal group calling themselves *The Sad Puppies*, the group's purpose to diminish what they see as a liberal bias in the selection of Hugo Award nominees.)[7] But analysis of the Newbery's conservatism is sincere criticism, not manufactured scandal. To our knowledge, no winner of the Newbery Medal has declined, much less denounced it, probably because there's little to be gained from such responses. Whereas adult authors can sometimes claim greater prestige or authority by not accepting certain awards, or by performing disdain or ambivalence toward them, the ethos of sincerity is just too strong when it comes to children's literature. Playing with scandal might risk the benefit to the child and to the common good—and soil the author's own reputation. Additionally, children's authors rely on ALA and other systems of prizing more than adult authors rely on any one prizing apparatus.

A recent surge of controversy around children's literary prizing suggests both an ongoing struggle over child-appropriateness and increased faith in the pluralist mission and power of prizes. The year 2007 saw a flare-up around Susan Patron's Newbery Medal-winning *The Higher Power of Lucky* (2006), which, to the consternation of some readers and reviewers, includes the word "scrotum" on its first page (the protagonist overhears a character relating a story about his dog getting bit on the balls by a rattler).[8] The scandal here was not simply that the first page of a *children's* book referenced part of the canine reproductive system, but rather that the first page of a *Newbery Medal-winning* children's book did. Kenneth discusses this incident—colorfully dubbed "Scrotumgate" and "The Great Scrotum Kerfuffle"—in an essay about the connections between prizing and anti-censorship work ("Not Censorship"). As he notes, Scrotumgate appears to have been manufactured by the media and specifically *The New York Times*, which exaggerated a polite and small-scale debate within the library community (on a closed listserv, no less) into a large-scale crisis; the *Times* article by Julie Bosman was entitled "With One Word, Children's Book Sets Off Uproar." Larry King and Barbara Walters weighed in. Eventually the *Times* issued an op-ed piece in defense of the book. *The Higher Power of Lucky* thus got a double boost in publicity, as both a prizewinner and a challenged book. While there's ongoing tension between the librarian's role as reading chaperone and the ALA's commitment to "the freedom to read," in this case the challenged book was already an ALA prizewinner, so no surprise that the ALA stood by its book. "In evaluating this modern enterprise that we call, sometimes fulsomely, children's literature," writes Smith, "librarians must make their decisions conscientiously, then be willing to defend them if necessary" (105).

Another example of the same sort: In late 2014, Raziel Reid's YA novel *When Everything Feels Like the Movies* was selected for a Governor General's Literary Award by the Canada Council. Reid's novel was inspired by the story of openly gay fifteen-year-old Larry King, who was shot to death in 2008 by a male classmate whom he'd asked to be his Valentine. Reid's protagonist Jude Rothesay is also gay, exuberantly so, and the book explores Jude's sexual fantasies and the queer possibilities of life. Barbara Kay wrote a rather negative review in the *National Post*, and helped launch a petition drive to recall the book's selection. Even reviewers more sympathetic to the book misdescribed Jude as "transgender" and registered other sorts of discomfort with the book's investigation of queerness. The Council affirmed the book's selection, and Raziel responded to Kay in a piece entitled "Smells Like Teen Dispirit," to the effect that Kay's attempted suppression only accentuated the book's urgency.[9] Here again we see the drama of would-be censorship and anti-censorship elevation. As with Patron's novel, prizing both brings about the controversy and then further legitimates, even inflates, the book's significance.

A different problem emerged in 2013, one that centered on potential drawbacks inherent in the seemingly more populist readers-choice-style prizes. Foreshadowing the 2015 Sad Puppies affair (for the Hugo Award is, in essence, a readers-choice award), the fracas erupted after conservative radio host and propagandist Rush Limbaugh won Author of the Year in the 2013 Children's Choice Book Awards. From a list of four finalists (all chosen from bestseller lists), children selected his bestselling *Rush Revere and the Brave Pilgrims: Time-Travel Adventures with Exceptional Americans* as the winner. Limbaugh's selection was something of a scandal in the children's book world. Outrage centered not around the qualities of the book, but around Limbaugh himself; librarians and other champions of children's books found a wolf in their midst. The choice was all the more shocking given that children (innocent children!) selected the book. As Roger Sutton noted immediately in the wake of this announcement,

> it's just people being mad that Rush Limbaugh won. Any inaccuracies [in Limbaugh's book] are beside the point, because the winner of this award is determined by popular vote. It really *is* a popularity contest. And if Rush had his Dittoheads auto-voting through the wee hours— well, welcome to the Internet.

In this case, the scandal is one of *failed* gatekeeping: Limbaugh infiltrated the world of children's literature.

A final example of scandalous prizing also underscores the sincerity of children's literature and likewise the identity politics and cultural positionings of the author. As June Cummins reminds us in her contribution to this book, at the 2014 National Book Awards ceremony, master of ceremonies Daniel Handler, author of the Lemony Snicket series, made a racist joke in presenting Jacqueline Woodson with the Award for Young People's Literature for her memoir *Brown Girl Dreaming*. "I told Jackie she was going to win," he remarked, "and I said that if she won, I would tell all of you something I learned about her this summer, which is that Jackie Woodson is allergic to watermelon. Just let that sink in your mind."[10] This unfortunate event set off a firestorm—it really did, we promise—and Woodson herself called the joke painful, writing in a *New York Times* op-ed that

> In a few short words, the audience and I were asked to take a step back from everything I've ever written, a step back from the power and meaning of the National Book Award, lest we forget, lest I forget, where I came from.[11]

She goes on to emphasize that Americans are not yet ready to laugh off racism as a thing of the past. She also makes clear her commitment to literature as a series of "mirrors for the people who so rarely see themselves inside contemporary fiction, and windows for those who think we are no more than the stereotypes."

Handler has since apologized and made reparations in the form of a $110,000 donation to the We Need Diverse Books Campaign. But the watermelon joke wasn't the only indication of white *ressentiment*. Earlier in the evening, Handler had also reportedly joked that he would never win a Coretta Scott King Award because he isn't black. And the rest of Handler's "watermelon joke" wasn't as widely reported.

Handler explained that when he discovered Woodson is allergic to watermelon, he suggested, "You have to put that in a book."

"*You* put it in a book," Woodson responded.

His retort: "I'm only writing a book about a black girl who's allergic to watermelon if I get a blurb from you, Cornell West, Toni Morrison, and Barack Obama saying, 'This guy's OK. This guy's fine.'"

So he put it in a speech instead. Bad idea. Some commentators have pointed out that Handler is himself Jewish, making even messier the identity politics of the scene.

Perversely, if also predictably, Handler's racist commentary drew quite a lot of attention to Woodson's win. But contrary to assumption, not all publicity is good publicity, especially if we mean *good* in the ethical sense. We're betting that for Woodson (and for many others), any increase in sales that might come from scandal isn't worth the cost. If the incident had any value, it may have been in forcing attention to the glaring problem of white privilege in publishing as in the broader culture. In her *New York Times* piece, Woodson observes that only three of the 20 National Book Award finalists were people of color. "The world of publishing has been getting shaken like a pecan tree and called to the floor because its lack of diversity in the workplace," she writes. These scandals seem rather different from the scandal, say, of Jonathan Franzen refusing his selection as an Oprah's

Book Club title, or the exposure of James Frey's *A Million Little Pieces* as partly fabricated.[12] While there's a whiff of the "new rhetoric of prize commentary" about these situations, they seem more motivated by sincere and impassioned commitments to identity and diversity. They reflect the broader shift away from generic and abstract rhetorics of literary excellence to more avowedly political or cultural ones, as with so-called identity-based awards, which arose with the progressive social movements of the 1960s and 1970s. The scandal in the Handler case is racism, and the ease with which it persists despite efforts to diversify publishing, children's literature, our very society. If prizing is a game, then it comes into sometimes painful conflict with more sincere expectations about the status and function of children's literature in a pluralist society. Or perhaps prizing has competing threads of sincerity and shameless self-promotion? Moreover, there are surely other ways in which the prizing of children's literature differs from the prizing of literature for adults.

Scholarly interest in children's literary prizing has picked up in the last several decades and especially in recent years.[13] The year 1998 saw the publication of Barker's "Prize-fighting" and also Ruth Allen's *Children's Book Prizes* (1998), a comparative treatment of 40 English-language prizes that raises some difficult questions about value and valuation.[14] In 2005 Laretta Henderson published an important study of the Black Arts Movement and the role of the Coretta Scott King Awards in relation to such, and in 2007 Elizabeth Webby wrote an article entitled "Literary Prizes, Production Values and Cover Images." Thomas Crisp (2011) has argued for strategic essentialism in the case of LGBTQ prizing,[15] and Gillian Lathey (also 2010) has analyzed "landmark translations" in the Batchelder and Marsh Awards, awards for the outstanding translation of children's literature. Recent articles by Carl Miller (2014) and our contributors Erica Hateley (2013) and Ramona Caponegro (2014) further evidence the upsurge of interest. The 2014 meeting of the Children's Literature Association saw fifteen talks on prizing specifically.

Prizing Children's Literature builds on this foundation, featuring new scholarship on book awards in their cultural, national, and institutional contexts, as well as meditations on the ongoing expansion of prizing as a cultural and commercial enterprise.

* * *

We have been interested for some time in children's literary prizing. Joseph has served as a founding judge for *The Lion and the Unicorn* Award for Excellence in North American Poetry, created by Lissa Paul and modeled on the British *Signal* Poetry Award. With his colleagues, Joseph read and evaluated submissions for the Award, and wrote annual evaluative essays, which both discussed the winners and meditated on the broader landscape of North American poetry for children—with that tag, "for children," very much under scrutiny. Joseph has used the Award and the accompanying essays to shape the collective understanding of what counts as outstanding poetry for children and why and how it matters. Kenneth chaired a 2006 MLA panel on children's literature prizing and published an essay the following year on the Newbery Medal as a test case for the broader enterprise. That article is a touchstone for many of the essays here, especially in its application of the insights of English and John Guillory. Our contributors, moreover, draw on their own rich and varied experiences with prizing. We all bring to the subject our own investments as well as expertise, not only as scholars but also as participants in prize culture—even as prize contenders. As editors, we hope that this book will be considered for the Children's Literature Association's Edited Book Award. For better and for worse, none of us is independent of prizing or its consequences. Any attempt to reform prizing must bear such in mind.

Comprised of fourteen chapters and this introduction, the volume focuses on prizing practices in Australia, Canada, and especially the United States. Conceived narrowly, a book about the prizing of children's literature might focus on the history and functions of significant prizes—a greatest hits approach. Conceived broadly, such a book might take up larger questions about literary and cultural value. This book steers a middle course, offering discussion of significant prizes, debates, and moments with respect to those big picture questions. We knew that there was no way to make *Prizing Children's Literature* representative or comprehensive, given the scale and complexity of prizing. There are hundreds of prizes in the English-language tradition alone, and hundreds of contexts and concerns that might be brought to bear upon those prizes. Interestingly, we received no submissions on the oldest and perhaps best-known American and British Awards: the Newbery, the Caldecott, the Carnegie, and the Greenaway. Discussions of the Newbery have so long dominated the scene that we are pleased *not* to include an essay devoted to such. And once we leave English-language prizing behind, the horizon expands dramatically. There is considerable research to be done in comparative prizing studies, building on the insights of scholars of translation and comparative children's literature such as Emer O'Sullivan, Gillian Lathey, and Riitta Oittinen. We gesture toward that research, but focus on English-language awards, which all too often pose as international.

Moreover, prizing is a topic that must be confronted obliquely as much as directly, and we have opted not to provide a strong theory of prizing or even a centralizing account in this introduction or elsewhere in the book. Instead, we have organized the book around the cultural work that prizing does, especially in the contemporary moment, grouping chapters into four general categories: those addressing the ideological work of prizes in enforcing norms and ideals beyond and alongside their stated purpose; those dealing specifically with "identity-based" prizing and cultural pluralism; those exploring the dynamic forms and parameters of prizing; and those attending to university-level practices of literary and academic prizing. The first two clusters are the largest, with four and five essays respectively. We have opted against formal sections, in the interest of emphasizing the topic's fungibility, and no doubt there are other equally sensible groupings. Contributors read one another's chapters, and there are rich interconnections throughout.

Essays in the first group stress not only the ubiquity of prizing but also its ideological dimensions and effects—some predictable, some more surprising. As they show, prizing is not simply voluntary, deliberate, and contained but also involuntary, diffuse, unconscious. The book opens with Clare Bradford's analysis of the ALA's Michael Printz Award (Chapter 1), theoretically an international prize with no nationality or citizenship specified for the author, but in practice dominated by American and (then) British titles, thanks to the requirement that contenders be first produced or distributed by American publishers. Bradford shows that Australian contenders for the prize must not be *too* Australian if they are to compete, ruling out more local or regional texts that might not resonate with American readers. The result, she observes, is a "world literature that does not so much transcend national origins as elide them." Examining the Mildred L. Batchelder Translation Award for the translation of children's literature, Abbie Ventura (Chapter 2) likewise underscores how Western and English-language works are heavily favored through translation and translation awards as "international" titles. The translation of already-prized titles thus constitutes a second or double consecration, she suggests, such that ostensibly international prizes contradict their mission of transnational enlargement. Ventura and other contributors make clear that prizing in the more narrow sense of title selection is only one in a series of evaluative steps or actions.

In her contribution (Chapter 3), Erica Hateley sees in three Australian national book awards for YA literature (The Children's Book Council of Australia Book of the Year Award, the Prime Minister Literary Award, and the Inky Award) an unconscious or unremarked prizing of hegemonic masculinity. This emphasis might surprise us, given the widespread assumption that YA writing is largely an affair about and for teen girls. Hateley reads the prizing of hegemonic masculinity as part of a defensive neoliberal logic of patriarchal assertion. The hard work of prizing, she proposes, underscores if also secures the precariousness of both masculinity and literary excellence. Joe Sutliff Sanders and his Kansas State University graduate student colleagues Katlyn M. Avritt, Kynsey M. Creel, and Charlie C. Lynn (Chapter 4) likewise discover a surprising ideological emphasis or trend. Studying winning titles for the two major U.S. prizes for children's non-fiction, the Orbis Pictus Award, and the Robert F. Sibert Award, whose stated purpose is to affirm quality non-fiction, Sanders and company detect a marked preference for books about the Holocaust and the Civil Rights movement, as well as a strong tendency in those books to humanize the perpetrators of atrocity.

Prizes were originally devices for creating and reinforcing literariness; they aimed to raise standards and recognize exemplary works. Gradually, however, prizing came to have other ends and motivations. "The most frequently voiced criticism of children's book awards," writes Barker, "is that the various winners are often far too literary, thereby encouraging and endorsing an elitist approach to reading" (55). So-called identity-based prizing gave expression to revisionist understandings of literature in a diverse and pluralist society. Essays in the second group of this collection address so-called identity-based prizing in cultural and national context, and in tension with more formalist rhetorics of distinction. Some commentators see an impasse between identity-based prizing and formalist prizing, while others see potential for productive dialogue or change. The conversation around identity-based prizing focuses attention on what prizing does more generally, and why, and to what effects. Discussions of prize reform often center on identity-based prizing.

Drawing on their experiences as prize judges, Robert Bittner and Michelle Superle argue in Chapter 5 that the rhetoric of excellence typically deployed in prizing too often leans formalist and ahistorical, making difficult any real engagement with or appreciation of diversity. As the broader literary scene continues to modernize, giving more priority to issues of social representation, prizing seems "the last bastion of aesthetics," to echo their title. In her contribution, June Cummins makes a related point (Chapter 6), acknowledging that very few books by diverse authors are published and awarded, and proposing that the contested notion of identity is a key problem. That notion trends both essentialist and constructivist, and those supporting and opposing identity-based prizing are often talking about very different things. Meanwhile, she notes, prizes that are ostensibly *not* identity-based in fact presume a white male normative identity, coded in/as "excellence": such is the power of hegemonic white masculinity. Cummins proposes that the Newbery Medal is indeed an identity-based award, and recommends that ALA judges learn about and draw on intersectionality theory, which emphasizes social activism as well as flexible formations of identity.

Like Cummins, Marilisa Jiménez García points out (Chapter 7) that identity-based prizing has not met the need for a diverse literature and indeed has contributed to the ghettoization of minority children's literature. For García, the literary prize is more problem than solution. She focuses on the Pura Belpré Medal for Best Latino Children's Literature, awarded by the ALA since 1996. While the Medal has succeeded in raising the visibility of Latino/a children's and young adult literature, thereby satisfying a particular "need," it has also reinforced literary segregation and made more difficult an integrated, holistic field of children's literature. The commodification of identity, she stresses, is a significant problem for all of us. Ramona Caponegro tackles the same set of issues (Chapter 8) but reaches a different conclusion in her case study of the Ezra Jack Keats (EJK) Award, designed to honor picture books by new authors and illustrators "in the tradition of Keats ... that reflect the universal qualities of childhood and the multicultural nature of our world." The award is thus imagined as an extension of Keats himself, a white author who wrote a ground-breaking (and prize-winning) text, *The Snowy Day* (1962), about a young African-American boy enjoying a new snowfall. Administered by a small foundation and the de Grummond Collection of Children's Literature, the EJK Book Award is more modest in scale if also more ambitious in intention, hoping to reconcile identity and excellence through a melting pot multiculturalism. Caponegro finds the EJK Award successful as a progressive prizing venture, in that it celebrates works of "incidental diversity" alongside more avowedly "issues" books.[16] Progressive prizes such as the EJK Award have pluralized the terms of distinction and can be useful tools for publicity and public-making. Such is the paradox that prizing represents, at once the stuff of distinction and democratization.

Concluding the second cluster is Barbara McNeil's essay on Canadian children's literature prizing (Chapter 9). Through a close reading of several winners of the Canada Governor General Literary Award, McNeil argues for the ongoing need for identity-based prizing. She argues that such prizing *can* alter the larger literary and social scene with the right kind of support. McNeil finds that Canadian identity-based awards have been an effective countermeasure to racist traditions of literature and prizing, thanks to the influence of the Canada Council's Equity Framework, which includes strong affirmation of racial and cultural diversity. English stresses in *The Economy of Prestige* that formalist prizes and identity-based prizes are caught in a feedback loop, each instantiation of one sort leading to the creation of its other. The essays in this section would seem to confirm but also challenge this assessment. Identity-based prizing has achieved certain kinds of visibility, it seems clear, and it has also productively troubled the privilege of formalist prizing; perhaps something like the Equity Framework would encourage an integration of formalist and identity-based prizing?

The boundaries of prizing have always been fuzzy, and the next two essays raise questions about what counts as prizing here and now. Peter Kunze (Chapter 10) focuses his attention on children's film, pointing out that the Academy Award for Best Animated Feature (first presented in 2002) is a *de facto* prize for children's literature, since animated features are often adapted from fairy tales and other child-associated, ostensibly family-friendly genres. Kunze argues for a consideration of this and potentially other film prizes in the examination of literary prizing. Drawing on her previous work on prizing and the bestseller lists, Rebekah Fitzsimmons (Chapter 11) makes a similar case in her analysis of the blockbuster as prize. First used to describe the powerful bombs of the British Royal Air Force, "blockbuster" has long been associated with films but now can also mean a blockbuster book or book series, such as *The Hunger Games* trilogy. The blockbuster, she holds, at once draws on classic strategies of cultural promotion and taste-making and explodes those strategies entirely. It is both prize and antiprize. Fitzsimmons argues that a hypercanon of blockbuster books is now displacing prize-winning titles as the landmark texts of children's and YA literature.

Essays in the fourth and final section address children's literary prizing in the academy. At the University of Southern Mississippi (USM) in Hattiesburg, children's literature prizing has long been part of a broader effort to promote the profile of USM's de Grummond Collection, one of the foremost such collections in the world. Since 1969 the USM Medallion for children's literature has been presented annually at the Children's Book Festival. In her case study of the de Grummond and the USM Medallion, Emily Murphy (Chapter 12) shows how prize-giving and festival-making grew out of founder Lena de Grummond's strategies for collection development and promotion. Prize and festival boost the visibility of archive and institution, she shows, and even help to create a contemporary children's literature canon. Collaborators Michael Joseph and Joseph T. Thomas, Jr. (Chapter 13) also focus on the prizing aims and ambitions of university workers. Their essay is a playful meditation not simply on the history of *The Lion and the Unicorn* Award for Excellence in North American Poetry but on the very possibility of children's poetry, expansively imagined. As they point out, the award refuses the notion of "best" even as it celebrates conceptual and stylistic excellence across a diverse range of work. Michael and Joseph complicate the observation that children's poetry is about "play," underscoring the richness of play and refusing more instrumentalist (even anti-intellectual) conceptions of children's poetry. The stimulation of criticism and scholarly work is one of the many goals of the Award and the annual discursive essays about Award contenders. Kenneth Kidd (Chapter 14) brings us home, as it were, turning to the literary and academic prizing activities of the Children's Literature Association (ChLA), an Anglophone scholarly organization made up mostly of North Americans. Kenneth gives special attention to the ChLA's Phoenix Award, a reparative prize designed to recognize a book published 20 years prior that did not (in the organization's estimation) receive the attention it deserved. He points out that prizing functions to create and shore up professional identity, sometimes against the wider publicity or circulation that prizing is also designed to ensure. Promoting the Phoenix Award too widely might push the award out of the organization's hands or might compromise its purpose, he speculates—although he notes that some in the organization have energetically countered that point.

We hope that others involved in prizing will likewise study their own professional and disciplinary investments in prizing. While the discussion about identity-based prizing is lively and significant, we worry that the prizing wars too often unfold like the canon wars of the 1990s. We *do* need diverse prizes, no question, and we certainly need a better understanding of prize identity politics. But we also need professional and institutional analysis. Who are the agents and players and stakeholders or prizing, including but not limited to those who select and administer prizes? How do particular systems or networks of value and evaluation work?

So that's a preview of the pleasures that await. We hope you enjoy and learn from these essays as much as we have.

Like prizing, scholarship has its own logic of proliferation, each new investigation making way for another. Thankfully, we do not risk saturating the field. The wonderful and exciting work this book does can only lead to *more* wonderful and exciting work. Another book on prizing children's literature might look different, and we expect that the book's gaps and failures will encourage others to pursue research on the topic. Looking back, we see interesting opportunities missed, which (like the roads taken here) reflect our own personal and professional orientations. For instance, if prizing can be understood as a venture in collective appreciation or elevation, what other forms of cultural work might count as prizing? There's a case to be made for fandom along these lines, which seems a populist sort of prizing (working in an alternative economy of literary creation and community) but with its own regulatory and promotional mechanisms. In *The Economy of Prestige*, English notes that the prizing landscape is littered with dead or dying prizes, so we might also ask, what children's literature prizes have died or failed, and why? A case study of a dead or dying prize might tell us much about the discontents of prizing. It's a fair if depressing generalization that the more socially progressive children's prizes are more vulnerable to changes in the culture or a loss in funding, akin to local independent bookstores or record shops. What excellent children's book awards are no longer presented?

Or conversely, what prizes need to die, and how do we kill them? The rhetoric of prize-saving looms so large that we rarely ask this question. "Successful" prizes are inevitably bound up with established institutional and professional value systems as well as the engines of commerce. Is there any way to stop, slow down, or reverse course if prizes are no longer doing what we want, or if we want something else? English underscores that mock prizes are prizes all the same, because they nearly always turn into legitimate prizes. The power of prizing would seem hard to challenge, especially if the prize really is, as English claims, "cultural practice in its quintessentially contemporary form." The wholesale refusal of prizing is probably beyond our means.

Not that resistance is futile. You'll recall, *to prize* once meant to seize legally a ship in combat, to confiscate its wealth, the noun form signifying both the captured ship and its ample booty (perhaps that's why prizes are so hard to stop, slow down, or reverse course: they are huge, treasure-laden vessels). With that older sense in mind, maybe we could set fire to certain ships rather than hauling them into port, sink them and their bulging chests of shiny medallions just off shore, leave them on the seafloor for future treasure hunters to explore, their gold better fit for museums than the market. Or, less drastically, we could simply reevaluate our own enthusiasm for prizes, including those for scholarship.[17] And then we might go public with the thoughts prompted by our reevaluation. Despite the dramatic image of foundering hulks and flaming hulls sputtering as fire meets wave, we're not calling for revolution. But we do hope to push the conversation about prizing beyond critiques of individual prizes and prizing contexts and toward a broader analysis of prizing as a cultural strategy and phenomenon. And if we can do that—however slightly—maybe we *do* deserve a prize.

Notes

1. On rewards of merit, see Fenn and Malpa (1994), and Reynolds (2008).
2. Ruth Allen points out that "the idea of awarding a medal or prize to a specific title" might be a "reaction to the industry which had built up around the provision of cheap 'prize books' for the many schools and churches of the English speaking world"—a sort of prizing vs. prizing scenario (5).
3. In October 2003, Oxford Brookes University hosted a conference on "Culture and the Literary Prize," convened by Daniel Leah of that university and Claire Squares of the Oxford International Centre for Publishing Studies. English was a keynote speaker.
4. See chapter 3, "The Logic of Proliferation" (50–68).
5. *Foetry*—which went offline in 2007—sought to shed light on what they deemed the quasi-nepotistic nature of poetry prizes, publishing detailed lists of mentor/mentee, professor/student, and lover/beloved relationships between the recipients of major poetry prizes and their judges. After closing shop, the administrators of the controversial site noted that it "has done all it can do in its present form. It has chiseled a small crack in the façade of the academic poetry industry, and allowed people to peer in on the poet-making machinery." See *Foetry*'s goodbye message.
6. Bonnie J. F. Miller offers pointed criticism of the Newbery in her 1998 "What Color is Gold?" but Nancy Larrick got there first, discussing racism in Caldecott Medal titles in her 1965 "The All-White World of Children's Literature."
7. The group was spearheaded by a crew of self-avowed "conservative" science fiction and fantasy authors including Brad R. Torgersen, Larry Correia, and Vox Day. Disappointed by an increasingly diverse body of Hugo nominees—authors whose works treat a variety of socio-political topics, including gender, race, and sexual orientation—The Sad Puppies complained about "social justice warriors" who substituted progressive politics for "quality." For an overview of their tactics see Gavia Baker-Whitelaw's article "How the 'Sad Puppies' Internet Campaign Gamed the Hugo Awards."
8. By Joseph's count there are six instances of the word "scrotum" in *The Higher Power of Lucky*. The last usage appears alongside the word "sperm":

   > After a moment Lucky said, "Brigitte, what is a scrotum?"
   > "It is a little sack of the man or the animal which has in it the sperm to make a baby," said Brigitte in her deep, quiet voice. "Why do you ask about that?"
   >
   > (132)

   Which is all to say that we should count ourselves lucky (thank a higher power?) that "scrotum" distracted us from what might otherwise have been called *Spermgate* or—worse—*The Great Sperm Kerfuffle*.
9. Raziel offers his own controversial comments about the narcissism of millenials, but that's another matter.
10. Handler's remarks were quoted in a number of major news outlets; see, for instance, Emily Yahr's summary in *The Washington Post*.

11. In a radio interview with Terry Gross on NPR's Fresh Air program, Woodson contradicts the recollection in her *New York Times* op-ed. When talking to Gross, Woodson says that she was so swept up in the moment that she missed the unfortunate joke that most of the audience attending the event caught in real time. She suggests that it was only after the cheering and celebration that she was made aware of her friend's ill-conceived attempt at humor:.

> You know it's so interesting [because at the time] we were all jumping up and cheering and, you know, there was a standing ovation [...] and [...] the chair of the committee had just said that it was a unanimous decision and then in the next moment she said 'Jacqueline Woodson' and so all of that energy was swarming around us. So [...] I kind of missed it all and [...] was just so elevated in the moment of having won this award. And I think [...] when the fury [at his comments] came down and when [the outrage] all just started flying around it was just kind of like, "Oh man."
>
> ("Jacqueline Woodson on Growing Up")

Later in the interview, Woodson takes great pains to communicate that her friendship with Handler was not permanently ruined by his unintentional racism, so while we hesitate to speculate too much on her motivation in articulating this version of the events, the narrative she weaves for Gross strikes Joseph at least as an act of generosity by a famously generous woman: that is, she communicates the pain Handler's words caused her while stressing that they didn't diminish the immediate joy she felt when her award was announced.

12. Most of us will remember the brouhaha that erupted after Jonathan Franzen publicly blanched at Oprah Winfrey's selection of his novel *The Corrections* as her 45th Oprah Book Club pick. Franzen recalls,.

> I'd been working nine years on the book and FSG had spent a year trying to make a best-seller of it. It was our thing. She was an interloper, coming late, and with an expectation of slavish gratitude and devotion for the favor she was bestowing.
>
> (Kachka 297)

13. Much of early scholarship focused on the Newbery and Caldecott Medals. See, in chronological order, Leo Miller (1946); Clark, Lennon, and Morris (1993); Houdyshell and Kirkland (1998), Jenkins (1996), Bonnie J. F. Miller (1998), and Kidd (2007). Other materials offered more plot summary and "booktalk" aimed at teachers and librarians; see Gillespie and Naden's *The Newbery/Printz Companion: Booktalk and Related Materials for the Award Winners and Honor Books* (Libraries Unlimited); *Children's Book Awards & Prizes* (Children's Book Council); Lee Klingman's *Newbery and Caldecott Books* (Horn Book) series, organized by decade (1966–1975, 1976–1985 and so forth).

14. There's also significant analysis of adult literary prizing, much of it dealing with particular national prizes (e.g. Lizzie Attree on the Caine Prize for African Writing, Sarah Bowskill on the Premio Cervantes) and/or the politics of language and language translation in a global culture (e.g. Susan Pickford on the Booker and Prix Goncourt).

15. For a different perspective on queerness and award-winning titles, see Ryan and Hermann-Wilmarth.

16. Caponegro reaches a similar conclusion in her excellent case study of the Jane Addams Book Award, noting that while "the notion of a competitive award for books that celebrate collaboration and community seems counterintuitive, the award serves a necessary purpose in promoting books that encourage peace and justice" (219).

17. And should this little book of ours win, say, the ChLA Edited Book Award, let us be the first winners both to anticipate and to comment upon our prize in the pages of the book yet to be so prized, yet even (as we write these words) to be published! And by way of generating scandal (before even the ballots are printed, much less returned), let us address the fine judges who will have deemed this book prizeworthy—and so deemed despite the title of this introduction—and answer, like the man in the story, "We must decline the soft impeachment." But we are sorry we need to.

1 Prizing National and Transnational
Australian Texts in the Printz Award

Clare Bradford

At the beginning of his study *Economy of Prestige*, James English observes, perhaps a little histrionically, that the practice of awarding prizes is "both an utterly familiar and unexceptional practice and a profoundly strange and alienating one" (1). In the field of children's literature as in other areas of cultural practice, more and more prizes are offered each year: national, state and city awards; prizes offered by foundations, individuals, professional bodies, universities, research centers, newspapers, and journals; awards for genres of production; and prizes for books that address particular topics. When English writes that prizing is both familiar and unexceptional and also strange and alienating, he touches on the complex interrelations of culture and economics that swirl around prizing, from the nomination of contenders to the administration and judging of prizes, award ceremonies, and the discourses that surround awards, increasingly through social media but also in the more traditional forums of newspapers and journals.

The domain of children's and Young Adult literature constitutes what Pierre Bourdieu refers to as a field with its own practices, habits, and hierarchies (*Distinction*). Within this field, cultural capital accrues to books that win or are named as honor books in various award systems. Literary awards are not reducible to the economic benefits that flow from them; rather, they endow winning titles with weight and value. Nevertheless, as English observes, the field of children's and Young Adult (YA) literature is notable for the effects of prizes on sales (360–1n35), particularly in the case of venerable awards such as the Newbery and the Caldecott Medals. Books that win these prizes do not merely sell better, but they stay in print longer than other books and are marked out as members of an illustrious "family" of prize-winning books.

The properties and practices of fields of production shape perceptions of cultural capital and the worth of prizes, quite apart from any monetary rewards that flow to authors. The Printz Award is located firmly within the profession of librarianship: it honors the memory of a revered school librarian, Mike Printz; it was instituted by the Young Adult Library Services Association, a division of the American Library Association, being first awarded in 2000; and it is sponsored by *Booklist*. This institutional location confers on the Printz a certain gravitas, so that it is not susceptible to the scandalous excesses of, for instance, the Academy Awards where public relations firms, lobbyists, and "awards consultants" seek to influence members of the Academy.

The Printz distinguishes itself from most other children's literature awards by its departure from the requirement that authors should be citizens or residents of the nation in which it is awarded. In contrast, major national awards such as the Newbery Medal, the Children's Book Council of Australia Awards, the Governor General's Literary Awards for children's literature in Canada, and the Esther Glen Award in New Zealand, all stipulate citizenship or at least residency. The charge of the Printz Award is to "select from the previous year's publications the best Young Adult book ('best' being defined solely in terms of literary merit) and, if the Committee so decides, as many as four Honor Books" ("Printz Award"). Much discussion around the Printz hinges on the diversity of the books and the fact that a number of winners and honor books are citizens of countries other than the United States.[1]

This impression of diversity is, however, not borne out when we look closely at the statistics of Printz Award winners, seen in Table 1.1 below. Of the fifteen winners from 2000 to 2014, eight come from the United States, five from the U.K., one from Australia, and one, Meg Rosoff, has dual U.S./U.K. citizenship:

Table 1.1 Printz Award Winners, 2000–2014

Country of citizenship	Number	Percentage
U.S.	8	53%
U.K.	5	33%
Australia	1 (*Jellicoe Road*)	7%
Mixed affiliation U.K./U.S.	1	7%

Table 1.2 Printz Honor Books, 2000–2014

Country of citizenship	Number	Percentage
U.S.	36	63%
U.K.	7	12%
Australia	7: Margo Lanagan, *Black Juice* Markus Zusak, *I Am the Messenger* Sonya Hartnett, *Surrender* Markus Zusak, *The Book Thief* Judith Clarke, *One Whole and Perfect Day* Margo Lanagan, *Tender Morsels* Craig Silvey, *Jasper Jones*	12%
Canada	3	5%
New Zealand	1	2%
Denmark	1	2%
Mixed affiliation	2	4%

The record of Printz winners thus points not so much to diversity as to how the selection processes of the award favor books from the United States and the United Kingdom. The pattern is only slightly different when we look at the Honor Books in Table 1.2, which include seven Australian titles:[2]

Apart from Denmark, represented by Janne Teller's translated work *Nothing* (an Honor Book in 2011), the countries represented here are, predictably enough, English-speaking former British colonies. All are nations in the North of the North–South divide, with well-established children's publishing industries.

The most crucial aspect of the eligibility rules relates to the provenance of titles. Award-winning books must be published or distributed by American publishing companies; they may be self-published, ebooks, or published in another country, but they "will not be considered eligible until the first year the book is available in print or distributed through a U.S. publishing house" ("Printz Award"). But the availability of books first published elsewhere is limited, since very few such books are taken up by U.S. publishers. In his analysis of prizewinners in music, cinema, architecture and literature, English observes that while the proliferation of prizes might suggest that more artists and authors might be expected to win prizes, in fact the reverse occurs, in that there is a tendency for "huge numbers of prizes to accrue to a handful of big winners" (334). In the field of children's and YA literature as well, one of the main predictors of success in awards is previous success. And it seems that authors' achievements as prizewinners influence U.S. publishers in their selection of books originally published outside the U.S., along with considerations about the extent to which such books are cognate with or complement their own lists.

Melina Marchetta's *Jellicoe Road* (2006), the only Australian Printz Award winner (2009), affords a telling example of these dynamics. This novel was first published in 2006 by Penguin Australia as *On the Jellicoe Road*. By the time Marchetta won the Printz, her earlier novels had achieved success in the Children's Book Council of Australia (CBC) Book Awards: in 1993 *Looking for Alibrandi* won the award for Book of the Year: Older Readers; and in 2004 Marchetta won the same award for *Saving Francesca*. In 2007, when *On the Jellicoe Road* was eligible for consideration in the CBC Awards, the novel did not appear in the lists of shortlisted or prize-winning books, or even in the CBC's publication of "Notable Books," the long list from which winners are selected. It is impossible to know why the novel did not succeed in the CBC Awards, since these awards are too well-mannered (or well-policed) for any intelligence to leak from the judges' deliberations. But Marchetta's previous novels had been sold into the desirable U.S. and U.K. markets, paving the way for the publication of *Jellicoe Road* by HarperTeen in 2008, and its success in the Printz Award.

In 2007, 87 Australian novels were nominated for the CBC Older Readers Award.[3] Two of the award-winning and shortlisted authors in the

CBC list for that year also appear in the Printz: Margo Lanagan, author of *Red Spikes*, the CBC winner, received a Printz Honor award for her short story collection *Black Juice* in 2006, and her novel *Tender Morsels* in 2009; and Judith Clarke's *One Whole and Perfect Day*, shortlisted in 2007, was named a Printz Honor book in 2008. The winning, honor, and shortlisted CBC books for 2007 are set out below in Table 1.3:

Table 1.3 2007 CBC Awards, Book of the Year: Older Readers

Winner	
Lanagan, Margo	*Red Spikes*
HONOR BOOKS	
Cornish, D. M.	*Monster Blood Tattoo Book 1: Foundling*
Dubosarsky, Ursula	*The Red Shoe*
SHORTLIST	
Bauer, Michael Gerard	*Don't Call Me Ishmael!*
Clarke, Judith	*One Whole and Perfect Day*
Shanahan, Lisa	*My Big Birkett*

Of the 87 books nominated for the CBC Older Readers Award in 2007, only fifteen (17%) were subsequently reprinted or distributed by U.S. publishers. That is, 83 percent of Australian YA books nominated in 2007 were not. As I have noted, prize-winning books are always more likely to find international publishers than other books; for instance, all the 2007 CBC winners and shortlisted books were republished in the United States.[4] But the small percentage of Australian books eligible for the Printz Award butts up against the idea that the Award celebrates "the best" Young Adult book published in a certain year. Katherine Bode remarks that

> we need to accept—and be concerned with and intrigued by—the way that the production and reception of literature (including 'evaluative criticism') is always already implicated in commercial systems; indeed, we need to acknowledge that the different forms of implication in such systems are constitutive of the processes of literary production and reception.
>
> (97)

The commercial systems at issue in the Printz Award are the decisions and choices made by U.S. publishing companies, which are implicated in the processes whereby some Australian novels are "consecrated," to use Bourdieu's term (*Distinction* xxvi), while others are rendered invisible.[5]

Whereas Bourdieu views awards as a manifestation of "the dominant taste" of different groups and classes, the American Library Association

(ALA) uses terms such as "excellence" and "quality" to identify the criteria on which Printz Awards are determined. As Bourdieu says, "each taste feels itself to be natural" (49), defining itself by its rejection of other tastes. The Printz policies and procedures pose the question "What is quality?" and responding with "We know what it is not"...: "Popularity is not the criterion for this award. Nor is MESSAGE" ("Printz Award"). In Bourdieu's terms, popularity and message are rejected as markers of taste. Having tied itself in knots by defining what quality is not, the Printz policy falls back on a rearticulation: "What we are looking for, in short, is literary excellence" ("Printz Award"). The Printz is, then, said to recognize an indefinable "excellence" that is nevertheless graspable by the Printz Committee.

Transnationalism and the Printz Award

If concepts of literary excellence are difficult to pin down, national inflexions in fiction are also elusive. Literary history has traditionally viewed the production and dissemination of fiction in terms of nationhood: how and why national imaginaries have shaped textual production and formed reading communities. More recently, however, scholars have addressed the multiple modes in which national literatures connect with the wider realms of international and global literature. One strand of this investigation has reinvigorated the concept of world literature, addressed in David Damrosch's *How to Read World Literature* (2008) and Pascale Casanova's *The World Republic of Letters* (2007). Damrosch proposes a model of reading in which readers who encounter works from a tradition different from their own "become aware of different literary assumptions made in different cultures" (4), thereby enlarging their appreciation of diverse approaches and concepts. A second scholarly direction, typified by Paul Giles's *Virtual Americas: Transnational Fictions and the Transatlantic Imaginary* (2002) and Wai Chee Dimock's *Through Other Continents: American Literature Across Deep Time* (2008) explores how national literature manifests multiple connections to diverse traditions and "deep time" through transnational relationships.

The Australian books that appear among Printz winners and Honor books belong to the vast body of texts produced in one place and subsequently unmoored from this location to find readers elsewhere. While Damrosch emphasizes the role of readers in the reception of "world literature," it is also the case that authors and publishers consciously seek to produce texts for international markets. Australia's population of 23 million cannot sustain the large-scale print runs common in the United States, so that in purely pragmatic terms these print runs and the readerships associated with them are highly desirable to Australian authors and publishers. As Lynda Ng observes, "in the current hyper-networked and globalized environment, we can discern 'worlding' as an active and conscious method used by contemporary Australian writers" (158). By "worlding," Ng refers to how texts reach beyond their national and local inflexions to attract global and international markets.

This way of thinking about texts chimes with theories of transnationalism that consider how nation-based texts negotiate with international and global contexts. Graham Huggan argues that Australian literature has always been transnational, "either derived from an apprehension of internal fracture…, or from a multiplied awareness of the nation's various engagements with other nations, and with the wider world" (viii). Given that Australian publishing occupies a small foothold on the periphery of world literature, it is not surprising that when Australian YA texts achieve success in the Printz, the Australian publishing industry accords such success a high profile. Thus, Penguin Australia, the publisher of *On the Jellicoe Road*, emphasizes the international reach of Marchetta's fiction:

> Melina Marchetta is one of Australia's most successful writers of young-adult fiction and is a best-selling and critically acclaimed author in more than twenty countries and in eighteen languages. In 2009 Marchetta won the prestigious Michael L. Printz Award from the American Library Association for *On the Jellicoe Road*.
>
> ("Melina Marchetta")

The first sentence of this profile establishes Marchetta's international success; the second defines this success in relation to the Printz Award and hence to the U.S. market.

The other side of Australian transnationalism resides in the appetite of the domestic market for international publications. From colonial times, Australian young people have encountered a mix of Australian texts and those from elsewhere, principally from Britain and the United States. Whereas few Australian YA books reach the U.S. market, Australian bookshops and libraries carry substantial numbers of American texts. Bode identifies a "defensively nationalistic" (81) response by Australian commentators to the globalization of the publishing industry, which, she says, is often "directed towards producing dread of [a] foreign influence or invasion" (81). Despite doomsday scenarios predicting the decline or end of Australian publishing, independent publishers in Australia continue to produce YA texts, as do multinational conglomerates such as Scholastic, Penguin, HarperCollins and Random House in their Australian manifestations.

The Australian texts that feature in the Printz comprise a sample of transnational production for young adults from 2006, when Margo Lanagan's *Black Juice* and Markus Zusak's *I Am the Messenger* were named as Honor Books. Lanagan's oeuvre ranges across realist and fantasy modes, but it is her fantasy texts, *Black Juice* and *Tender Morsels*, which have achieved Printz distinction. Like so much Young Adult fantasy, these texts manifest a preoccupation with European traditions: *Tender Morsels* responds to and contests the Grimm brothers' version of "Snow White and Rose Red," while the ten short stories in *Black Juice* locate their narratives in fantasy settings in which elements of premodern, modern, and future times and cultures mingle. Zusak's *The Book Thief* evinces another style of transnational production, since this novel speaks to the author's experience as a second-generation Australian whose parents migrated from Austria and Germany. In *The Book Thief* Australia enters the narrative only in the book's last few pages, when the narrator, Death, visits the protagonist, Liesel Meminger, in Sydney. Here, just before her death, Death shows Liesel the "dusty black book" (583) in which she wrote her account of her life in Nazi Germany. The Australia of *The Book Thief* is empty of meaning or narrative; it is merely the place from which, after many years, Liesel revisits the story of her girlhood. In contrast, the action of Zusak's *I Am the Messenger* occurs squarely in Australia, in the "suburban outpost" (6) of an unnamed city; but when the nineteen-year-old protagonist, Ed Kennedy, compares himself to other nineteen year olds his imaginings lead him to three wildly different figures: Bob Dylan, Salvador Dali, and Joan of Arc, all of whom have by the same age established themselves as identities or artists.

Ed's invocation of Dylan, Dali, and Joan of Arc works in a somewhat similar way to the citational practices that Judith Clarke deploys in *One Whole and Perfect Day*, where characters attribute significance to figures and texts remote from their own lives: Emily Bronte, Alice B Toklas, Robert Burns. Such citations are, as Ken Gelder notes, "an expression of proximity, of literary sociality, where texts are put into relationships with other texts, just as places are put into relationships with other places, with varying degrees of precision and imprecision" (5). The transnational frameworks of these novels, like those of Lanagan's fantasy fiction, produce meanings accessible beyond the nation. Nevertheless, representations of national and local contexts often elude readers when texts enter global markets. To cite just one example: in Clarke's *One Whole and Perfect Day*, much of the action occurs in the sprawling region of Western Sydney, signaled in the names of suburbs such as Lidcombe, Blacktown, and Toongabbie. The protagonist, Lily, thinks that her grandfather Stan is "a bit of a racist..., or at least the sort of person who thought a decent Aussie was the best kind of person in the world" (4). The phrase "a decent Aussie" is code for "a white Australian" as distinct from a person of Asian or Middle Eastern ancestry, and carries particular potency in the novel's setting because the Western Sydney region, an area inhabited by large numbers of migrant groups, has historically been prone to racial tension. The novel's depiction of Stan both suggests and also interrogates the notion that Stan is indeed "a bit of a racist," but the complexity and ambivalence with which it treats Stan's orientation to the world are unlikely to be evident to readers outside Australia. Emily Apter refers to this effect as "untranslatability" (584), that elusive and ungraspable something which cannot readily be communicated in language but which is nevertheless encoded in depictions of places, cultures, and relationships.

Another dimension of transnational relationships lies in the global commonalities of genre fiction. Thus, Craig Silvey's *Jasper Jones* and Sonya Hartnett's *Surrender* conform to the conventions of Australian Gothic, which projects contemporary experience onto a landscape redolent with intimations of the violence of colonialism and its aftermath. Both these novels feature dysfunctional families in small, remote towns where young protagonists encounter violence or death, and where outsiders are punished for their difference. The horrors of the past are visited on contemporary protagonists, much as American Gothic concerns itself with ghostly and monstrous elements that rehearse dark aspects of the nation's history.

In summary, the Australian texts that have succeeded in the Printz are Australian but not *too* Australian; they are readily swept into the celebratory ambit of the award and its insistence on the significance of Young Adult literature. As I read the descriptions of Printz winners and honor books on the Young Adult Library Services Association (YALSA) website, I am struck by the fact that because the books' U.S. publishers are listed following their titles and the names of authors, these texts might almost be regarded as "world literature," but a world literature that does not so much transcend national origins as elide them. World literature envisaged in this way comprises texts that present their American readers not with the shock of the new and the unfamiliar but with a sense of recognition in that their themes and narratives overlap with the codes of American YA literature.

Only occasionally does the YALSA website allude to the settings of the realist Australian books in its lists, and these allusions are strangely one-dimensional. The action of *Jasper Jones* is said to occur in "the oppressive heat of small-town 1960s Australia" ("Printz Award"), as though the entirety of Australian small-town life in the 1960s is defined by "oppressive heat." Marchetta's "lyrical writing" in *Jellicoe Road* is said to "[evoke] the Australian landscape" ("Printz Award"). The novel is set southwest of Sydney; the landscape it describes suggests this geographical region, but it is no more "the Australian landscape" than Jasper Jones's town is "1960s Australia." In comparison, the geographical locations of U.S. texts are defined in relation to states and cities: Clare Vanderpool's *Navigating Early* is said to begin "at a Maine boarding school" ("Printz Award"), while *Where Things Come Back* is set in Cullen Witter's "stiflingly dull Arkansas town" ("Printz Award"). If "Maine" and "Arkansas" were replaced by "American" in these descriptions, a similar effect would result: "America" would present as a monolithic and internally consistent entity.

A Tale of Two Books: *Jellicoe Road* and *The Red Shoe*

To succeed in the Printz Award, it seems, then, that Australian books need to avoid an emphasis on local or national concerns. Fantasy fiction like Lanagan's, as well as Hartnett's heightened realism, is readily assimilated into a YA world literature; invocations of Australian culture in *Jellicoe Road*,

Jasper Jones, One Whole and Perfect Day, and *I Am the Messenger* can be glossed over, subsumed into narratives of identity formation. But what of books that consciously (and self-consciously) address aspects of nationhood and Australianness; a novel, for instance, like Ursula Dubosarsky's *The Red Shoe* (2006), a CBC Honor book in 2007? Books that travel readily between cultures and nations are often said to possess "universality." Rather, as I have suggested, such texts are often coded in ways that overlap with the assumptions and practices of diverse readerships. As Paul Sharrad says, "we all like to consume the other as a mirror in which to see our own concerns more clearly, or a window through which we can obtain touristic views of exotic difference" (27).

Jellicoe Road offers both these perspectives, locating much of its action in relation to tropes surrounding one of the most durable settings in children's literature, that of the boarding school. Narratives featuring this transnational institution have circulated since *Tom Brown's Schooldays*, in texts produced in Britain and former British colonies, and they embody tropes that include rivalry among Houses, parental absence, relations between students and locals, and combat through sport. *Jellicoe Road*'s treatment of the boarding school sustains the tradition of the House system, naming its Houses after Australian rivers: Murrumbidgee, Clarence, Murray, Hastings, Darling and Lachlan. "Murrumbidgee" is the only exotic signifier among this cluster of Anglo place names, thus simultaneously gesturing to and minimizing difference.

The school, on the edge of Jellicoe, a small town in the south of New South Wales, is run by the state but is selective, so that intelligence is a prerequisite. Taylor Markham, the first-person narrator and the leader of Lachlan House, explains "it's not about money or religion" (19); a tenth of the students are wards of the state, the rest being the children of locals or of environmentalists who desire a country experience for their offspring. Discarding the elitism of *Tom Brown's Schooldays* or Holden Caulfield's Pencey Prep, the Jellicoe School is represented as a microcosm of an idealized Australia, an egalitarian society innocent of hierarchies based on class or race. The setting is near enough to British and American models to be comprehensible outside Australia, different enough to be intriguing.

Teachers are almost invisible in *Jellicoe Road*, so that structures of power default to a system where the young are in charge. This structural feature aligns with Taylor's first-person, present-tense perspective, a narrative strategy that enables tight control: not only is Taylor's the only contemporary voice we access, but her account of events leaks out as it occurs, moment by moment. Taylor's narrative is interspersed with excerpts from a novel drafted by Hannah, her aunt, about a group of five children who met at the Jellicoe School two decades before the contemporary setting, which also focuses on five young people. Part-romance, part-mystery, and part-melodrama, the momentum of *Jellicoe Road* derives from its progressive disclosure of connections between the two sets of characters, and the emotional fallout of this disclosure.

The most strikingly transnational feature of *Jellicoe Road* is its deployment of cultural references. From the 7/11 store where Taylor is abandoned by her drug-addicted mother, to the Kenny Rogers songs favored by Ben, her deputy House leader, and the McDonalds she visits in Sydney, the novel privileges American over Australian references, so catering to two readerships: Australian YA readers familiar with American popular culture; and American readers for whom these references locate the novel in a world only tangentially Australian. In this sense the narrative reaches out to an American audience; its American references and citations constitute a prominent component of its transnational appeal.

A key aspect of the novel's symbolic register lies in its multiple references to Harper Lee's *To Kill a Mockingbird*, a novel that has been a staple of Australian secondary school literature programs for many years. Early in *Jellicoe Road*, Taylor Markham ends up in the local jail following a skirmish between the Townies (local young people), the Cadets (a private school quasi-military troop) and the Jellicoe School students. The school principal John Palmer, who collects Taylor from jail and returns her to the School, offers her a crucial piece of information about the whereabouts of Hannah, her aunt, who has disappeared from Jellicoe to Taylor's distress. He tells her that Hannah is in Sydney taking care of a friend, saying:

> "[Hannah] calls her friend, 'Mrs. Dubose.' That's all I know."
> Mrs. Dubose.
> "Have you heard of her?" he asks.
> "Yes," I say sleepily. "She lived in the same street as Jem and Scout Finch."
>
> (105)

The figure of Mrs. Dubose is woven into both the novel's narrative strands. In Hannah's manuscript, set in the 1980s, Narnie (Hannah's childhood name) takes an overdose of Panadol. To stop her from falling asleep, Tate (Taylor's mother) relates the plot of *To Kill a Mockingbird*, explaining that in the novel Atticus Finch punishes Jem for vandalizing Mrs. Dubose's camellias by requiring him to read to the old woman every day for a month as she withdraws from her addiction to morphine. At the end of *Jellicoe Road* Hannah nurses Tate while she dies of cancer after years of addiction and prostitution. Taylor speculates that her mother wants to die "beholden to no one. Like Mrs. Dubose" (396) but learns that Tate is motivated by her desire to die clean for her daughter. The incorporation of Mrs. Dubose into these stories of overdose and addiction taps into the canonical status of *To Kill a Mockingbird*, claiming moral seriousness by association.

I referred earlier to *Jellicoe Road*'s blend of fictive modes: romance, mystery, melodrama. The melodramatic elements of the novel manifest in what Peter Brooks describes as "a mode of excess,"[6] encapsulated in its proliferation of extreme events. The 1980s narrative incorporates a calamitous car accident that kills four adults and a child; the accidental death of Hannah's brother Webb at the hands of Fitz, another of the five; Tate's descent into drug abuse; various suicide attempts. In the contemporary narrative, Taylor is oppressed by memories of her precarious early life with her mother; and an episode when Fitz fatally shoots himself before her when she is fourteen. Several characters are attributed with suicidal thoughts; a serial killer lurks about the area and kills two young people; an electrical fire almost destroys Lachlan House; and Tate dies in Hannah's house in Jellicoe. The appeal of melodrama, as Brooks notes, is that it provides a "heightening of existence" (ix), insisting on the significance of the ordinary: "in the right mirror, with the right degree of convexity, our lives matter" (ix). Melodrama also, I would argue, travels readily across national boundaries because its themes and approaches are familiar through globalized literature, media, and film.

Like *Jellicoe Road*, Dubosarsky's *The Red Shoe* was first published in 2006 and was subsequently republished in the U.S. Whereas *Jellicoe Road* was consecrated by its Printz success, *The Red Shoe* received brief notices in U.S. review journals and is relatively little known outside Australia.[7] The novel is set in 1954 in Sydney. Its narrative involves personal and family crises; but *The Red Shoe* extends its reach to national politics, following the so-called Petrov Affair, during which two USSR secret agents defected from the Soviet embassy in Canberra and sought asylum in Australia. The protagonists and focalizers of the novel are three sisters, six-year-old Matilda, 11-year-old Frances, and 15-year-old Elizabeth, who live with their mother and seaman father in Palm Beach in the north of Sydney, next door to the safe house where Vladimir Petrov is installed following his defection. Having served in the Second World War, their father suffers from what we now know as post-traumatic stress disorder, but which is downplayed in the 50s setting as "nerves."

The traumatic event at the center of *The Red Shoe* is an unsuccessful suicide attempt by the girls' father when the family goes on a picnic on Boxing Day, 1954. His action disrupts the surface calm of a familial and political climate where emotion is repressed or denied, and the novel foregrounds the three girls' varying responses to trauma. The narrative is studded with allusions to texts ranging from Hans Christian Andersen's story "The Red Shoes" to the Audrey Hepburn film *Roman Holiday*, so exemplifying a transnational imaginary. But the novel is also determinedly and concretely local, incorporating excerpts from Sydney newspapers, detailing the development of the Petrov Affair and reporting on scandals, weather events and the poliomyelitis epidemic of 1954: "Test for Polio: Yellow Tinge to Skin" (137). *The Red Shoe* is not one of those texts described by Damrosch as "so culture-bound that they can only be meaningful to a home-grown audience" (2), since the novel ranges across local, national, and transnational elements. Its deft evocation of a Cold War setting relies on local inflexions, citing warnings about nuclear war, the dangers of communism, and the imminence of global destruction, but within the context of international politics. Like historical fiction more generally, *The Red Shoe* refracts the past by filtering it through the perspective of the present; in particular, its treatment of the sense of entrapment experienced by girls and women in the 1950s looks to a future in which the three sisters will enjoy agency and independence. Yet metafictional and iconoclastic versions of history are by no means foreign to the Printz, as is clear from the fact that Volumes One and Two of M. T. Anderson's *The Astonishing Life of Octavian Nothing* were named Honor Books.

The ALA press release announcing *Jellicoe Road*'s Printz Award lingers on Marchetta's CBC success: "Melina Marchetta lives in Sydney, Australia, and is the award-winning author of two previous novels," describing the novel as follows: "This roller coaster ride of a novel grabs you from the first sentence and doesn't let go. You may not be sure where the ride will take you, but every detail—from the complexities of the dual narrative to the pangs of first love—is pitch perfect" ("Printz Award"). *Jellicoe Road* is "pitch perfect" because it is perfectly pitched to a transnational audience through its deployment of narrative approaches and cultural references. If the Printz Award takes up some of the discourses of world literature in its claim to reward "the best" of YA fiction, this is a version of world literature that irons out difference. In comparison, the lack of attention paid in the U.S. to *The Red Shoe* is perhaps attributable to the fact that this novel is thoroughly grounded in Australian cultural history. English's observations about the effects of prizing on sales of children's and YA books suggest that scholars should be conscious and critical of how commercial systems influence literary production and reception, and of the role of prizing in these commercial systems. Those of us who train the teachers, librarians, and scholars of the future might well ensure that our students are challenged to examine the discourses, agendas, and practices of prizing, so that they will know better than to believe that prizes are awarded to the "best" books.

Notes

1. See, for instance, Michael Cart, "A New Literature for a New Millennium?" 29; Patricia Bloem, "International Literature for U.S. Children and Young Adults" 210; Kendra Marcus, "Buying and Selling International Children's Book Rights" 55.
2. The "mixed affiliation" category applies to authors who move between countries: Lucy Christopher (United Kingdom/Australia), and Christine Hinwood (United Kingdom/Australia).
3. See "The Children's Book Council of Australia Judges' Report 2007" (5) in *Reading Time*, the CBC's journal.
4. *The Big Birkett* was republished by Delacorte Press as *The Sweet, Terrible, Glorious Year I Truly, Completely Lost It*.

5. While I focus on the small proportion of Australian books republished in the United States, the same applies to books from Canada, the U.K. and New Zealand, the other nations whose books feature in the Printz, and even more markedly to translated books, exemplified by Teller's *Nothing*. See Marcus, who notes that:

> Given the already flooded children's book market in the United States, and the fact that so many very fine books are also published around the world, American editors are presented with the unfortunate dilemma of deciding which few foreign books would most likely survive and be successful here.
>
> (54)

6. See Peter Brooks, *The Melodramatic Imagination: Balzac, Henry James, Melodrama, and the Mode of Excess.*

7. *The Red Shoe* received brief notices in *The ALAN Review*, *Kirkus Reviews* and *The Horn Book Guide to Children's and Young Adult Books*, but not in the *Bulletin of the Center for Children's Books*. The *Horn Book Guide* refers to Vladimir Petrov as "Australia's Soviet ambassador" ("Intermediate Fiction"), so promoting him to a position well above his relatively junior status as Third Secretary of the Soviet embassy in Australia.

2 Prizing the Unrecognized

Systems of Value, Visibility, and the First World in International and Translated Children's Texts

Abbie Ventura

Introduction

In "Prizing Children's Literature: The Case of Newbery Gold," Kenneth Kidd notes that the Newbery Medal claims universality through a culturally selective and arguably narrow set of ideals about literary excellence. In this essay, I build on Kidd's argument by examining literary prizes for translation, which reflect more than challenge the dynamics of privilege and especially the hegemony of the English language. I focus on the ways in which translated texts, children's or adult, prized or otherwise, do not fare well in the U.S., and on how a literary prize for translations can do little to create gold or elevate the status of the text in terms of sales and visibility. I also show how texts that favor normative Western cultures and ideologies dominate prizes for translated children's books. International prizes, while minimally recognized, often contradict their own mission of transnational enlargement, not from bias within the award systems per se, but rather because of translation publishing conditions. "Domesticated" translations are favored over "foreignizing" translations, thus privileging authors and texts from Highly Developed Western nations. Using several high profile international and translation children's awards, I supply quantitative data on the winning nations' Human Development ranking[1] (as determined by the United Nations' Human Development Index), and apply this two-pronged focus, the first concerning a translation's invisibility and the second concerning a text's First World representation, to the American Library Association's Mildred L. Batchelder Translation Award. In this analysis, I 1) outline the ways in which not all prizes are successful; 2) demonstrate how translated texts are few in numbers; 3) discuss how awarded texts privilege normative Western ideologies, thus limit a construct of international; and finally 4) address how such a limited international construct manifests among five of the more dominant international and translation awards for children's literature, including the Batchelder. Throughout, I maintain that the Batchelder Award cannot make visible what is invisible; awards can only amplify visibility. I argue, too, that translation and international prizes are often limited in their construction of "international" and therefore do not offer a true sense of global and varied childhoods, their ostensible purpose.

When Prizing Cannot Work: Translation Studies and Children's Literature

In "Tradition and the Individual Talent" (1919), T.S. Eliot argues that a literary text is only recognized for its contributions when the text and the author engage the parameters of the existing tradition of value. It is from this insight that I posit that, while scholarship has been dedicated to the economy of prizes and the cultural and economic capital bestowed upon the recipients of such awards, the prize itself must first be prized, or consecrated, by systems of dominant cultural value and cultural production. James English continues this thread in "Winning the Culture Game: Prizes, Awards, and the Rules of Art" stating that, "There is no form of cultural capital so ubiquitous, so powerful, so widely talked about, and yet so little explored by scholars as the cultural prize. Prizes and awards fairly dominate the cultural landscape these days" (109). My argument focuses on English's use of the word "fairly" and interrogates Kidd's claim that "Literary prizing has been a remarkably effective mechanism for publicity, sales, and scandal, if not always for the production of Literature" (166). English's argument looks specifically to the cultural prestige of the Booker Prize; likewise, similar scholarship on literary prizes has focused on the dominance of awards or, more appropriately, awards that dominate. I address the texts and prizes that exist outside of the 'fairly domina[nt]' cultural landscape, and the instances in which an award cannot dominate. Kidd closes his prizing essay with the insight that, "The debate about prizing and its value(s) seems another version of the canon wars" (183). In this way, I discuss first not the prizes associated with translated texts, but the very nature of the international and translation canon, first in the general adult market and within the children's genre specifically.

Translation studies is an important aspect of literary criticism and cultural studies, yet translated children's literature is often not considered in this field.[2] This phenomenon connects to two key features: the first deals with the lack of attention given to international children's literature in terms of numbers (that is, the number of translated texts available on the English language market in relation to English language texts, as well as the number of English texts that are imported to non-Anglophone nations) and the support of these texts via the American Library Association, as well as other dominant literary apparatuses. The second issue deals with contemporary concerns of translation theory, including globalization, authorship, cultural identity, heterogeneity, and marketing.

Lawrence Venuti discusses the role of the translator, and lack of recognition given to the translator, in his seminal work *The Translator's Invisibility: A History of Translation* (1995); also spotlighted in his analysis (without specification in his title), however is the invisibility of the translated text itself. The University of Rochester's online journal *Three Percent: A Resource for International Literature* is dedicated to this study, its title derived from the percentage of texts on the U.S. market translated from another language. The journal understands that translation is crucial to developing an international genre, and maintains an ethics of responsibility for cross-cultural literary exchange, as explained on the website's front page:

> reading literature from other countries is vital to maintaining a vibrant book culture and to increasing the exchange of ideas among cultures. In this age of globalization, one of the best ways to preserve the uniqueness of cultures is through the translation and appreciation of international literary works.
>
> (n.p.)

Of books published in the U.S., only 3% are translations and only 0.7% are literary fiction or poetry (interestingly, these numbers do not include children's translated texts).[3] While the children's genre does face a bias here, being excluded by one of the few resources actively developing the international genre and encouraging publishers to expand translated titles, the work of *Three Percent* highlights the ways in which international, and more specifically, translated texts do not have much of a visible presence on the U.S. market, both in adult and children's sectors. Venuti expands on this issue of (in)visibility:

> Since World War II, English has been the most translated language worldwide, but it isn't much translated into, given the number of English-language books published annually. In 2000, according to UNESCO statistics, 43,011 books were translated from English throughout the world, followed by 6670 from French, 6204 from German, 2431 from Italian, and 1973 from Spanish.
>
> (11)

Again, children's books do not appear to factor into these numbers, and the number of children's literature translations is at an even lower one percent, according to Carl Tomlinson in "The International Children's Movement" (2003).[4]

Focusing specifically on children's translations, Gillian Lathey aptly phrases this similar invisible phenomenon in *The Translation of Children's Literature* as "the halting and uneven travels of children's texts" (4). Despite its invisibility and unevenness, the presence of an international children's genre can be traced to the mid-twentieth century and the work of Jella Lepman and the International Board on Books for Young People (IBBY). Tomlinson details,

> The International Children's Literature Movement was founded primarily through the efforts of Jella Lepman, a German Jew who fled the Nazi Holocaust of World War II but returned to her devastated homeland immediately after the war. [Children's] books, Lepman

believed, would build bridges of understanding among the children who read them.

(68)

Through this work, IBBY was founded in 1953, clearly linking translated texts to a type of ethical activism: "[IBBY's] general mission is to promote international understanding and world peace through children's books" (Tomlinson 68). Like *Three Percent*, IBBY emphasizes the ways translations foster cross-cultural dialogue, as well as encourages "the publication and distribution of quality children's books, especially in developing countries," as explained in the "What is IBBY?" section of its webpage; it should be noted, though, of the 74 National Sections that make up IBBY in the present day, only six are countries with a Low Human Development Index, i.e. developing countries.[5] Despite IBBY's overall ambitious and noble mission of cultural exchange, "Relatively fewer children's books are imported to the United States today than in the eighteenth and nineteenth centuries. It is also due to the [...] difficulty of selling many of these books in this country" (Tomlinson 70). Venuti goes on to label this a trade imbalance, and because the translations themselves are invisible—three percent for the adult market and one percent for the children's—the awards themselves are invisible. In this case, they cannot raise visibility, increase sales, or be considered a form of cultural capital.

International and Translated Children's Book Prizes

Walter Dean Myers writes in his 1985 essay, "The Black Experience in Children's Books: One Step Forward, Two Steps Back" about, "the crying need for children's books reflecting the Third World experience" (222). Myers' use of Third World does not correlate to a geographical Global South or developing country; instead, Myers uses Third World as a way of expressing difference, marginalization, and diversity within U.S. borders to demonstrate the chasm between the lived experiences of ideologically dominant and privileged childhood and these neglected voices. The concepts he draws attention to in this seminal piece, First and Third World experience, and, moreover, how he uses them are of incredible relevance to a conversation on international children's literature; that is, the actual Third World is not present in the genre, both nationally and internationally. I highlight this invisibility with quantitative data based on the United Nation's Human Development Index, a resource which no longer uses the terms First, Second, Third, or Developing World, instead favoring the four categories of Very High, High, Medium, and Low Human Development from the three criteria of health, education, and income. I use the United Nations and their Human Development Report first because of its comprehensive and quantitative aspects, but also because of the ways in which the Index highlights systems of difference, privilege, and oppression (though the UN does not use such language). Acknowledging, too, that the HDI method is flawed in places, especially in regards to favoring Gross Domestic Product, excluding environmental issues, and calculating the HDI differently for different countries, I rely on this model because of the philosophical and ethical activism located in the creation of this method. Pioneered by Pakistani economist Mahbub ul Haq, this system was developed in order to measure the individual citizen's well-being; he argued that previous systems "failed to account for the true purpose of development—to improve people's lives" (Burd-Sharps n.p.).

Thus, by using the UN Human Development Report, I maintain that international and cultural diversity in children's literature is exclusively defined by representation of the First World, as is seen through the statistical breakdown of countries and author nationalities recognized via literary prizes. I argued in the previous section that these books remain largely invisible, and that is indeed true; but if one were to try to locate an international children's book, the most visible are the ones most culturally and economically recognized—that is, those sponsored by large organizations that do have cultural capital: the American Library Association and IBBY, for example.

As discussed earlier, translated international texts are largely invisible in terms of marketing and promotion: there are no bookstore displays dedicated to these titles nor do they warrant articles or reviews in the same way the American Library Association's Newbery and Caldecott Medal winners and honors do in premier journals of children's literature. In many ways, international prize lists are the primary and only way to locate international texts; in my own ethnographic research and experience with accessing international titles, I have relied on such lists and the occasional teacher-run weblog dedicated to international books. I have found that the recipients of the Hans Christian Andersen Awards (both the Writing Award and Literature Award), the Astrid Lindgren Memorial Award, and the American Library Association's Mildred L. Batchelder Translation Award, as well as texts on the international book list published through the United States Board on Books for Young People (USBBY), largely make up this literary body for Western readers—that is, they are the most visible and accessible.[6]

IBBY sponsors the first two awards I outline. While they are not prizes for the act of translation in particular, they are nonetheless concerned with children's literature on the international stage and they have more industry visibility than most international awards.[7] The first and third items of IBBY's Mission Statement connect to the establishment of an international genre: "to promote international understanding through children's books" and (as noted above) "to encourage the publication and distribution of quality children's books, especially in developing countries." Founded in 1953[8] in Zurich, Switzerland and made up of 74 National Sections in the present day, IBBY (along with their United States division, USBBY) is able to do little to accomplish these goals and represent children's texts in so-called developing countries. As they acknowledge:

> [The] right to become a reader is not equally available around the world [...] This is due to the structure of the publishing industry as well as to the more general economic forces with which we all contend. Publishers from the great colonial powers Britain, France and Spain continue to live off their former colonies, and along with companies from the USA, they are the world's great exporters of books [...] The frightening reality is that the vast majority of the world's book production comes from a handful of multi-media conglomerates.

With this recognition, and with the United Nation's Human Development Index, the following data on the winning books demonstrates how a true sense of internationalism does not exist on international lists, prized or otherwise, and so any award meant to recognize this would be limited in its scope.[9]

The Hans Christian Andersen Writing Award, often referred to as the Nobel Prize for children, is based out of Denmark and was founded in 1956 (1966 for the companion Illustrator's award, which is not included in this examination); awarded every two years to a living author who has "made a lasting contribution to literature for children and young people," this award is not specifically designed to recognize the work of translation or for international understandings. However, the award criteria do recognize and affirm IBBY's overall commitment to children's books as vehicles of cultural understanding: "Cultural differences in literary aesthetics will be taken into account and appreciated" (IBBY.org). Of the 30 authors recognized, they represent a total of 21 countries: with the exception of Brazil, with a High HDI, all of the countries have a Very High Human Development Index,[10] and only two authors are from countries in South America, Argentina, and Brazil (though they are not countries recognized as part of the Global South).[11] The countries represented more than once with this award are the United Kingdom (three wins); Sweden (two wins); Germany (two wins); U.S. (five wins); and Brazil (two wins). Presented by the IBBY, we see in this data breakdown that international is limited to economic superpowers.

Not to be confused with the Hans Christian Andersen Writing Award is IBBY's newly developed (2010) Hans Christian Andersen Literature Award; the purpose of this award is "to celebrate Andersen's influence on writers throughout the world by selecting award winners, whose writings can be linked to Andersen's name and authorship through genre similarities or storyteller-artistic qualities" and is one of the larger children's literature awards with a prize of kr 500,000 (US$85,000) (IBBY.org). The four winning authors/nations for this award represent a more even distribution of nations than the HCA Writing Award: J.K. Rowling from the United Kingdom (Very High); Isabel Allende from Chile (Very High); Paulo Coelho from Brazil (High)[12]; and Salman Rushdie from India (Medium). Still in its infancy, this award does show the promise of more broadly defining "throughout the world," but currently exists with a limited scope of international like IBBY's other prominent international children's literature award.

The third international children's literature award I wish to briefly consider before examining the Batchelder more intensively is the Astrid Lindgren Memorial Award (ALMA). Established in 2002 by the Swedish Arts Council, the prize is five million SEK, or roughly US$714,000. This is the most amount of money associated with a children's book award (though it does not necessarily double the sales of the text as is the case with the American Library Association's Newbery Medal—a prize that does not come with a cash prize) and the third richest literary prize in the world, of any genre. This type of economic capital lends itself to a type of cultural capital, and so the authors/nations represented on this award list help to further define what is included in the international canon. ALMA honors Swedish children's author Astrid Lindgren by awarding authors of "the highest artistic quality and in the deeply humanistic spirit associated with Astrid Lindgren" (ALMA.se/en/). In addition to humanism and high artistic quality, the award criteria also emphasizes that "it shall be awarded irrespective of the laureate's nationality" (ALMA.se/en/). While such a disclaimer may be more intended to emphasize that Sweden will not be given preferential consideration, it ultimately seems a superficial disclaimer, as only a handful of nationalities tend to be represented on such lists. That said, of the fourteen recipients, twelve nations are represented: ten are Very High nations; one is a High HDI nation (Brazil); and one Medium (Palestine). The two repeat nations are the United States and Australia; coupled with the repeat wins for the United States and the United Kingdom in the previous awards discussed, it seems true that "It is safe to say [...] that the great majority of imported English-language books come from Great Britain, Canada, and Australia." (Tomlinson 70). Such examples show the way in which these prizes only represent a handful of select nations in their configuration of international; in that way, a global sense of international does not exist. This is not about the quality of the texts or the authors' contributions to the field, rather, it concerns how we understand international: we are prizing a half-definition of international and therefore the prize means little. Likewise, the American award for best translation of an international children's text, the Batchelder Award, follows this pattern.

A Case Study in the Batchelder

The American Library Association's children's Batchelder Award, officially titled the Mildred L. Batchelder Translation Award, explicitly links the issue and act of translation to the construction of a truly international sensibility by encouraging the "international exchange of quality children's books" (ALA.org). While the Award is specifically titled for translation, and its criteria speak more to the act and quality of translation than to cross-cultural exchange, the award was meant to honor retired ALA librarian Mildred

Batchelder whose work was "[...] to eliminate barriers to understanding between people of different cultures, races, nations, and languages" through children's books (ALA.org). Furthermore, the Award formally recognizes the U.S. publishing house, and not necessarily the author or translator of the text, an unusual practice for translated texts (ALA.org).[13] While the award criteria are about translation, the establishment of this award is very much concerned with the "international" and Batchelder's belief that "[...] children of one country who come to know the books and stories of many countries have made a beginning toward international understanding" (ALA. org). The award was founded in 1966, marking the year that Batchelder retired from the American Library Association; reflecting on her career and the role of children's books in facilitating cultural dialogue, Batchelder's comments reflect an early twentieth-century attitude toward the importance of translated works:[14]

> To know the classic stories of a country creates a climate, an attitude for understanding the people for whom that literature is a heritage. When children know they are reading in translation the same stories that children in another country are reading, a sense of nearness grows and expands. Interchange of children's books between countries through translation influences communication between the peoples of these countries, and if the books chosen for traveling from language to language are worthy books, the resulting communication may be deeper, richer, more sympathetic, more enduring. I accept and believe in these assumptions.
>
> (Tomlinson, *Children's Books* 15)

However, there has been limited cultural interchange in the type of countries represented on this awards list. Of the 77 books that have been recognized as winners and runner-ups from 1968–2013, fifteen countries in total have been recognized; eleven of those fifteen have a Human Development ranking of Very High (VH), and the remaining four countries have High (H) rankings. The countries are Germany (VH), Norway (VH), Greece (VH), Netherlands (VH), Russia (H), Denmark (VH), Sweden (VH), Japan (VH), Israel (VH), Italy (VH), Spain (VH), Turkey (H), France (VH), Brazil (H), and Lebanon (H). This breakdown seems to enforce Venuti's idea that "The aim of the translation is to bring back a cultural other as the recognizable, the familiar, even the same" (14). He speaks, of course, about the act of translation itself and the linguistic and ideological choices made by the translator; however, that desire to reproduce familiarity is a deliberate choice by publishing houses. In this way, these literary prizing organizations are only able to evaluate and prize what the publishing house has selected as translation-worthy. Lathey elaborates on this and explicitly says that translation practices by publishing houses rest "on assumptions that young readers will find it difficult to assimilate foreign names, coinage, foodstuffs, or locations, and that they may reject a text reflecting a culture that is unfamiliar" (7). The Batchelder list erases the very nature of both the translation and the international, i.e. cultural difference. Like the Newbery, the Batchelder is part of what Kidd calls the "canonical architecture of children's literature" because of the dominance and prestige of its sponsoring organization, The American Library Association (169). However, to return to the first argument of invisible translations, the Batchelder Award does not, like the Newbery, "[…] more than double the sales of a book, as well as increase sales of the author's other books" nor does the Award "[…] keeps titles and authors in circulation for decades" (Kidd 168).

Such circulation can be found on both industry and social media bestseller lists and book reviews: comparing reviews and ratings on the Amazon, Barnes & Noble, and Goodreads websites of Batchelder titles to Newbery titles, as sales information is often difficult to locate and unreliable, I maintain that consumer-critic reviews function as a grass-roots version of the bestseller list. I have chosen to look at Uri Orlev's 1985 Batchelder-winning *The Island on Bird Street* (1981) and Christine Nöstlinger's 1979 Batchelder-winning *Conrad: The Factory-Made Boy* (1975). Of the 77 possible honors and winners, I selected these because both have won more than one of the more visible international awards I outlined earlier, therefore would hypothetically have reached a wider audience as a result: Orlev won the Batchelder in 1985 and the Hans Christian Andersen Writing Award in 1996, while Nöstlinger has been awarded the Batchelder in 1979, the Hans Christian Andersen Writing Award in 1984, and the Astrid Lindgren Memorial Award in 2003.

I am relying solely on these texts' popularity and the idea that "Popularity began to take precedence over expert recommendations or reviewers' opinions [in the 1950s] when deciding what book to buy, even in children's literature" (Fitzsimmons 90). And so, in Table 2.1, I am comparing the popularity of *The Island on Bird Street* to the popularity of the 1985 Newbery Winner, Robin McKinley's *The Hero and the Crown*, and to the 1996 Newbery Winner, Karen Cushman's *The Midwife's Apprentice*. These two years represent major awards for Orlev and certainly a promotion of his titles through them.

Table 2.1 Popularity Comparison Between *The Island on Bird Street*, *The Hero and the Crown*, and *The Midwife's Apprentice*

	The Island on Bird Street	The Hero and the Crown	The Midwife's Apprentice
Amazon	37	312	185
Barnes & Noble	5	101	97
Goodreads: Ratings	538	30,775	26,680
Goodreads: Reviews	62	1,266	1,053

Observe in Table 2.2 that the same pattern of Newbery winners vastly out-ranking Batchelder titles, is true for Nöstlinger and the three corresponding Newbery winners to her three awards, 1979's *The Westing Game* (Ellen Raskin); 1984's *Dear Mr. Henshaw* (Beverly Cleary); and 2003's *Crispin: The Cross of Lead* (Avi).

Table 2.2 Popularity Comparison Between *Conrad: The Factory-Made Boy*, *The Westing Game*, *Dear Mr. Henshaw* and *Crispin: The Cross of Lead*

	Conrad: The Factory-Made Boy	*The Westing Game*	*Dear Mr. Henshaw*	*Crispin: The Cross of Lead*
Amazon	3	1,037	225	325
Barnes & Noble	0	947	181	208
Goodreads: Ratings	430	81,530	19,915	12,286
Goodreads: Reviews	40	5,262	859	1,284

What this data shows, besides the popularity of the Goodreads site, is the cultural capital of the Newbery and the way in which translation and inter-national awards have not bestowed the same type of cultural capital on the works of Orlev and Nöstlinger, and that the Newbery and Batchelder are on opposite sides of the ALA success spectrum in terms of sales, pub-licity, and public interest. It is also not an issue of currency, as this pattern holds true of the 2014 Batchelder title, Truus Matti's *Mister Orange*, and the 2014 Newbery title, Kate DiCamillo's *Flora & Ulysses: The Illuminated Adventures*: Matti has three Amazon reviews to DiCamillo's 293; 1 to 29 for Barnes & Noble; 96 to 11,683 for Goodreads ratings; and 31 to 2,126 for Goodreads reviews. If all prizes carried equal cultural capital, these titles would be as well-known and as well-reviewed (in terms of numbers, not content of reviews) as Newbery titles. Of course, this data is subject to scrutiny, as it does not concretely tell us if the Batchelder awards are actually being read—it only tells us these titles are not being reviewed at the same rate of the Newbery. But given Fitzsimmons' argument about the taste-making function of the bestseller list, I do believe these charts indicate the Western reader's reception of international and translated texts. These are texts from dominant High Human Development nations, and so do not encompass a global sense of international, and, even after being prized, they are not being read/reviewed by the consumer-critic.

I close this piece by shifting from the particulars of the prizing argu-ment to the wider cultural implications of these realities. This is a much larger conversation that encompasses more than issues of invisibility and prizing: what all of this suggests is that more under dominant Western pub-lishing trends, international is a limited and singular concept, and national literatures are difficult to establish in developing countries, and nearly impossible to export to the wider international market. In "The Spectacle of the 'Other'" Stuart Hall asks, "Can a dominant regime of representation be challenged, contested or changed?" (340). I use his call to action to refigure the cultural manifestations of international, but also to elaborate upon it to raise the question, "what if we are unaware of the dominant regimes of representation?" emphasizing both the marginalization of translations and non-normative Western nations in the children's genre. This essay highlights those dominant regimes, so that as we analyze these prized global representations of childhood, we may ask the questions: What isn't translated into English and why? Why translate or read translations? When do we already read translations unaware? Why select a particular work to translate, to read, to teach? Why prize a particular work? These are questions that must be considered, and answered, before a translation award may have a serious impact on a children's text; until then, such prizes exist outside the fairly dominant landscape of today's prizing culture. However, as Andrea Davis Pinkney acknowledges about identity-based awards in "Awards That Stand on Solid Ground,"

> These awards are a gateway to progress. They provide a door for authors and illustrators into the world of children's literature, a world that, despite its increasing diversity, still too often maintains a quiet inference that is racism in its most subtle forms.
>
> (535)

The international and translation awards I consider here likewise function as gateways even as they perpetuate a subtle racism. However, we must answer these questions concerning translation and (in)visibility first, in order to allow a fully global construction of international to permeate the children's genre. While international and translated children's book awards do not prize texts in the sense of increasing their sales or visibility, they do increase our own awareness about (and, perhaps, our activism toward) the inequality and imbalance in children's literary cultures of the world.

Notes

1. All rankings are taken from the United Nations' 2012 *Human Development Report* (published in March 2013).
2. This is to say that translation studies scholars often ignore children's texts in their data, analyses, and critical readings; the scholarly treatment of translated children's texts happens almost exclusively by established children's literature scholars, who are also translation scholars. Gillian Lathey's *The Translation of Children's Literature* (2006) and *The Role of Translators* (2010) are such examples, and that I rely on later in this argument, as are Göte Klingberg's *Children's Fiction in the Hands of the Translators* (1986), Emer O'Sullivan's *Comparative*

Children's Literature (2005), and Jan Van Coillie and Walter P. Verschueren's *Children's Literature in Translation: Challenges and Strategies* (2006).

3. In the *Three Percent* database, they do not even include the more visible children's translated titles from 2008 through 2013 (winners of the ALA's Batchelder Translation Award). The one exception is Sun-mi Hwang's *The Hen Who Dreamed She Could Fly*, published as a children's book in Korea, but remarketed by Penguin in the U.S. as an adult self-help book, thus its inclusion in this database.

4. "According to [children's book experts], for the past several decades the number of [translated] children's books published in the United States, compared to total annual children's book production, has been about 1 percent" (Tomlinson 70).

5. Those countries are Afghanistan, Haiti, Pakistan, Rwanda, Uganda, and Zambia and texts from these nations have yet to be recognized on any of the IBBY "best of" lists or through IBBY-sponsored awards.

6. Other major international prizes for children's literature not examined in this essay include the UK Marsh Award for Children's Literature in Translation and the Deutsche Jugendliteraturpreis (German Youth Literature Prize).

7. *The Children's Literature Association Quarterly* makes note of the winners of the HCA Writing Award in their regular "Awards, Prizes and Organizations" section; *The School Library Journal* covers the HCA Writing Award process along with featured articles on the nominees; and *Publishers Weekly* features stories on the award winners each year.

8. IBBY's Hans Christian Andersen Author's Award was established in 1956; the Illustrator's in 1966; and the Writing Award in 2010.

9. The following is from The United States Board on Books for Young People's (a division of IBBY) 2006–2014 book list titles, though this is not an awards list; I include this in order to showcase a variety of representations of international: 96 percent of children's books included on the USBBY's 2006–2014 lists are from countries with a Very High Human Development Index (or, are First World countries). This means, of the total 348 titles on this list, 334 are from Very High nations; 1 is from a High nation; 4 are from Medium nations; and Low HDI nations are not represented in any way. Furthermore, access to these international texts favor First World countries and publishing houses: 74 percent of the Very High nations can be purchased through either Amazon or Barnes & Noble websites (not including second-party sellers), while only 54 percent of the Medium HDI nation texts from the list can be purchased on these sites.

10. Bohumil Riha won the award in 1980 from the former Czechoslovakia. The United Nations does not list the status of this nation in terms of Human Development at this time; I am including it as a Very High HDI, the Czech Republic's current ranking.

11. The Global South is defined here as more of a socio-economic divide and less of a geographical location, and encompasses Africa, Latin America, and developing parts of Asia. Their lack of representation is, of course, connected to the very economic conditions IBBY discusses in terms of multi-media conglomerates dictating publishing trends.

12. Coelho was presented an honorary award in 2007, before the award was formally established.

13. The PEN American Center's Translation Awards, some of the most prestigious and established in the field, recognize and prize the act of translation and the work of the translator.
14. This attitude is not limited to the early twentieth century; however, more attention was given to translated works in the aftermath of World War I in the hope that cultural exchange could prevent such an atrocity from occurring again. The PEN American Center was founded in 1922 to promote translated works and the Rockefeller Foundation developed an international focus in its Humanities Division in the 1930s.

3   The Guys *Are* the Prize
Adolescent Fiction, Masculinity, and the Political Unconscious of Australian Book Awards

Erica Hateley

In a discussion of multiculturalism in Australia, Jon Stratton and Ien Ang strike on a telling formulation when they describe the cultural practice of such policymaking as the production of *"public fantasy*—a collective narrative fiction" of national identity (152). In this chapter, I borrow the notion of a collective narrative fiction to explore the cultural practice of Australian book awards, which, by their text selections, make of individual literary works public fantasies and national narratives both collective (grouped choices within award categories or years) and cumulative (grouped choices over time).[1] Attending to the winning titles of three national Australian book awards—the Children's Book Council of Australia (CBCA) Book of the Year Awards; the Prime Minister's Literary Awards (PMLA); and the teen-choice Inky Awards for adolescent fiction—makes clear a sustained interest in gender as part of desirable Australian subjectivity. The collective and cumulative narratives produced by these awards between 2010 (the first year in which all three national prizes for adolescent fiction were awarded) and 2012 suggest that Australian adolescence is defined first and foremost by hegemonic masculinity. Troublingly, this definition is not only the norm but is also normative in recent Australian award-winning adolescent novels in which to strive for the hegemonic masculine ideal is sold as desirable.

Contemporary Australian young adult (YA) literature is marked by particular codes of masculinity, in line with what Kimberley Reynolds sees as the emergence of the YA genre being "shaped and masculinized by its rejection of childhood and femininity" (73). And, while it may be true that the field of YA literature is now widely populated by female characters, marketed to female readers, and addressed to an implied reader who is feminine (Reynolds 74), the selections made by the CBCA Awards and PMLAs suggest an ongoing commitment to masculinity as the *raison d'être* for YA literature. An interest in masculinity as both desirable and dangerous can be traced not only in individual titles chosen, but also in the narrative and thematic elements present across award winners.

The choices made by the CBCA Awards and the PMLA are thrown into relief by the selections made during the same period by the Inky Awards. Where the top-down awards selected adolescent novels with male protagonists, which were thematically engaged with masculinity, the national teen-choice

book award went to novels with female protagonists, and which were thematically engaged with issues of female agency and the limitations or dangers
of patriarchal stereotypes. Reading across these awards demonstrates that
"literary merit" may be less significant than perceived "social merit" in "top-
down" (adult institution addressing young reader) awards seeking to shape
adolescent experiences and preferences, as opposed to the "bottom-up"
(young reader addressing adult institution) award, where selections seem to
reflect adolescent experiences and preferences. This is not to assert a naïve
faith in teen-choice awards as unmediated expressions of youth culture
and agency, any more than to read a novel is to assert a naïve faith that it
expresses an unmediated expression of a given author's intentions, but is to
suggest that top-down awards may be ideologically constrained by an understanding of youth literature as having a social function beyond the aesthetic.

Although Australia has no single personification of its citizenry—no Uncle
Sam, no John Bull—it figures national subjectivity and asserts core values
via an ongoing investment in potent stereotypes of embodied masculinity,
which are mobilized in the service of a desirable nationalism. Archetypal
figures of the Anzac, the stockman, or the surf lifesaver are continuously
recycled, not least for their silent alignment of (white, heterosexual) masculinity with ideal Australianness.

Australian sociologist R.W. (now Raewyn) Connell's theory of "hegemonic masculinity" makes such contradictions and tensions visible. Connell
has been at the forefront of masculinity studies in recent decades, largely for
her critiques of gendered experiences in neoliberal educational and social
contexts. Drawing on extensive sociological work undertaken in Australia,
Connell writes:

> Hegemonic masculinity can be defined as the configuration of gender
> practice which embodies the currently accepted answer to the problem
> of the legitimacy of patriarchy, which guarantees (or is taken to guar-
> antee) the dominant position of men and the subordination of women
> [...] hegemony is likely to be established only if there is some corre-
> spondence between cultural ideal and institutional power, collective if
> not individual.
>
> (77)

The selection of adolescent novels by major Australian book awards is one
of the means by which a desired correspondence between cultural ideal
and institutional power is articulated and possibly even achieved. When
explored in novels, the configuration of gender practice referred to by Connell manifests as a

schema, shaping what a character is like, how he behaves, and how
he interacts with other characters. Only a couple of elements of the

schema need be adduced for readers to instantiate the whole schema, because audiences recognize it from other texts—other novels, magazines, TV soaps, Hollywood films, and the like.

(Romøren and Stephens 219)

In Australia, the schema for hegemonic masculinity includes: heterosexuality; a flexible Whiteness, or Anglo-Australianism; a privileging of homosocial bonds (often described as mateship); a privileging of physical over emotional expressiveness; a rejection of "high" culture in favor of interest—and, most desirably, high-achieving participation—in organized sports; and explicit avowals of normative Australian political ideologies such as faith in egalitarianism and social equity, but implicit discourses of racism, isolationism, and militarized defense of Australian territory.

However, hegemonic masculinity—like the patriarchal order it indexes and shores up—must be flexible enough to absorb and accommodate historical, cultural, and social shifts while retaining authority. Recent Australian YA fiction is one cultural formation which bears witness to, and often seeks to secure, patriarchal social order. Thus, the individual books and the corpus generated by the awards offer fruitful examples of "the multiple paths that lead to the unmasking of cultural artifacts as socially symbolic acts" (Jameson 20). As per Jameson's account of the political unconscious of cultural forms, this chapter assumes that book awards derive their social force precisely because their ideological content and effect *is* unconscious; that both the books and their selection are manifestations of wider social and cultural norms which may not be immediately apparent to particular authors or award judges, but which reflect and shape dominant understandings of what constitutes desirable subjectivity at a given moment in time. Although neither the CBCA nor the PMLA profess any social agendas beyond a presumed allegiance to the literacy myth as constituent of nationed subjectivity, the adolescent literature prized by each in recent years implies an agenda (conscious or otherwise) of identifying books about and for young men. Their selections may also confirm that "In Australia, it seems that public discourse about boys, particularly that produced and maintained through the media, has contributed spiritedly to an unexamined, unsophisticated approach to a boys' education agenda" (Alloway 586).

Seen in this light, the fact that from 2010 to 2012 the CBCA Awards and PMLA each selected YA novels which not only feature male protagonists (predominantly white, cisgendered, heterosexual male protagonists) but which tell stories *about* masculinity looks less like coincidence or conspiracy, and more like a confirmation that Australian book awards are embedded in a wider ideological move to recuperate deeply problematic modes of masculinity as the ideal or exemplary version of contemporary Australian subjectivity.

National Australian Prizes for Adolescent Literature

The venerable children's book awards in Australia are the Children's Book Council of Australia's annual Book of the Year prizes. First awarded in 1946 to a single title, the CBCA's awards program has developed sub-categories and has, since 2001, been given in five such categories: Younger Readers, Older Readers, Picture Book, Early Childhood, and the Eve Pownall Award for Information Books. The Older Readers category was first introduced in 1987, and has consistently veered toward upper adolescence in its implied readership.

Judges of the CBCA Awards are drawn from the membership of the CBCA itself: each state branch of the organization provides a judge who serves as such for two years.[2] The presence and amount of cash accompanying the CBCA Awards has long been varied and obscure: the CBCA Awards "value" is seen as primarily symbolic, even as claims to increased sales for award-winning titles are routinely made. What can be safely asserted is the pedagogical impact of the CBCA Awards: school library standing orders suppliers routinely include shortlisted CBCA titles in their programs, and the awards themselves are announced in and yoked to, the annual Book Week program which is widely celebrated in Australian school libraries as a flagship literacy festival.

While Australia's states have for many years run Premiers' literary prize programs, many of which include categories for young readers, the establishment of a *national* prize for Australian children's literature with the political and economic weight of government behind it only took place in 2008 when the Prime Minister's Literary Awards appeared. Driscoll notes that in addition to the substantial cash prize attached to them the PMLAs "carry symbolic heft as official endorsements of the value of literature in Australian society" (72), and that the awards offered a kind of safe political capital in their connection with the "uncontroversial social and educational goal of literacy" (73). Indeed, the PMLA made its commitment to this literacy agenda explicit when in 2010—a year after Driscoll's article—it added to the roster specific categories for Children's and Young Adult literature.

There has occasionally been some crossover of titles between the PMLA's Young Adult category and the CBCA's Older Readers category (as can be seen in Table 3.1), but the awards proper have gone to different books. Nonetheless, as will be discussed below, the awards have thus far trodden very similar thematic and ideological terrain in their selections. While these similarities *could* seem to suggest that contemporary Australian YA literature has a more general homogeneity, the selections made by teen judges of the Golden Inky Awards suggest otherwise. In turn, it would seem that the CBCA Awards and the PMLAs have much more in common than either program might care to admit.

As with the state-level Premiers' book awards, Australia has no shortage of state-level children's choice awards. However, the Inky Awards are notable as a readers' choice award, which is administered by the State Library of Victoria, but is national in scope and focused on adolescent literature. First awarded in 2007, the awards recognize an international YA title with a Silver Inky, and celebrate an Australian title with the Golden Inky. The Inkys are judged by a panel of six teenaged readers, and the panel tries to achieve coverage of all six Australian states, and a range of ages and genders. The annual longlist of ten titles is generated from titles suggested via the State Library of Victoria's teen reading web portal, *Inside a Dog*. While it is clear that the Inkys are committed to young people's participation in as much of the process as possible, they nonetheless note that some adult mediation takes place: "with the Centre for Youth Literature staff acting as the filter for coordination and eligibility" ("Guidelines").

Given the long-recognized connections between literacy and social agency, it is unsurprising that one locus of cultural anxiety has been boys as readers, or rather, as incapable or reluctant readers. I have argued elsewhere that constructions of reluctant boy readers serve the interests of neoliberalism and patriarchy, most immediately by rendering literacy a seemingly apolitical aspect of subjectivity (Hateley 172). In the present context of education and literature, this manifests as a preference for young men asserting individualism and independence in order to counteract or even defeat systemic feminization (such as that which is attributed to schooling and literary cultures). In this imaginary scene of masculine development, then, a young male would attain literacy in a feminized environment, but would achieve maturity and thus reap the rewards of said literacy, by escaping and/or transcending feminine institutions and social formations in favor of agency and autonomy.

As with many contemporary Western nations where patriarchal norms have come under increasing pressure from emergent identity politics and social-justice movements such as feminism, multiculturalism, queer rights, Aboriginal activism, and so forth, schooling has emerged as one "safe" space for expressing anxieties about masculinity and "to position boys and men as the new disadvantaged" (Alloway 584). The selections of the top-down book awards are presumably made in order to increase participation of Australian boys as readers who are popularly and pedagogically being constructed as "deficit" or "at-risk" subjects, even when sociological and economic research shows that this is not the case. The chosen titles often depict the 'constraints' and 'oppressions' of a feminized schooling system, and offer narratives of masculine emancipation from such systems. Of course, they also offer cautionary tales of unthinking or untrammeled autonomy, and thus conform to a very limited definition of acceptable or desirable masculinity. If it is the case that male students are alienated by formal schooling, it may well be that the most immediate audience for these award winners are those female students who are seen as enthusiastic and capable readers. In other words, the lessons of masculinity taught by these novels and endorsed by awards programs, may well be consumed by those subjects least likely to benefit from them. But then, an ideological analysis would assert that it is precisely those who are subordinated or oppressed by hegemonic masculinity who need to accept and internalize the legitimacy thereof.

The Award Winners

Table 3.1 Winning Titles from National Australian Adolescent Book Awards, 2010–2012[3]

Author	Title	Year of Publication	Year of Award	CBCA: Older Readers			PMLA: Young Adult Literature		Inky (Golden)	
				Winner	*Honour*	*Shortlist*	*Winner*	*Shortlist*	*Winner*	*Shortlist*
Christopher, Lucy	*Stolen*	2009	2010			*		*	*	
Condon, Matt	*Confessions of a Liar, Thief and Failed Sex God*	2009	2010				*			
Metzenthen, David	*Jarvis 24*	2009	2010	*						
Crowley, Cath	*Graffiti Moon*	2010	2011		*		*			
Hartnett, Sonya	*The Midnight Zoo*	2010	2011	*						
Moloney, James	*Silvermay*	2011	2011							*
Bailey, Em	*Shift*	2011	2012							*
Gardner, Scott	*The Dead I Know*	2011	2012	*						
Newton, Robert	*When We Were Two*	2011	2012			*	*			

While it is beyond the scope of this chapter to discuss all nine award-winning adolescent novels in detail, the shared themes and narrative concerns of these books shed light on the wider ideological values of the awards.

Both Bill Condon's *Confessions of a Liar, Thief and Failed Sex God* (2009) and David Metzenthen's *Jarvis 24* (2009) read like templates for contemporary Australian adolescent masculinity. The fact that Condon's *Confessions* is set in 1967 only emphasizes these novels' shared project of rendering masculinity as ahistorical. Both novels code schooling as an irrelevant impediment to growth for their male protagonists: an experience to be escaped and/or survived.

In *Confessions*, Neil attends an all-boys Catholic school, which provides an institutional context shaped entirely by homosocial relations. Tellingly, even in this environment, the most significant lessons learned at this school are the domain of the sports field or the confessional rather than the classroom. The sports field emphasizes physical strength and ability as a marker of success, and the confessional provides a theater for the imposition of social norms versus interior desires. In each space, boys learn lessons of self-policing. When Neil sees his best friend commit suicide by stepping into traffic, he is propelled into a self-motivated maturation. Neil's measures of success are maintaining a friendship with a boy who has been expelled from school, the loss of his virginity, establishing a more equal peer relationship with his elder brother, and leaving school to enter the workforce without having completed his certificate. The masculine subjectivity prized by Neil is homosocial, heterosexual, non-intellectual, and untrammeled by institutions.

Despite a culture of willful self-reliance having lead to one schoolmate getting wrongly expelled and another committing suicide, Neil remains committed to what he calls the "stone wall": "Every single bloke I know feels the same way. You cop the strap and you deal with it yourself" (Condon 134). This ethos of self-reliance is closely linked with a projected adult masculinity, and as Neil chooses to tank his school math exam he experiences a cathartic move toward autonomy: "I gulp in freedom, and I run" (Condon 218).

In *Jarvis 24*, protagonist Marc exemplifies the constant vigilance and self-surveillance that constitute and confirm acceptable masculinity. The novel is marked by foregrounded examples of adolescent masculinity as a paranoid performance staged to cement homosocial bonds, maintain peer relationships, procure romantic or sexual encounters, and most importantly, to neither be, nor be perceived as in any way, "gay." Marc's self-consciousness about this, though, at least suggests that the wider social pressures on young males to be engaged in homosocial relationships but not homosexual ones may contribute to widespread homophobia: "I also worry, now and again— perhaps because I often find myself comparing myself to other guys, their clothes and physiques—that I might be a bit gay" (Metzenthen 4). Marc's heterosexuality is repeatedly affirmed in the novel by his overt interest in young women, and his forming a friendship with Mikey, a young gay man. Mikey is an able tradesman, and thus disrupts symbolic connections between labor and sexuality. More importantly, Mikey's feelings of alienation from his family and experiences of homophobic violence, serve to educate Marc (and the reader) about the consequences for individuals of socially normalized homophobia. Nonetheless, Mikey serves as a figure of 'not me' for Marc's self-definition, so even as Mikey's presence in the novel lessens Marc's homophobia it nonetheless affirms ideal male subjectivity is heterosexual, or at least, not gay. When compared with other novels, though, Metzenthen does attempt to engage the paradoxes created by hegemonic masculinity for adolescent subjects.

Marc escapes the constraining feminization of school in general and English class in particular when he undertakes work experience at a local car yard. The differences from his affluent upper-middle-class home life, and his private school education, allow Marc to mature toward manhood. Marc's socio-economic privilege is as great as his gendered and sexual privilege: readers are asked to believe that Marc has never before met a single mother, a lesbian, or a gay man before working at the car yard. Without sacrificing any such privilege, though, Marc's time in the car yard gives him the chance to undertake practical, hands-on work, which provides him with the kind of satisfaction that at school he has only really found on the football field. The manhood to which Marc aspires is quite traditional. He sees himself as a footballer and as a "minder" of women (Metzenthen 254).

The transition from school to work life is also the developmental context for Scot Gardner's *The Dead I Know* (2011). Gardner's novel tells the story of Aaron Rowe, who must reconcile a traumatic event from his own childhood—the reader learns along with Aaron that he has repressed the memory of his father shooting his mother before committing suicide when Aaron was five years old. The novel covers the period of time immediately after Aaron has left the last of many high schools that have failed him, and is beginning a career as a trainee funeral director. His boss, John, tells Aaron:

> Your school counselor, Andy Robertson, is a close friend. We're from the same church. When we discussed you, he warned me that you could be reticent, moody and unreachable. That you struggled with every aspect of schoolwork and no amount of personal intervention changed that.
>
> (Gardner 98)

That John follows this up with a paean to Aaron's achievements and abilities in the workplace signals both that school was constraining Aaron, and that John will serve as a much-needed male mentor just as Aaron's guardian—his grandmother—is being hospitalized for dementia.

The heightened emotional landscape of the novel is shaped by Aaron's own nightmares and sleepwalking which result from his repressed trauma, and his new work in a funeral home, where he (and thus the reader) are confronted with a number of deaths, mournings, and questions about mortality. Aaron's psychological journey from repressed trauma to emotional growth is mirrored in his economic journey from poverty to wage-earning and from living in a caravan park to a room in the funeral home. The novel further emphasizes these developments with Aaron's increasing mastery over his own body: Aaron sleepwalks and often wakes up in places without knowing how he arrived there and without any sense of what he may have been doing while asleep. Even when awake, though, the socio-economic liminality of the caravan park is emphasized by repeated depictions of the bathrooms at the park being a space of violence and danger, reaching a nadir when Aaron is beaten and urinated on by another resident: "Westy unzipped his fly and hauled his penis out. He stretched it and flapped it from side to side, took aim and relieved himself on the floor, on my leg, my hip, my stomach" (Gardner 142). When Aaron recovers and confronts the memory of his parents' death, he stops sleepwalking, and is at the same time, offered a room in his employer's home. The final scene of the novel shows Aaron driving "home" with his new symbolic family, sure that "We'd all be okay" (Gardner 208).

A similarly heightened landscape for the exploration of adolescent masculinity is found in Robert Newton's *When We Were Two* (2011), which follows sixteen-year-old Dan Wheelan and his younger brother on a journey across rural New South Wales with an eye to joining the Australian army and serving in WWI. Dan and his younger brother Eddie are escaping a violent, abusive father, and seek positive male role models and acceptance throughout their picaresque journey. Dan's negotiation of mature masculinity and fraught experience with father figures is explicit:

> While my father never taught me anything much, never sat me down and explained things, I have a feeling that without him I would've missed out on learning the most important lesson of all. You see, indirectly, it was my father who taught me what not to be. The very idea that one day I might grow up to be like him seemed almost impossible to bear, so I began to look at him different, in reverse, and model myself on everything he wasn't.
>
> (Newton 73)

Eventually, Eddie dies from a stroke of some kind, and Dan buries the past along with his brother at the Australian coast.

The historical setting of *When We Were Two* not only connects Eddie's coming-of-age with the national mythology of Australia's coming-of-age in WWI, but enables a social landscape where white/Anglo masculinity is the default position of agency and authority. After meeting and then escaping from negative role models—the violent father, a pedophilic traveling salesman, and a henpecked police informant—the two boys fall in with a group of men who are traveling to the coast to enlist. Among this group, Dan makes peace with his self-attributed complicity with his younger brother's suffering at the hands of their father, realizes that he has no need of further connection with his mother or any of his past, and prepares to enlist in the army himself. Even as the novel celebrates the idealized masculinity of the men who are going to war, it must balance this celebration with an acknowledgment that (thankfully) war is not a constant state for Australia. *When*

We Were Two strikes this balance by constructing war as a context that highlights an ideal masculinity that is actually forged domestically:

> I'm sure there have been plenty of men who have gone to war just like them, ordinary men with sunken chests and hairy backs who have taken to killing without the blink of an eye. But these men from Walcha don't seem capable of killing. These men are husbands and fathers, simple men with hearts of gold.
>
> (Newton 143)

Thus, the reader of *When We Were Two* has available to them the kind of masculine subjectivity for which Dan strives, and which—it is implied—helped Australia's victorious efforts in WWI.

The shared concerns or ideas about adolescent masculinity which may be traced in these novels, and which thus characterize the cumulative narrative of the awards programs which identified them as the best of their years, include: formal schooling as at best an imposition and more often an active impediment to masculine development or maturation; the dangers of feminized spaces and figures of authority and discipline (mothers, teachers, etc.) and an accompanying anxiety about a lack of male role models; the 'natural' expression of masculinity through sports, sex, criminality, and cars; a rejection of any expression of sexuality which is not emphatically heterosexual; a desire for heteronormative pathways through life (most consistently, the expectation of marriage and reproduction in accordance with capitalist values).

Generally speaking, then, these books do not seek to critique or disrupt hegemonic masculinity. Their selection by awards judges serves as a kind of cultural investment in boys as readers which mirror the kinds of political and economic investments Alloway critiques:

> Put boldly, there is a real investment risk in throwing money at advantaged boys for whom school literacy practices and for whom the outcomes of schooling are still promising, if not privileged, while more deserving students experience the effects of a diluted national effort.
>
> (Alloway 597)

The symbolic labor of 'reuniting' masculinity with literacy, within and by means of approved literary texts, even in texts that disavow the relevance of schooling to masculine subjectivity, is disingenuous.

Of course, this group of novels is not entirely homogenous in its exploration of adolescent masculinity and education. A more nuanced vision of learning—its meaning and value—is offered by Crowley's *Graffiti Moon*. Here, an emphasis on masculine autonomy remains, and the novel also seems to suggest that normative schooling practices fail both Ed and Leo because they cannot 'be' their creative selves (Shadow and Poet) at high school. However, rather than set up dichotomies of school/not school,

Graffiti Moon explicitly identifies non-normative schooling as valuable to these young men. Ed has had a positive school experience learning from his art teacher Mrs. J., but his lack of literacy attainment renders much of his school time a challenge at best. He "escapes" from school in favor of an artistic apprenticeship model of development with his mentor Bert and is even considering the possibility of non-traditional entrance to a university course in fine arts (Crowley 207). Leo/Poet, it is revealed, has only taken up the criminal enterprise which shapes the novel's central plot to pursue his artistic interests: "I needed the five hundred dollars for a poetry course. My gran wanted me to take a TAFE [Technical and Further Education] poetry course on Saturday mornings" (Crowley 233). In these ways, the novel values education (especially artistic education) for young men, and seems suspicious of normative schooling's capacity to deliver such education, but offers alternative pathways rather than opposing desirable masculinity to education.

The Golden Inky Awards

If the winning booklists of the CBCA and PMLA awards read like parables of hegemonic masculinity, the Golden Inky selections offer far more nuanced engagements with issues of gender and agency. These three novels all display deep consciousness of the challenges and risks associated with normative gender—their female protagonists all confront the consequences of hegemonic masculinity, for themselves and their peers. Their concerns with the constraints placed on young people by patriarchal norms throw into relief the insistent commitment to those same norms demonstrated by the CBCA and PMLA choices.

In Lucy Christopher's *Stolen*, a young British woman, Gemma, is kidnapped from Bangkok airport and taken to a remote farm in outback Australia. Her captor, Ty, conforms in a number of ways with hegemonic figurations of Australian masculinity: he is strong, self-sufficient, rugged, and can live off the land. In the tradition of John Fowles's *The Collector* (1963), *Stolen* extends patriarchal logic to its end: the forcible taking ownership of a woman in the service of establishing a self-contained kingdom, wherein the woman's purpose is companionship, cleaning, and (presumably) breeding. So, even as Gemma experiences a range of conflicting emotions about Ty, the reader of *Stolen* cannot easily fit its plot into romance conventions or unproblematically celebrate Ty as an embodiment of desirable masculinity. The novel demonstrates ways in which Gemma is equally constrained by those who rescue her:

> I tell them what they want to hear. I tell you really are a monster, that you are screwed up. I tell them I don't have any feelings for you other than hatred. I go along with everything the police say I have to say. And I've written the statement they want me to write. I try to believe it all.
>
> (Christopher 294)

Stolen critiques hegemonic masculinity and patriarchy by making them the centerpiece of a story told by a female who is both objectified and victimized by it.

James Moloney's *Silvermay* (2010) also explores the effects of masculine norms on non-male adolescents. This fantasy novel interrogates codes of masculinity by following a *female* protagonist who sets off on a quest involving stolen babies, missing swords, competition for crowns, and magical powers. While Moloney obviously traffics in the genre conventions of high fantasy, his protagonist is deeply conscious of how such narrative traditions shape thought and action:

> Heroes are men who win battles with nothing more than courage and the swords in their hands. That's what I remember from childhood stories. Now and then, a woman, or even a girl, is the brave one who fights off enemies or leads her people to safety in the face of heart-stopping danger. A heroine whose spirit and deeds make her stand out like a proud flame for all the rest to admire.
>
> On this journey, I learned there is another kind of heroine.
>
> (Moloney 98)

In *Shift* by Em Bailey, critique of patriarchal culture is mobilized by way of a heightened narrative of girl–girl relationships and rivalry. When Olive returns to her high school after having attempted to kill herself, she finds that her social status has gone from elite to marginal. As she navigates her new social world, it is revealed that her one true friend, Ami, is imaginary, and her new friend Miranda, may be a sociopath. While Olive feels "like I was in the middle of my own romance novel" (Bailey 269), as with *Stolen* and *Silvermay*, the conventions of the romance genre are never allowed to circulate without complication here.

What may be most telling about the selections made by the Inky teen judges is less their seeming disinterest in fables of hegemonic masculinity, or even their interest in genre stories which explore the darker sides of life, than the struggle to narrate the self which is present in all three texts. Gemma is determined to articulate her experience free of interference from either her captor or her rescuers; *Silvermay* asserts "I have a story to tell" (Moloney 2); and, in *Shift*, Olive's battle for survival is a battle to be able to see and speak the truth of her experience. There may well be some resonance here with young people choosing for themselves the books of greatest value in their quest to make sense of the world.

For the PMLA and CBCA Awards, there is an irony to selecting novels which will likely be used as curricular resources in secondary schools and which presumably are intended to engage reluctant or at-risk adolescent men, but which tell stories about how problematic and constraining secondary school is for young men. There is a deeper philosophical critique, however, which may be inferred from this irony: *education* is not constructed as negative in these novels, *schooling* is. Perhaps the most troubling myth of hegemonic masculinity (re)produced in these texts is that of the autonomous masculine subject who is educated most effectively either by himself, or by participating in traditionally male spaces and experiencing traditionally masculine activities. Insidiously, then, these novels contribute to an understanding of education as desirable and masculine, but of schooling as constraining (but fine for young women).

By consistently prizing such narratives, book awards programs seem simultaneously to be endorsing the social values espoused by these texts and attempting to incorporate them into the very systems of cultural evaluation and education they are critiquing. It is as though by embedding stories of how constraining schooling is for young men, these books will help those same young men 'survive' the experience of school. The circularity of such gestures is the circularity of book awards in general: if books were *intrinsically* great, there would presumably be no need for awards; if hegemonic masculinity were *truly* achievable, it would not need continually to be (re)inscribed. Nonetheless, the hegemonic masculine remains the prized subjectivity of agency, autonomy, and authority.

Notes

1. This research was supported by the Australian Research Council under the Discovery Early Career Research Award (DECRA) scheme. My thanks to Amy Cross for her assistance in preparing this piece.
2. The CBCA positions itself as analogous to administering bodies of children's book awards in the United States, where the ALA administers the Newbery and Caldecott Medals (not to mention an array of other annual book awards for children's literature), and in the United Kingdom, where CILIP administers the Carnegie and Greenaway Medals. Crucially, however, the CBCA is *not* a professional body in any of the ways that ALA and CILIP both advocate for, and make accountable, library professionals in their respective countries. This is not to suggest that CBCA members are not experts or professionals in the field of children's literature, but to note that the CBCA Awards are not tied necessarily to a particular professional domain or context.
3. Table 3.1 shows that there has been some level of consensus between awards at the shortlisting stage, if not at the final prizing. Christopher's *Stolen* (2010) appears on the shortlists for all three awards, suggesting its appeal to the adult judges even though it was only the teen-choice judges who ultimately prized it.

4 How Award-Winning Children's Non-fiction Complicates Stereotypes

Joe Sutliff Sanders, Katlyn M. Avritt, Kynsey M. Creel, and Charlie C. Lynn

James Loewen has famously complained that children's textbooks frequently whitewash the sins of history in order to please school boards. The result, he argues, is a version of history that is too boring to be useful or even interesting. But textbooks are not the only non-fiction for children. *Trade* non-fiction routinely addresses topics such as exploitative child labor, sexist governmental policies, hate groups, the environmental impact of consumer capitalism, natural selection, and even sex. Further, the two major awards for non-fiction—the Orbis Pictus (established by the National Council of Teachers of English in 1989) and Robert F. Sibert (established by the American Library Association in 2001)—seem particularly interested in non-fiction that grapples with controversy. Indeed, in the years during which the field has enjoyed both the Orbis Pictus and the Sibert, roughly a third of the total awards have been given to books that focus extensively on the Civil Rights Movement and the Holocaust, historical moments filled with the sorts of villains that, Loewen argues, school boards hate to see.

The four authors of this chapter worked together to gain a broad overview of the villains in non-fiction about these periods and favored by these two awards, and what we found was both encouraging and disturbing. When award-winning non-fiction for children addresses these two events, it inherits a cast of characters whose identities are already familiar: white Americans of the 1950s and 1960s and Germans of the 1930s and 1940s play the role of villain (or at least the passive beneficiary of prejudice), and black Americans and European Jews play the role of victims, or, if they're lucky, heroes. Children's non-fiction that tends to win the two major American awards of the field frequently goes out of its way, though, to complicate those familiar roles. Specifically, these books very often humanize the people whom one would normally expect to see presented as monstrous. This chapter takes as its subject books that have focused on the Civil Rights Movement and Holocaust and that have been a medalist or an honor book for either award. We find that award-winning children's non-fiction shows a remarkable insistence that the villains—and for that matter, the heroes and victims, too—of these two historical periods are more complicated than one might expect.

Throughout this chapter, we will use the term "humanize" to talk about a specific psychological process signaled by traceable rhetorical patterns. We are drawing especially on a field, defined by Henri Tafjel and others, about how stereotypes work. That is to say, to use the terms favored by social psychologists, we are interested in how in-groups (the people making or maintaining the stereotypes) talk about out-groups (the people characterized by the stereotypes). In general, we read any rhetorical move that homogenizes the membership of an out-group as a move that dehumanizes the members of that group; by the same token, we regard contrary rhetorical moves, such as those that individualize members of the out-group from one another or provide what psychologists call "stereotype-inconsistent" information about members of the out-group, to be humanizing. The terms "humanize" and "dehumanize" are not widespread in psychological theories of stereotyping, but Daniel Bar-Tal's term "delegitimization" says much of what we see to be the dehumanizing work of stereotypes. He writes, "Delegitimization may be viewed as a denial of categorized group's humanity" (170). Bar-Tal's work is especially useful to us because he points to the use of stereotypes not just on victimized groups, but also groups of people who have come to be understood as oppressive: he lists as potential out-groups, for example, "Nazis, fascists, imperialists, colonialists, capitalists, and communists" (173).[1] From Bar-Tal's perspective, a perspective that informs our own study, an in-group need not be a small group of bigots—say, white supremacists—but might also be a majority group who maintain an uncomplicated view about another group—say, a modern America smugly satisfied with the superiority of its level of racial tolerance as compared to that of white society of the 1960s. In our essay, the in-group is generally the presumed audience of children's non-fiction: a vaguely liberal, inquisitive audience who can be counted on to assume that racial oppression is bad. The out-groups are sometimes monstrous villains, but they are also sometimes a broader white society that benefits from the passive hatred of which Nazis and members of the Klan are more visible actors. When many psychologists—including David J. Schneider (326–7), Amy S. Harasty (282), and Janet B. Ruscher (241)—explain stereotyping, they emphasize how in-groups "emphasize outgroup members' homogeneity" (Ruscher 244). Combining this consensus about stereotyping with Bar-Tal's notion of delegitimization provides a theoretical framework for looking at how award-winning children's non-fiction humanizes both the victims and the victimizers in stories of America's recent past.

Homogenizing the White Community of *Birmingham Sunday*

Winners of these two awards certainly do sometimes portray the oppressive classes in ways that avoid humanizing them, and the example of one book can demonstrate what such a portrait looks like. Larry Brimner's *Birmingham Sunday* (2010, Orbis Pictus Honor in 2011) recounts the story of the September 15, 1963 bombing that took the lives of four girls in a Birmingham church. The book makes clear that the violence perpetrated that day was not an isolated act of injustice, but part of a larger system of segregation that put the lives of black Americans in danger while benefiting the broader white community. Much of the power of the book comes from its careful, lingering accounts of the four girls, rendering them as sharply defined individuals whose loss is specific and human; as a result, the in-group position offered to readers of Brimner's book is one that accepts as tragic these girls' deaths.

Contrast with such humanization the portrait Brimner paints of Birmingham's white community. Brimner routinely presents Birmingham whites as an out-group, either avoiding complications in that group or declining to develop white characters who do not fit the larger mold. The effect is one that is probably inaccurate—surely there was some diversity of white opinion even in Birmingham in 1963—but, at least to some extent, politically satisfying. For example, Brimner tends to make generalizations about white southern citizens, grouping them together as being like-minded. He writes, for example, that "white southern politicians usually ran on campaign promises to uphold and enforce these Jim Crow laws ... [as] many white southerners were filled with fear, resentment and hatred" (9). Words such as "usually" and "many" imply a diversity of opinion within the white community, but Brimner avoids sharing the voices of dissent that would make the diversity tangible. Hints at white individuals who disagree with the status quo do appear elsewhere in the book, but Brimner avoids giving them the detail necessary to make them convincing counter-examples—the stereotype-inconsistent examples of which psychologists speak—to the overall narrative of white opposition to segregation. For example, when Brimner discusses the role of the Ku Klux Klan, he states that "patrols were usually enough to intimidate blacks—and any whites who supported them—into quiet submission" (9). Adding the white supporters between dashes recognizes the existence of white people who opposed segregation, but it fails to name them or in any other way convey them as solid individuals. He does this again when he says that although Fred Shuttleworth and his wife "were not attacked, a white supporter was beaten" (15): the white supporter is nameless, without history or any solid presence in the narrative. The historical events show diversity in white opinion, but when white people with divergent views appear on the page in *Birmingham Sunday*, they are not individuals, not developed with the same humanity that the black heroes and victims of segregation are developed. In these ways, *Birmingham Sunday* suppresses the sorts of complications that would humanize the white people of Birmingham, the out-group that benefits from the segregation that laid the ideological groundwork for the bombings.

And probably that is as it should be. After all, *most* of United States history is told as the story of white people as individuals, struggling against adversity and leaving behind a heroic history worth studying. The primary importance of what happened in Birmingham in September, 1963, is not what the bombings meant to white people, so perhaps it is ultimately to the good that the white community members portrayed in a book about the bombings are swept into a faceless, nearly homogeneous group. However, the fact that *Birmingham Sunday* stands out as an exception to the trend in award-winning non-fiction means that the question of when and how to humanize the people in children's non-fiction is a legitimate one. Given that, as *Birmingham Sunday* demonstrates, children's non-fiction doesn't *have* to humanize the white people, segregationists, and other members of the oppressive classes in scenes from the Civil Rights Movement and Holocaust, it is all the more remarkable that in general, non-fiction honored by these awards routinely does so.

Humanizing by Developing the Inner Worlds of Out-groups

The simplest method by which these books humanize the oppressive classes is providing glimpses into the thoughts of their individual members. This is a common trope in Susan Campbell Bartolletti's *Hitler Youth* (2005, an honor book for both awards in 2006), which, by taking young Nazis as its subject, frequently opens spaces for humanizing the oppressive group, a technique that would have been ill-suited to Brimner's book about the murdered victims of oppression. Bartoletti offers this example of a young Nazi: "He believed what his Nazi education had taught him: that the leader was always right and that Jews were the enemy of Germany. 'Why else would our government declare them to be non-Germans?'" (59) The conclusions of Bartoletti's character are of course abhorrent, but in tracing the thought processes of the individual, Bartoletti animates a very human decision-making process and complicates the homogeneity of the villainous group of Nazis. She offers these insights not as a means for justifying the groups' actions, but for individualizing a Nazi voice. She also communicates a less-familiar side of the war by explaining the emotions of Germans who suffered through Allied bombing raids. "We became very bitter," says one of Bartoletti's Nazis about the bombing of cities, going on to confide that "Bombs were dropped on the helpless civilian population. Residential areas were their sole targets" (87–8). As the book continues, Bartoletti further complicates the homogenization of the Germans as a group by highlighting their differing levels of complicity and even knowledge. "It's hard to know how many Hitler Youth were aware of the atrocities being committed in the concentration camps," Bartoletti explains. "It is known that the news reached home. Yet many German people dismissed the stories as too horrible to be true. They did not believe that Jews were being mistreated" (101). By letting outsiders into the minds of the "villains," the disharmony between individuals complicates the group as a whole and begins to fracture the group identity that overwrites the individual subjectivity of the Nazis.

Besides showing the inner ideas and observations of the villainous group, humanization also increases when differences in opinion cause disagreement within the group. In Cynthia Levinson's chapter "Views from the Other Side" from her book *We've Got a Job* (2012, Orbis Pictus Honor in 2013), about children's marches in Birmingham, a sidebar provides several quotations from white residents of Birmingham. These quotations show a variety of opinions ranging from pro-segregationist to sympathetic toward civil rights. For example, one quotation reads, "We've got to accept integration. Not that I want to but it's here." The sentiment here is resigned, and its ideas are familiar: change is coming, and I don't like it, but I'm tired of fighting. Another quotation is more mixed: "You can't blame the Negro for what they are trying to do. Sooner or later they are going to win, but they aren't going to school with my children." This quotation again features resignation, although it also includes a note of dedication to continuing prejudice, anticipating the white flight that often follows integration. But the most sympathetic view comes from an anonymous school teacher who says,

> All these years ... there should have been social exchange between colored and white children ... To me the solution is very simple: just treat human beings as human beings. But to many of these people Negroes are not human beings. Please do not use my name ... if you do I will lose my job.
>
> (96)

The sentiment of this quotation is surprising in the context of the rest of the story, as a member of the oppressive class voices actual support for integration. Indeed, this quotation goes so far as to claim that integration springs from a common sense, humane philosophy. It closes by highlighting the danger the speaker faces her- or himself, painting this member of the out-group as threatened by segregationists in ways reminiscent of the dangers faced by black southerners.

These three quotations, displayed alongside each other in the sidebar, complicate the homogenized group, but the space in which they do so carries conflicting messages. Is it more important that the voices are placed immediately next to each other (emphasizing the conflict between them) or that they are in a space that is literally marginalized (the sidebar)? Providing conflicting ideas from the members of the group humanizes that group by rendering them heterogeneous; does doing so in a sidebar imply a reluctance to let that complexity into the main narrative? There isn't really any way to know. Still, as we read this book in the larger context of the pattern of humanizing the oppressive class, we realized that the ambiguity of a sidebar that marginalizes the humanization of these Birmingham whites mirrored our own ambivalence over how to treat these white voices in a story that, we felt, ought to be about black voices.

Elsewhere, both *Hitler Youth* and *We've Got a Job* develop further the pattern of complicating members of the oppressive group by showing diverse opinions, in these cases by showcasing examples of children challenging their parents' political beliefs. Bartoletti, for example, shows how one young girl "couldn't understand why her parents didn't support a great man like Adolf Hitler, who said that a person's money and titles didn't matter. All that mattered was whether a person contributed to the well-being of the people" (6). Elsewhere, Bartoletti provides the example of Henry Metelmann: "I was prepared to struggle for, to kill, and, if necessary, to die for my Fuehrer and country," he says. "While my parents worried about the threatening clouds of war, I believed my Hitler Youth teaching that war was a necessary cleansing process for the human race" (73). The opinions the children hold in Bartoletti's book are awful, and the book makes no attempt to make them more palatable, but the conflict between child and parent over the ideas forces the point that the ideas were not natural or indigenous to wartime Germans. *We've Got a Job* portrays a similar conflict, but in this case the children hold the more attractive position. When white students such as Charles Entrekin and Pam Walbert entered college and were exposed to a different set of mores while studying alongside black students, they became aware of a reality in which their parents' racism could not hold. Levinson writes how "Charles 'woke up' in college and then had a 'tremendous fight' with his father who called him a traitor to his race and threw him out of the house" (98). Walbert describes her realization of her parents' racism and the false stereotypes of blacks, saying, "It's like finding out everyone you ever loved or respected had lied to you" (98). These instances of children developing different opinions from those of their parents show individual emotional responses and conflict within both the children themselves and their families, further humanizing the group of oppressive people. This strategy is part of the larger strategy used by award-winning works of children's non-fiction: complicating the homogeneous portrait of members of the non-minority groups.

Humanizing through Positive Examples

These books also go out of their way to present members of the oppressive classes who are actively good, thereby providing stereotype-inconsistent examples that frustrate an easy classification of those who benefited from oppression. Take for example Russell Freedman's book about the Montgomery, Alabama marches, *Freedom Walkers* (2006, Orbis Pictus Honor in 2007). Freedman makes a point of noting the work of white southerners who were especially positioned to benefit from segregation but acted instead with kindness. Freedman quotes Jo Ann Robison, who was a black passenger on the buses and who said that "There were some fine, courteous bus drivers who were kindly disposed and carried out the laws of segregation without offending the riders" (9). Freedman also supplies more glimpses of white support of black boycotters: "Sympathetic whites, both men and women, stopped and picked up pedestrians. Young white drivers would stop and allow walkers to 'pile in'" (55–6). And Juliette Morgan, a white librarian, wrote the *Montgomery Advertiser* to say,

> It is hard to imagine a soul so dead, a heart so hard, a vision so blinded and provincial as not to be moved with admiration at the quiet dignity, discipline, and dedication with which the Negroes have conducted their boycott [...]. One feels that history is being made in Montgomery these days.
>
> (quoted in Freedman 56)

These examples show the complicated nature of race politics in the Jim Crow South and imply that skin color alone is not enough to categorize friend or enemy.

John Fleischman's *Black and White Airmen* (2007, Orbis Pictus Honor in 2008) also features several examples of white individuals standing up for the rights of African-Americans in the United States military. This book relates the story of two World War II pilots—one the Tuskegee Airman John Leahr, the other Herb Heilbrun, a Caucasian bomber pilot—and depicts the rigid segregation of the armed forces as well as the fight against it. Leahr and other black service members faced segregation in military units and training as well as exclusion from many choice military jobs, yet Fleischman breaks away from his central narrative of the problems of segregation to convey several instances of white servicemen standing up for the rights of black servicemen. For example, Colonel Noel F. Parrish, a native southerner, was the Tuskegee program's commanding officer. He originally felt that segregation was "part of the natural social order," a belief shared by many at the time who felt that segregation was not really something to question or even consider (85). But Parrish eventually came to believe that "there can be no consistent segregation policy because segregation is itself inconsistent and contradictory ... a segregated outfit always has a phony feel about it" (85). Fleischman uses Parrish's change in personal philosophies to complicate the oppressive white male position in the segregated military. Fleischman elsewhere records how many other white individuals also took a stereotype-inconsistent stance in response to a "mutiny" of 101 black officers refusing to sign a formal order forbidding them from entering the white officers' club. The black officers were taken into custody, but "eventually, cooler heads prevailed" when "twelve senators, four congressmen, the White House, and a young black lawyer for the NAACP named Thurgood Marshall came to the defense of the mutineers" (130). The combination of black and white champions of these black officers shows the blurred lines between the two groups, demonstrating that the views and stances on segregation were significantly varied, with the actions of some spotlighted members of the non-minority group acting in support of the group against which most other white people discriminated.

Other award-winning works of children's non-fiction also make a point of portraying exceptional members of the oppressive class who fight alongside members of the minority groups. Ann Bausum's *Freedom Riders* (2006, Sibert Honor in 2007), for example, follows the stories of John Lewis, a black southerner, and Jim Zwerg, a white man, as they travel through the country on the freedom rides testing local compliance with the Supreme Court's ruling that intrastate buses could not be segregated. Bausum focuses on Zwerg but indicates that he was only one white member of the rides. She animates his inner feelings about the freedom rides, explaining that Zwerg wrote in his journal that he expected "jail, extreme violence, or death" (44). By conveying Zwerg's anticipation of such a bleak outcome, Bausum makes Zwerg, a white male, not only an individual, but a highly sympathetic one, serving to humanize the white population through him. She also points out that white participants of civil rights protests, including the freedom rides, tended to receive the most extreme beatings and were specifically targeted as "nigger lovers," which furthers the complication of the white male character type by encouraging readers to empathize with and feel compassion for these whites (32). Bausum points to one momentous example of such a beating. After a riot in Montgomery, Zwerg was beaten until unconscious, and from the hospital, he released a televised statement that "segregation must be stopped ... We'll take a hitting. We'll take beating. We're willing to accept death" (51). Bausum argues that Zwerg's televised statement served as a "clarion cry for action," and that as a result, people across the country "dropped what they were doing and headed off to join the Freedom Rides. Black and white, young and old, students, professors, members of the clergy, rabbis, Quakers, Northerners and Southerners, males and females alike" joined the protests (53). Zwerg is not just an individual with clear opinions and even fears, not even just heroic, but a centerpiece around which cooperative opposition to segregation formed and expanded. Therefore, Bausum's account of his participation in the freedom rides works to fracture stereotypes of white people as unilaterally opposed to segregation.

As we explored this pattern, we again found ourselves torn. The selection of these stories complicates totalizing conceptions of identity, but does it also unfairly amplify or even exaggerate the role of remarkable but very special exceptions? What does the emotional warmth that these books hold for these stereotype-inconsistent members of the empowered group ask of its readers? What, in short, is the work of breaking up stereotypes of groups that have already enjoyed enormous privileges?

Humanizing through Sentimentality

The partnership between white and black integrationists is given with particular warmth in Ruby Bridges' *Through My Eyes* (1999, Orbis Pictus

Medalist in 2000). Bridges' book is an autobiographical account of her struggle as the first black student at the William Frantz Elementary School in New Orleans. When she began attending, the majority of white parents withdrew their children from the school. Still, Bridges points out that "a few families took the risk" (26). Bridges uses "risk" here, again showing that these white individuals were aware of the dangerous situation into which they were entering. Since it is an autobiographical account, Ruby's use of "risk" also shows that she sympathized with and felt gratitude toward these families, even if, as the rest of the book accurately conveys, her personal risks were greater. The use of "families" rather than "parents" also implies that the effort to end segregation was being spread throughout generations, with children being educated on the injustice of the system. She gives the example of Pam Foreman, the daughter of a Methodist minister who felt that "integration was morally and spiritually right" (26). He walked his daughter to and from school every day, and Bridges recalls that he was taunted "without mercy" outside the school (26). Ruby shows Foreman and his family, like Zwerg and other white participants of the freedom rides, accepting abuse despite the lack of any personal gain that Foreman would have acquired if integration were completely accepted. This serves to complicate the oppressive class, as she shows three types of white families: those who opposed integration, those who did not oppose it but still refused out of fear to send their children to school with Ruby, and those similar to the Foreman family, who took the risk despite threats and personal violence.

Bridges also challenges the stereotype of white people in the south in her portrayal of her teacher, Barbara Henry. As a result of the segregationist policies of the school administrators and the great majority of the parents, Bridges was the only student in Henry's class. Still, Bridges felt it was "fun and felt sort of special. [Henry] was more like my best friend than just an ordinary teacher. She was a loving person, and I knew she cared about me" (40). Bridges' warm description of her teacher and their relationship paints their connection as personal, almost domestic. Henry was a native northerner, and her class with Bridges was her first at William Frantz, but Bridges reports that Henry felt just as deep a bond as did her young pupil. "I grew to love Ruby and to be awed by her," Henry said. "It was an ugly world outside, but I tried to make our world together as normal as possible" (23). Both Bridges and Henry use the word "love," which brings a new motivation for the white characters of these books who fought for civil rights. While most other white characters who joined the battle for equal rights did so for moral reasons, Henry's seem to be both moral and emotional. Henry's sentiment for Bridges is further shown when she moves back to Boston after Bridges' first year, as she recalls that "for years I thought about Ruby. I have one teeny photo of her, with her front teeth missing, and I guarded it my whole life" (52). Henry says that she "guards" this picture, demonstrating the intense bond that stretched across barriers, even she taking on something of a maternal quality. By Bridges' second year, the protests had stopped and Bridges was able to join an actual classroom with both black and white students. While the harsh protests during Bridges' first year at William Frantz depict a villainous characterization of whites, people like Barbara Henry and Lloyd Foreman destabilize the split between in-group and out-group during this period of the fight for civil rights.

One white person in particular garners a surprising amount of attention across award-winning children's non-fiction: Eleanor Roosevelt. As with Bridges' teacher, Roosevelt takes on a decidedly sentimental role. Bridges herself makes special note of a letter of encouragement sent by Roosevelt. "We received stacks of encouraging cards and letters," Bridges recalls. "Even Eleanor Roosevelt wrote me a note. She was the widow of Franklin Roosevelt, the former president of the United States. Mrs. Roosevelt's note was my mother's favorite, and she looked at it again and again" (37). Bridges' narrative carries tones that echo in many similar accounts in other books about civil rights. This quotation labels Roosevelt's position as the widow of the president, and the word "even" further emphasizes how the Bridges family perceived Roosevelt's gesture as extraordinary because of Roosevelt's lofty status. Yet more significant is the extreme fondness Roosevelt's gesture elicits. Not only is the note a favorite, but the former first lady takes on a tinge of sentimentality as the author of the note that became the favorite of Bridges' *mother*, who "looked at it again and again." Eleanor Roosevelt figures as a woman highly placed in the structures of American privilege at the same time as she is someone on whom the oppressed people in the narrative look with profound fondness. Fleischman paints a similar picture of Roosevelt in his history of the segregated American flying forces. Although black pilots were routinely held to be inferior, Fleischman recounts a story in which the first lady visited the training fields at Tuskegee and, much to the dismay of her guard detail, gave the black instructor, C. Alfred "Chief" Anderson, an opportunity to prove the rumors false. "I always heard that Negroes couldn't fly," Mrs. Roosevelt said to Anderson. "I wondered if you'd mind taking me up" (62). Fleischman reports Roosevelt's words with contractions, implying an easiness and personality that show Roosevelt inviting familiarity with the black instructor. When Anderson replies, as Fleischman puts it, that he would be "delighted," the book provides another example of a member of the oppressed class whom Roosevelt has charmed through her evidently ingenuous display of kindness. And her personal connection with these members of the oppressed groups again portrays her as an ally, fighting against prejudice with black people who suffered from discrimination at the hands of a system that routinely benefited the first lady.

Roosevelt's sentimental portrait is further advanced in two award-winning books about the great vocalist Marian Anderson. Pam Muñoz Ryan's picture book *When Marian Sang* (2002, Orbis Pictus Medalist and Sibert Honor in 2003), for example, tells of how Anderson, who had developed an international reputation but struggled to build a career in America because she was black, was denied permission to sing at Constitution Hall, the grand venue managed by the Daughters of the American Revolution (DAR), of which Roosevelt was a member. "Enraged fans wrote letters to the newspaper," Ryan explains of the reaction to the DAR's decision. "In protest, Eleanor Roosevelt, the first lady of the United States, resigned from the organization that sponsored Constitution Hall" (n.p.). Again, the prose focuses on Roosevelt's powerful position. Here, the text does not linger over Roosevelt's kindness, but that might be because Ryan's book is a picture book and has fewer words to spare over secondary characters. Russell Freedman's biography of Anderson, on the other hand, repeatedly showcases Roosevelt's kindness. Freedman, much like Bridges, links Roosevelt's kindness to a mother figure, in this case, Anderson's mother, Anna. The first lady, Freedman explains, asked Anderson to perform at the White House and specifically to bring her mother along. Freedman tells the story from the viewpoint of Anderson's accompanist, Kosti Vehanen:

> After Marian's recital, the first lady took Anna Anderson by the hand and led her over to meet the president. "I shall never forget seeing these two ladies enter the room," Vehanen wrote. "Mrs. Roosevelt's manner was sure and free, as becomes a woman of the world, happy to welcome the mother of America's best-known singer. In all of Mrs. Anderson's being, there was evident the feeling that this was one of the greatest moments in her life. Her face reflected her gratitude and the pride she felt."
>
> (45)

Freedman later writes that Roosevelt "had worked tirelessly since coming to Washington to promote racial equality" and points to an incident in 1939 when she used her position to thwart segregationist rules at an auditorium in Alabama (54). Elsewhere, in detailing Anderson's historic concert on the Washington Mall, Freedman notes that "The first name among the prominent sponsors listed in the program [for Anderson's legendary outdoor concert] was 'Mrs. Franklin D. Roosevelt,'" but the first lady was not in fact in attendance. "As the most famous, and controversial, woman in America," he explains, "she did not want to draw attention to herself and upstage Marian Anderson" (63). Eleanor Roosevelt's appearances in these books give examples of how award-winning children's non-fiction humanizes white people, even those who most benefited from a society grounded in segregation, in narratives that might otherwise find it easy to vilify them. Despite counter-examples such as the Daughters of the American Revolution, who remain faceless and pointlessly stubborn in their refusal to let Anderson sing at Constitution Hall, Roosevelt is a figure who links white privilege with kindness, power with activism on the behalf of the oppressed.

Eleanor Roosevelt and Barbara Henry are important individual stereotype-inconsistent examples because of their sentimental partnership with black Americans, but they and the other examples, when taken as a whole, also serve another important role in humanizing white communities. Ruscher has argued that stereotypes tend to emphasize "group-level rather than individual-level descriptions" (256), and thus, any focus on specific individuals has the potential to disrupt stereotypes. However, Miles Hewstone argues that research indicates that the in-group must see those individuals as common, even typical, for them to be effective counter-examples. He argues that "the most effective strategy" for disrupting stereotypes "is to link disconfirming information explicitly to (proto)typical outgroup exemplars and to disperse that information across multiple outgroup members" (210). It can hardly be argued that Roosevelt, Henry, Zwerg, and the other stereotype-inconsistent examples of these books succeed in portraying white people as *typically* inclined toward partnering with oppressed minorities, but the proliferation of such figures across the field of children's non-fiction might fit the strategy of which Hewstone writes. It is for this reason that the pattern of individual white people who do not fit the stereotype is important *as a trait of award-winning* books. According to psychological research, presenting a stereotype-inconsistent example that the in-group (vaguely liberal, inquisitive readers who can be counted on to see racial oppression as a bad thing) perceives as too individual, too specific can lead to a further hardening of stereotypes as the in-group reconfigures its stereotype to account for exceptions that, as it were, prove the rule. But because children's non-fiction that wins awards—and thus is more likely to be bought, discussed, and taught—provides so many of these individual stereotype-inconsistent examples, it has the potential to reach a critical mass, to demonstrate that the outgroup cannot accurately be characterized as fitting the existing stereotype.

Humanizing the Heroes and Victims

As counterintuitive as it might be to include efforts to humanize members of the oppressive class, though, award-winning children's non-fiction frequently goes a step further, also complicating the roles of hero and victim typically assigned to members of oppressed groups. Two examples can be found in *Terezin: Voices from the Holocaust*, by Ruth Thomson (2011, Orbis Pictus Honor in 2012). In this text the Nazis are the obvious villains, Jews the obvious victims, and the in-group position the book offers is likely to be one aligned with the Jews, but *Terezin* complicates the stereotype of Jews as victims by noting places where Jews were complicit in their own oppression. For example, Thomson explains that "The Nazis appointed a Jewish Council of Elders to run life in Theresienstadt" (18). This council became the group that had to pick who would be sent to the camps. Thomson does not paint the elders as villains, but their role as victims is complicated by the tragic, collusive authority given to them. "The Elders," Thomson writes, "had to make up the transports of people, not the Germans" (30). The fact that the elders were responsible for transports of their own people severely complicates how this one particular group of oppressed people is portrayed, destabilizing the easy "us–them" dichotomy that underwrites stereotyping. Similarly, in *Surviving Hitler* (2001, Sibert Honor in 2002), Andrea Warren discusses the guards, referred to as "kapos," who helped run the camps. Warren writes, "The kapos were another story. All of them were prisoners, some Jewish" (63). Warren first introduces the "kapos" not as guards, but as prisoners. This alerts the reader first that they were the fellow prisoners of the people they guarded. Still, "The kapos in the different barracks had special privileges and could steal food before it reached the prisoners" (64). By showing that these prisoners were corrupt and hurt the other prisoners, Warren further complicates the image of the Nazis' victims.

One book in particular uses the same strategy to complicate integrationists of the civil rights movement: *Claudette Colvin* (2009, Sibert Honor in 2010), Phillip Hoose's story of a teenage girl who refused to leave her seat on a Montgomery bus long before Rosa Parks' famous act. But instead of rallying around her, many members of the black community in Montgomery turned against Colvin: "the attention was directed in the wrong way," he explains. "Kids were saying she should have known that would happen, that she should have got up from her seat" (51). In this case, the book presents a diverse view of the African-American community, one that is not commonly seen in civil rights stories. Hoose not only presents the community's reaction as wrong, but quotes one of Colvin's black classmates as later confessing that "We should have been rallying around her and being proud of what she had done, but instead we ridiculed her" (51). Such self-reflection further complicates how we are asked to interpret her peers, and the use of first-person point of view from a character other than Colvin adds a solidity to the portrait of a community member who worked against the tale's heroine. And neither were Colvin's peers the only members of the black community who failed to support Colvin: Hoose also singles out the NAACP. When Parks, after Colvin had already been arrested and tried, refused to give up her seat on a bus, the NAACP decided to use Parks instead of Colvin as the centerpiece of their bus boycott. Naturally, Parks' story is a triumph of the civil rights movement and one of the most significant victories of social justice in American history, but Hoose also emphasizes the betrayal his own heroine perceived. "I felt left out," he quotes Colvin as explaining. "I was thinking, Hey, I did that months ago and everybody dropped me" (61). Including Colvin's thoughts, her pain, and her perception that the community as a whole abandoned her, strikes a discordant note with the rest of the story of the Montgomery bus boycott, complicating the otherwise homogeneous tale of victimization of the black community.

Conclusion

On the whole, we find this trend in award-winning children's non-fiction positive, but we recognize (indeed, we've raised amongst ourselves) likely objections to it. From our perspective, books that argue against the homogenization of political, racial, and social groups into heroes and villains, victims and victimizers are increasingly important in a time when the trend of popular discourse seems to be toward pleasing entrenched opinion bases. A more negative—but, we must recognize, legitimate—perception of this pattern in children's non-fiction is that these versions of history, often told from the perspective of the oppressed, have been politically diluted through the inclusion of examples of good members of the oppressive classes. Considering the battles still being fought over whose history is told and whose history is obscured, it is possible to interpret this trend in award-winning children's non-fiction as regressive. Even more pessimistically, it is possible to interpret the trend as motivated by nothing more noble than sales. After all, the majority of the money spent on children's books comes from white pockets (and public pockets managed by white-friendly policies). Perhaps non-fiction's tendency to tell stories in which oppressive groups are humanized is at heart nothing more than an appeal for greater sales among sensitive members of those groups.

However, there might be a redeeming quality to the humanizing strategies of award-winning children's non-fiction even if those strategies have only base motivations, and again, Bar-Tal's work on delegitimization is key to understanding that quality. His essay examines not just how in-groups delegitimize out-groups, but also why, and he concludes that one of the main reasons in-groups work so hard to maintain homogenized views of out-groups is that doing so helps maintain "uniformity" within the in-group itself. He points out that groups tend to form because the members of the group have similar ideas, including ideas *about other groups.* When members of an in-group begin to think differently, of course, the life of the in-group is threatened. Therefore, not only do stereotypes work to homogenize the members of out-groups, but they also work to homogenize the members of the in-group, "to create," as Bar-Tal puts it, "uniformity of beliefs, attitudes, and behaviors." To some extent, the danger of such a process is minimal: in-groups can identify a certain behavior and the people who commonly engage in that behavior as monstrous, and if that behavior includes oppression of other human beings, on the whole, social justice is probably the winner. However, Bar-Tal also argues that in-groups use delegitimization, what we have called dehumanization, as a way to police the thoughts of the members of the in-group, to diminish "the possibility of considering alternative beliefs." "Since members of the delegitimizing group seek to receive positive rewards and to avoid negative sanctions," Bar-Tal finds, "they often conform to the group's pressure" (178).

It's possible, then, that whatever the motivations of award-winning children's non-fiction that makes a point of humanizing groups of people who have already enjoyed privilege, the result of humanizing these out-groups is also to prompt the possibility of, to fuse a notion from psychology with a notion from Bakhtin, a more dialogical in-group. By humanizing history's monsters, heroes, and victims, children's non-fiction might be able to foster an atmosphere in which more alternative beliefs can be considered.

Note

1. Bar-Tal does not use the term "out-group." Rather, he calls such groups "political groups which are considered totally unaccepted by the members of the delegitimizing society" (173).

5   The Last Bastion of Aesthetics?

Formalism and the Rhetoric of Excellence in Children's Literary Awards

Robert Bittner and Michelle Superle

One of the challenges that complicates prizing in children's literature is the breadth of our professional field. The work of children's literature occurs in classrooms, libraries, bookstores, garrets, corporate corner offices, and the ivory tower—to name but a few of the main locales. Teachers, librarians, book buyers, writers, editors, academics, and reviewers—not to mention children themselves—all approach children's literature in unique ways. While some of the aforementioned parties share methodologies at times, the often substantially different theoretical lenses used by various groups affect their beliefs about the value and purpose of children's literature. These differences can affect prizing, especially when a jury is composed of members from a single group. Children's choice awards, infamous for celebrating animal stories and joke books, are an obvious example. Perhaps a more telling case is Canada's prestigious Governor General's award: the "Children's Literature, Text" category is judged by children's writers, and the winning books are renowned for their edgy, innovative, boundary-pushing qualities. The Newbery Medal, on the other hand, is administered by the American Library Association (ALA), juried primarily by librarians, and often comes under fire for winners' lack of diversity in gender, class, and race.

We have observed such disciplinary and theoretical tensions in our experience as judges of several major and minor awards: Robert has served on the Michael L. Printz Award, the Newbery Medal, the Stonewall Award, and the Sheila A. Egoff Award committees, as well as on the TD Canadian Children's Literature Award; Michelle has served twice on both the TD Canadian Children's Literature Award and the George Ryga Award for Social Awareness in Literature. As literary scholars with theoretical training, we arrived at jury meetings armed with our usual arsenal of broad, complex critical criteria, ready to proceed with the business of analyzing and evaluating children's books as usual (Michelle is a feminist scholar trained in post-colonial literary theory and currently developing a child-centered critical approach to children's literature; Robert specializes in queer, trans, and gender theories). However, we were surprised by the different rules we would be required to follow in the jury box—rules that seemed inexplicably old-fashioned to us. There was no place to deploy our customary theoretical arsenal; instead, we were restricted to looking for "excellence" by reverting more than a generation of scholarship back to strictly formalist criticism.

While we do not intend, here, to join the chorus of voices denouncing the prize winners per se (and we are proud to stand behind the winners and finalists selected for each of the prizes we helped to judge), we do question the processes involved in prizing. We contend that selection processes, particularly those related to defining the criteria used to identify both jury members and winning texts, must be updated to reflect the diversity that has become a shared value across sub-disciplinary groups in children's literature. We recognize that prizing has historically been an elitist endeavor separate from quotidian proceedings in the field and understand that its very purpose is to elevate "greatness," but we suggest that greatness must be redefined—or rather, defined.

The primary criterion for identifying prize winners in many major awards—"excellence"—seems to invite the application of formalist modes of literary criticism that divorce themselves from biographical, political, and sociological considerations, focusing instead on observable elements within works of literature. Such approaches were prevalent in the mid-twentieth century, when New Criticism dominated North American literature classrooms. According to this evaluation system, meritorious works are defined by their aesthetic qualities: they display a complex relationship between content and form and exhibit unity among parts of the whole. But since the canon wars and the rise of cultural materialism in the 1980s, such values have been widely transformed in literary analysis and criticism through ideological considerations related to gender, race, class, and other social variables. While some techniques of formalism, especially close reading, are widely used and remain useful, strictly formalist approaches have been augmented—and in our opinion, improved upon—through the development and application of newer theoretical approaches. These various approaches, especially feminist, queer, and post-colonial literary theories, place less emphasis on aesthetics in favor of discussing politicized, ideologically driven elements of texts such as access to press, use of voice, and issues of representation—to name but a few of the award criteria we have tried to engage with in our own prizing work.

These more politicized values are also powerful forces in the wider examination and assessment of children's literature, particularly in its classroom application today, where issues of multiculturalism and social justice are paramount concerns. Even so, some children's literature scholars have noted skeptically that aesthetics deserve their hard-won place. For example, Kenneth Kidd asks, "Will our emergent interest in children's culture be indulged at the expense of the literary tradition we [children's literature enthusiasts] have worked so hard to champion?" ("Children's Culture" 146). We recognize the importance of the literature itself and the formalist components involved (analysis of structure, form, tone, unity, and imagery, among other literary devices); however, we argue that a critical preoccupation with both aesthetics and ideology is not mutually exclusive. As Heather Dubrow points out in the Foreword to *New Formalisms and Literary Theory*, formalist modes of literary criticism are not "apolitical," nor need they be understood as incompatible with "materialist agendas" (xiii). Along with Verena Theile in the same volume's Introduction, we begin with "an emphatic acknowledgement that there is no such thing as historicity or interpretation without form and aesthetics" (8). We suggest that attempts to separate children's literature from the ever-evolving culture surrounding children would be of great detriment to discussions occurring within the existing structure of many children's literature prizes. We question, therefore, why gender, race, class, and other social variables aren't given the importance in the arena of prizing that they are in other areas of children's literature.

We believe that such misaligned values in the field are problematic, particularly given the plethora of complex, interconnected ways in which prizing is bound up with avenues of promotion, distribution, criticism, and application in classrooms and libraries. As Kidd points out, both prizing and censorship of children's literature "clarif[y] what is and isn't legitimate in a culture" ("Not Censorship but Selection" 198) and need "to be understood not as an isolated action or singular event but rather as part of a complex set of exchanges and leverages within the cultural field" (199). Ignorance of these nuances resulting in a too-ready faith bestowed by the general children's literature community upon the prizing process (trusting small panels of experts to objectively identify the year's best offerings) is alarming. While blind acceptance, along with celebration and widespread elevation of winners into prominence, are commonplace practices, enough dissenting voices cry out with skepticism (in both formal scholarly publications and informal blogs) with the process to highlight dissatisfaction.

In a discussion of the John Newbery Medal and public response to its winners, Kidd suggests that this prestigious award "has come to embody our ambivalence about distinction in the wake of progressive social movements, canon reform, and widespread faith that literature, especially that for children, should be an equal opportunity employer" ("Prizing Children's Literature" 169). Kidd demonstrates how the historical foundations of one of the oldest children's literature awards are at odds with contemporary values, and he thoroughly discusses the ways complaints about the award tend to focus on the dissatisfying end results of the process—particularly winners that fail to reflect the diversity now prioritized in children's literature scholarship and publishing. But it is also important to understand the ways the process itself is often seen as outdated, elitist, and guilty of promoting a more limited, traditionalist value system—one which ignores the new and necessary ideological components discussed earlier—that "link[s] texts to a tradition of merit" (169). Pushback tends to be discussed "on the grounds that it [the Newbery] doesn't ... sufficiently promote the common good, or that its ideology of distinction is incompatible with a democratic program of literary citizenship" (169). It seems clear, then, that only by updating prizing processes can children's literature awards align with current values in related scholarly and critical fields.

But before moving on to strategies for updating prizing processes within a more contemporary context, it is important to identify the problematic elements contributing to outcomes often met with skepticism, such as that major prizes like the Newbery have "slowly and inadequately adapted to social change" (Kidd, "Prizing Children's Literature" 182). In the following arguments, we show that while our assertions echo some of Kidd's, the same questions and concerns he highlighted still remain unaddressed years later. A foundational issue at the root of the problem is that major children's book prizes in North America, such as the John Newbery Medal in the United States and the TD Canadian Children's Literature Award in Canada, rely on a sort of circular logic to establish winners because they fail—often intentionally—to define, specifically and objectively, terms of evaluation. The authors became aware of this surprising omission through our experiences as judges of children's literature prizes. These experiences propel us to explore the absences we have observed of various forms of ideological and aesthetic evaluation—particularly feminism, gender studies, queer theory, and a recognized "child-centered" value system. In particular, we are concerned that such approaches seem generally reserved for awards with particular social or political leanings. Our frustrations have inspired us to ask: if more contemporary, politicized criteria are being used to judge literary merit in various areas of literary scholarship, including classrooms, syllabi, and professional publications, then why is it so difficult to bring these values to prizing processes? And why are they more acceptable in awards defined by a "social or political vision"?

Criteria for assessment are significant contributing factors in the disconnect we have identified. Many prizes select winning books for their "excellence," yet that term is defined nowhere in supplementary materials provided to judges, nor is it clearly and specifically defined in disciplinary handbooks. This vagueness might seem to create space for any interpretation of excellence, but what we observed in practice was a privileging of formalist values related to unity among literary elements rather than broader socio-political considerations. And when we looked to various sources of expertise in the field, we found little help: well-known, frequently used texts that examine literary criteria and textual criticism, such as *From Cover to Cover* (Horning, 2010) and *Keywords for Children's Literature* (Nel and Paul, 2011) contain no definitions of "excellence" or "distinguished" in relation to literary merit. And this is despite the goal of *Keywords*, for example, to "respond to the need for a shared vocabulary by mapping the history of key terms and explaining how they came to be used in conflicted ways" through clarification of words with "blurred" meanings that confuse "cross-disciplinary conversations" (Nel and Paul 1). Perhaps it is understandable that literary excellence—a seemingly straightforward concept—stand aside to leave room for heavy hitters such as "Race," "Class," "Gender," "Queer," "Censorship," "Childhood," and other important terms explored in *Keywords*, that complicate evaluation and analysis of children's literature. These and other keywords point to this authoritative text's preoccupation with materialism, which is explored in the volume through the lenses of various literary theories and thus reflects current children's literature scholarship as it is practiced by some of our most respected thinkers. But there is, perhaps, an implication by omission that those involved in the assessment and scholarship of children's literature seem to possess a shared, apparently intuitive understanding of excellence.

Joseph Thomas, in his "Aesthetics" chapter in *Keywords*, addresses this issue, reminding readers that "the discipline of children's literature was shaped in a theoretical milieu suspicious of objective claims of aesthetic value" (5). He notes that "[t]he tendency in the discipline of children's literature to avoid aesthetics can also be traced to traditional aesthetics' rather limited focus—its inclination to concern itself with 'fine art' to the exclusion of the 'popular' [...]" (7). Thomas also points out that abandonment of New Critical approaches to literary analysis allowed children's literature to become "a space for literary study in the first place" (8). And while this is important to acknowledge in light of children's literature studies as a discipline, it is equally important to recognize that the opposite seems to be true in the realm of children's literature prizes, where aesthetics and New Critical values are favored.

Unlike "aesthetics" and other keywords noted above, "excellence" remains undefined in mainstays for literary scholars, such as the *International Encyclopedia of Children's Literature* (Hunt 1996), the *Oxford Encyclopedia of Children's Literature* (Zipes 2006), or *A Glossary of Literary Terms* (Abrams 2008). Similarly, the seemingly obvious concept of "excellence" receives no specific attention in various works designed to help parents, librarians, and teachers with their work, such as *The New Republic of Childhood* (Egoff and Saltman 1990), *A Guide to Canadian Children's Books* (Baker and Setterington 2003), or *Children's Literature in the Elementary School* (Huck 2003). At best, assessment criteria are described in terms similar to these: "High literary quality has been the determining feature in our first round of selection. What do we mean by high literary quality? Usually, we experience stories through four elements—style, character, plot, and setting" (Baker and Setterington 3). Tellingly, though, Baker and Setterington acknowledge the limitations of their formalist approach and justify their exceptions, which seem to be based on materialist considerations:

> We have also included many stories that have some, but not all, of the outstanding literary and artistic qualities outlined above. These are works that seem to be particularly useful and successful in exploring certain issues or in meeting the needs of certain kinds of readers [...]

they are certainly enriching and can often lead a child into reading stories of greater depth and intellectual nourishment.

(5)

One notable exception to this disciplinary silence occurs in *The University in Ruins* (1996) by Bill Readings, which offers a thorough critique of "excellence." Although his argument refers broadly to academia, his analysis of the term itself can be applied here. Readings argues that "excellence" is difficult to use as a criterion "because excellence is not a fixed standard of judgment but a qualifier whose meaning is fixed in relation to something else" (24). This subjectivity in relation to "excellence" translates to the world of prizing and is what caused us to examine the issue in the first place. Joseph Thomas and Michael Joseph's "Apologia" for *The Lion and the Unicorn* Award for Excellence in North American Poetry provides a telling example of this phenomenon (Chapter 13, this volume). The authors avoid spelling out a definitive description of excellence while relying on circular logic that insists "[e]xcellence is excellence, whether we are talking Mozart or The Slits, Jack Kirby or Rembrandt, Shel Silverstein or Marilyn Nelson" (183). They do, however, admit the shortcomings of a criterion lacking objectivity by conceding that

> prizing involves a negotiation between the excellent, the wicked, the self, and the structure by which the award, perhaps every award, is given: one must praise excellence, set it in dialectical relation to the wicked, and while drawing upon one's own experience and the lexicon and grammar of prizing, deny that one is acting on behalf of the self or behalf committee, or even the community: one is properly acting as a lone and disinterested agent of excellence.
>
> (184)

Similar to *The Lion and the Unicorn* poetry prize, many other major award jury criteria and manuals are no better at describing or defining excellence or related criteria. If one takes the time to read through the entire Newbery Medal manual, for example, it becomes obvious that while there are many rules and regulations surrounding the process of choosing a winning book, the criteria are just as undefined as those we observed in the smaller, more thematic awards we have also juried. Similarly, the TD "award recognizes excellence in Canadian children's literature," and identifies the "most distinguished book of the year in French and English" ("TD Canadian Children's Literature Award" n.p.). More specifically, the "quality of criteria for excellence" includes: "Quality of the text and illustrations (if present), interpretation of the theme or concept, presentation of information including accuracy, clarity, and organization," and "appropriateness of style and presentation" (n.p.). This shortlist is the sum total of prizing criteria: it focuses on formalist elements, provides no footholds for materialist considerations (aside from "accuracy"), and leaves a stunning amount of room for judges' subjective interpretations of "quality" and "appropriateness."

The problem is that seemingly objective formalist descriptions of quality belie how individual literary preferences can be, leaving an enormous amount of liberty for personal taste to be masked. Literary critics now recognize that "[r]ather than an absolute standard of literary value, there are multiple centers of value from which to assess a text" (Lundin 111). So while it may seem obvious that readers of varied backgrounds (in which we include all social variables, even age), would recognize excellence when they see it, the reality is much more complex due to their individual experiences, and backgrounds, not to mention their values—both ideological and aesthetic. When selection criteria are left vague, political values can be hidden—a situation that was exposed by the canon wars: "Recent critics have stressed how the literary canon favors works by white European men from the middle and higher classes to the exclusion of most works by women, popular artists or writers from other cultures or races" (Ross 516). This is relevant to the prizing process because as Kidd notes, children's literature prizes, particularly the major prizes such as the Newbery, are "part of the canonical architecture of children's literature" ("Prizing Children's Literature" 169); indeed, he contends that the "debate about prizing and its value(s) seems another version of the canon wars" (183).

Many people—even those immersed in the study of children's literature through its various sub-disciplines—are unaware of the criteria provided for award juries to consult while making decisions about what constitutes the "best" in each award category. In our own experiences as judges, we were initially surprised by the lack of specificity we perceived when first studying the materials we were given. For instance, the Stonewall Award, conferred by the ALA, is given very little in terms of concrete criteria outside of the award's mandate, which is to recognize books of "exceptional merit relating to the gay/lesbian/bisexual/transgender experience" ("Stonewall Book Awards" n.p.). Similarly, the Sheila A. Egoff Children's Literature Prize, conferred by the BC Book Prizes, is "[a]warded to the author(s) of novels, including chapter books, and non-fiction books, including biography, aimed at juveniles and young adults, which have not been highly illustrated" ("About BC Book Prizes" n.p.). The criteria for each award are broad and undefined, but the awards themselves are more specific and thematic—the Sheila A. Egoff Prize is given only to authors from British Columbia, and the Stonewall Award is bestowed specifically upon books with LGBTQ content. Our concern, however, is more focused on major awards such as the Newbery Medal, another ALA award, and the TD Canadian Children's Literature Award, which is administered by the Canadian Children's Book Centre—namely, larger awards with no specific thematic or ideological goal in place.

The work we perform as judges differs dramatically from the kinds of evaluation and assessment of children's literature we do regularly as reviewers, scholars, and instructors. As literary academics, we believe that excellence in literature is marked not only through the formal components of a work, such as strong characterization, but also through explorations of various ideologies, cutting edge themes, and experimental style. Further, our training has taught us that unique social and political elements in conjunction with solid literary elements make strong writing conspicuously excellent, and that authenticity of those ideas needs to be considered in any assessment of quality. Unfortunately, due to the vague, undefined idea of "excellence" that is prioritized in the award process, there is no real foundation for negotiating based on ideological criteria. For instance, Robert's own academic pursuits and research within various areas of gender and sexuality studies allowed him to highlight sometimes overlooked ideological aspects of a number of novels under consideration for the 2014 Newbery Medal—but in order to do so he had to take a personal stand, and the points he raised were given no special or powerful consideration because there was no official infrastructure to support such points.

We agreed not to discuss our work as judges on many of the award committees and promised not to disclose specific details of selection negotiations. As such, it is difficult to provide concrete examples of the kinds of competing values we have seen at play—and perhaps it is this very secrecy that hinders more open discussion and a more productive space for change. However, Michelle has also served as a juror for the George Ryga Award for Social Awareness in Literature prize (awarded to a book of any genre written by a British Columbia author, published in British Columbia, or focused on a British Columbian issue—including, but not limited to, children's literature) and has made no such agreement. An example from that award's negotiations will suffice to illustrate the basic principles we are discussing here.

Assessment for the Ryga award is only marginally more specific than those previously discussed, pointing clearly to the award's focus on social justice: "In keeping with George Ryga's status as a marginalized Ukrainian Canadian who was deeply concerned with justice, the judges will select an outstanding work of both literary and social value that opens up discussion of social and cultural issues" ("Criteria for Entry" n.p.). Keeping these criteria in mind, while serving on a jury of primarily white men, Michelle argued for an ambitious creative non-fiction work of social history by Sylvia Olsen. *Working with Wool* (2010) is a feminist examination of the contributions Aboriginal women knitters have made to their families and communities on Vancouver Island since the early twentieth century. Showcasing respectfully obtained, impressively synthesized primary materials including interviews and photographs, the book develops a careful examination of the intersectionalities at play in oppressing Aboriginal women on multiple levels—as well as their resilient insistence on empowering themselves through the best means at hand (in this case, knitting sweaters in high demand and highly valued in the market place). Michelle fought hard for the book, but it was saved from complete defeat only by intervention from the feminist mediator facilitating the selection process.

As a result of that pointed intervention, *Working with Wool* was grudgingly accepted as a token on the shortlist—the only book written by a woman, and one of two specifically related to women's issues—pitted as an adversary against a book of photography about Vancouver's Downtown Eastside that contained virtually no written text (despite the fact that the award was bestowed specifically for *literary* merit). In the end, the shortlist was expanded to accommodate *Working with Wool*, but Michelle's co-jurors were unrelenting in their devaluing of the work's literary merit: they offered no evidence or analysis for its alleged inferiority and simply repeated their claim that the book of photography was better written. In this situation, an essentially unsupportable circular argument in favor of perceived (yet undefined, unsubstantiated, illogical) aesthetic value functioned to exclude a writer (and topic) of female, Aboriginal origin precisely as canon-protecting mechanisms of the past once did. Even the specific criteria mandating consideration of social justice could not overcome the jurors' biases and personal preferences. But this was 2011, and Michelle's co-jurors behaved as though the canon wars had never occurred—refusing to acknowledge the development and importance of much more recent—and widely accepted—critical approaches to evaluating literature.

It is clear that while criteria are foundational to the problems we have identified, they are not the whole problem. Another important consideration is the jury selection processes within both the major awards and smaller specialty prizes. In the following section, we examine the role of jurors. But before continuing with our critique and exploration of future possibilities, we must recall some of the history and purpose behind some of the awards we've been discussing. The first and most notable award, of course, is the Newbery Medal, founded by Frederic Melcher in the 1920s with explicit goals:

> To encourage original creative work in the field of books for children. To emphasize to the public that contributions to the literature for children deserve similar recognition to poetry, plays, or novels. To give those librarians, who make it their life work to serve children's reading interests, an opportunity to encourage good writing in this field.
>
> ("How the Newbery" n.p.)

Shortly after its inception, the Newbery was already under attack: "In 1925, people were complaining that these were books kids don't want to read," says Horning (Maughan n.p.). In addition to questions of popularity, the Newbery has also been criticized for a variety of perceived shortcomings throughout the decades, most especially those related to lack of diversity among winners. Lindsey Chapman reports that

[i]n 1996, *The Horn Book Magazine* published an editorial about the Newbery Medal, pointing out that for ten years prior, only white authors had received the honor. Additionally, the winning books were written for middle-grade students and only featured white protagonists.

(n.p.)

And in his article, "Study Finds Less Diversity in Newbery Books," Dave Itzkoff examines a Brigham Young University study on diversity in winning Newbery books from 1922–2007. The study found that the majority of winning texts feature white male protagonists from two-parent households (n.p.).

In response to the above study and criticisms, Pat Scales, the president of the Association for Library Service to Children at the time, reminded readers that "ethnicity, gender, nothing of that is necessarily taken into consideration." She also noted, however, that "[w]e owe kids good stories that reflect their lives and give them a more global view" (qtd. in Itzkoff, n.p.). But how can an award promote literature with a more global view while at the same time being held back from considering specific elements of ethnicity, gender, class, family makeup, and dis/ability during deliberations? This is not to say that specifically focused discussions of ideology do not enter into deliberations; we can attest from personal experience that they do. But in the end, we have observed that such discussions more often lead to the exclusion of a book from further discussion, rather than the promotion of a book to the top of the list.

In "Not Censorship but Selection," Kidd argues persuasively that

> [c]ensorship clarifies what is and isn't legitimate in a culture, leading to further debate about worth and often transforming the original standards and expectations. So does prizing, which celebrates in part through exclusion, and might itself be understood as a form of censorship, not simply its inverse.
>
> (198)

He goes on to connect assumptions about literary merit with the fascination with and desire for "classic" children's literature: "Presumably the emphasis on literary merit as opposed to social value in the ALA's statement 'The Freedom to Read' is both residual, a carryover reverence toward the 'classics,' and also strategic, an assertion of literature's relevance or timeliness" (204).

As we discussed earlier, our own academic specializations (and subject positions) have given us the ability to bring unique perspectives to the various committees on which we have served. While we would never assert that all committee members on selection committees need doctoral—or even graduate—degrees, we do believe that personal and cultural backgrounds, as well as professional qualifications and specializations of individuals need to become a greater part of the process for appointing jurors or choosing candidates for election ballots. As literary scholars working within diverse arenas of research, and during our service as children's literature prize jurors, we were surprised by the lack of theoretical and ideological approaches applied by our co-jurors, particularly those with backgrounds in education and information sciences. Often our colleagues became preoccupied with age-appropriateness and literary unity, considerations we ourselves had understood as more outdated, while we prioritized issues of child empowerment, inclusiveness, and authentic cultural representation.

Debates regarding composition of awards committees are active, especially in online forums: "Yolanda Scott, editorial director at Charlesbridge, said that [...] the children's book world—writers, publishers, librarians—is predominantly white and female. But [Roger] Sutton said that the governing organizations do try to mix it up when choosing committee members" (Spurlock and Boss n.p.). Much like the judging criteria discussed earlier, the choosing of jury members only becomes specific with the more specialized awards. For the Newbery Medal, the jury makeup consists of "Eight (8) [ALA] members to be elected annually [...], a chairperson to be appointed by the president, and six (6) [ALA] members appointed by the president" ("John Newbery Award Committee Manual" 9), whereas the Stonewall Award requires more specificity: "Membership [in the committee] is balanced with female-identified and male-identified members" ("Stonewall Book Awards Committee" n.p.). While prioritizing style and form over ideology has been the norm since the beginning of children's book prizes, children's literature more broadly is becoming ever more diverse and engaged with various social issues. Selecting jurors who are familiar with various ideologies and represent a variety of cultural experiences should be a priority moving forward. Perhaps improvements in the selection of jury members will create more pressure to update selection criteria in larger awards.

But arguments for and against vague terminology in awards criteria have been made for decades. As far back as 1942, Clara Breed was already defending the vague terminology of the Newbery Medal, arguing that "[b]ecause creative talent cannot and should not conform to any pattern, the words 'most distinguished' were wisely undefined and unqualified, so that no limitations were placed on the character of the book" (724). We propose, however, that assessing further ideological components such as gender, sexuality, race, and class should not be looked at as a limitation, but rather as a way of increasing and promoting greater representation within literature for children. It seems obvious and logical to us that "excellence" and "most distinguished" don't have to mean a flawless plot and perfect structure, but rather more engagement with social themes, since promoting excellently written books with troublesome thematic elements is, at the very least, problematic in a pedagogical sense, especially since major literary prizes such as the Newbery and the TD Canadian Children's Literature Award are responsible for influencing the direction of children's literature through promotion and exclusion, affecting purchasing habits in libraries and classrooms as well as in individual home environments.

According to Anita Silvey's article, "Has the Newbery Lost Its Way?" (2008), there was at least one particular year in which a Newbery committee chose a book for seemingly ideological reasons, which ended up creating much discussion. In 1953, the Newbery Medal was given to *The Secret of the Andes* (1952) instead of *Charlotte's Web* (1952), and although the official position of the committee will never be publicly revealed, one member did note that "she preferred the former because she hadn't seen any good books about South America" that year (40). Discussions around these sorts of winning books over the "popular" books, is what has led to the creation of more and more awards over the years—including children's choice awards—each of which is better able to focus on a specific social or political goal.

In *The Economy of Prestige* (2005), James English notes that prizing generates "a 'logic of proliferation' within the relational field of culture. Each new prize makes possible yet another" (166). This is the very reason that so many politically- and socially-minded children's literature prizes have emerged over the last 25 years—the exception to this being the Coretta Scott King awards, which began in 1969—including the Pura Belpre Award (1996), the Asian/Pacific American Award children's literature category (2001), the Lambda Literary Awards children's and youth literature category (2001), the Schneider Family Book Award (2004), the American Indian Youth Literature Awards (2006), and the Stonewall Book Awards (which date to 1971, but saw significant expansion in recent years). This is just a small sample of the awards that are building on the issues of diversity that various critics believed were/are not being addressed by the larger awards that are often unable to award as many diverse titles due to their mandate of general literary excellence.

There are, of course, many concerns about the proliferation of numerous small awards as a direct result of concern over the selection processes of larger awards. In "Why Did That Book Win?" (2014) Spurlock and Boss documented portions of the conversation on the topic, including insights into specialized awards:

> [Martha] Parravano acknowledged this year's winners of the "big" awards are quite white—both characters and creators. Sutton shared a concern that perhaps too many creators of color are being slotted into working on books that would be eligible for the Coretta Scott King, for instance, which doesn't allow them to break out to other things.
>
> (n.p.)

Of particular interest in the above dialogue is the concern not only about the role of creators of color within the prizing community, but also within the larger publishing community. If creators of color are less likely to win the larger awards, then perhaps their publishers will be asked to work on projects better suited for specialized criteria of "diversity" awards, as Sutton states. Further, as Marilisa Jiménez García recognizes in her contribution to this volume, "[e]stablishing medals such as the Belpre addresses a 'need' while propagating a kind of specialized segregation" (106).

In discussing and examining larger awards that often ignore specific social and political ideologies in the decision-making processes each year, it is perhaps too easy to look at the other awards, such as those noted above, and take the position that at least there is recognition of diversity in children's literature, even if it is not prominent in the Newbery selections. The problem with this, however, is that such a position ignores the prestige of these larger awards. Kidd, for instance, notes that

> Although the [Newbery] Medal carries no cash prize, it can more than double the sales of a book ... Whereas the average shelf life of a children's book today is roughly eighteen months, many Newbery titles are still in print, and most can be found in public and school libraries.
> (168)

As such, the books that are purchased by librarians, teachers, parents, and other organizations will often be winners with a big gold sticker on the front, before there is even a consideration of the other award winners, if of course, funds are still available at that point.

The difficult and paradoxical position of the larger awards remains. They promote "excellent" literature, but this excellence is limited to an aesthetic scope and is of no help in molding a new, more inclusive landscape of children's literature unless more attention is paid to other awards with social and political leanings—or until prestigious awards such as the Newbery and TD Award are tasked with a more specific mandate that requires a systematic interrogation of specific ideological components of the texts under consideration. It is with this in mind that we have examined the roots of some clashes resounding in the arena of prizing children's literature, a high stakes game in which certain books are celebrated, elevated, and highlighted at the expense of others, while at the same time covert statements on what is meaningful in contemporary childhood are issued.

Major awards such as the Newbery and TD rely on nebulous criteria which make the selection process vulnerable to subjective personal taste while simultaneously excluding specific consideration of politicized or ideological concerns. Meanwhile, what has become some of the most crucial work in children's literature—valuing diversity, cultural specificity, and respectful representations of race, sexuality, and other social variables—is ghettoized to "special" awards prioritizing authenticity and countering cultural appropriation, such as the Coretta Scott King or the Lambda awards, suggesting that it is possible and/or necessary to separate excellence and representation.

We are making the argument here not that ideology should be prioritized over aesthetics, but that they should not, indeed cannot, be separated. Thus excellence must be redefined—or more accurately, defined—to appropriately reflect the literary values of a pluralistic, inclusive society. For example, such a definition might deem excellent a book's ability to foster the empowerment of child readers, especially through their creativity, critical thinking ability, and willingness to respectfully collaborate with people of any/every shape, size, color, orientation, and background; all of this can and should be accomplished through beautiful storytelling.

Not only do award criteria require revision to reflect current values in the discipline of children's literature, but there should also be a more systematic and careful selection process for amassing committees—a process that reflects the need for varied ideological approaches, as well as a diverse array of backgrounds (both socially and academically). When selecting committees, award administrators should vet jurors based on personal and professional backgrounds to ensure that diverse values are considered, represented, and applied. These two changes implemented together should result in an updated approach to the processes governing children's literature prizes.

In turn, this larger change could help modernize prizing from its traditional roots—raising children's aesthetic appreciation of literature, to a more contemporary approach in line with current values in the field—using children's literature to help children understand and facilitate empathy and social justice. We acknowledge that some of these matters have been discussed in previous years, but we assert that it is necessary to continue arguing for change as contentious issues remain unresolved. The changes we suggest seem both sensible and in keeping with the larger field of children's literature. What has been seen as aesthetics versus ideology has long functioned as an inherent tension between those who write and publish (and often those who prize) and those who theorize and critique within an academic context. Inevitably, however, some overlap needs to occur in order to update the processes of prizing. We are confident that by changing the terms and practices of prizing, awards can indeed support engagement with social change.[1]

Note

1. This article was composed throughout 2014 and reflects our perceptions and beliefs at that time. However, 2015 has been recognized by *School Library Journal* as "a watershed year for diversity" in their March 2015 commentary on the year's ALA Awards: "Initial reactions to the winners have centered around diversity of all varieties. There's the happy proclamation [...] that the winners were 'all diverse!'" (Lindsay n.p.). The statistics are significant—"In the previous three years, the Newbery and Caldecott committees recognized just one person of color between them. This year: five" (Lindsay n.p.)—and we hope this is the beginning of a productive new trend.

6 The Still Almost All-White World of Children's Literature

Theory, Practice, and Identity-Based Children's Book Awards

June Cummins

Late in April in 2014, author Aisha Saeed noticed that the line-up of the children's literature speakers for the upcoming BookCon conference consisted entirely of white male authors. In exasperation, she tweeted: "No diverse authors at #BookCon None. Nada. Zilch. #nowords http://bookriot. com/staff-contributors/ ... ... #weneeddiversebooks @BookRiot."[1] Saeed was the first person to use the hashtag "weneeddiversebooks," but she certainly was not the first to make that call. As the subsequently developed "We Need Diverse Books" website explains, authors Ellen Oh and Malinda Lo had been tweeting about the lack of diversity in children's book publishing even earlier. Now they amped up their call for action, a call "Several other authors, bloggers, and industry folks" answered.[2] The voices of Oh, Lo, and Saeed created a movement that extended beyond Twitter, a movement that demanded consideration of identity in publishing. The "We Need Diverse Books" campaign was thus born, making such a splash that it was written up in the *Los Angeles Times*, NPR, and *Publishers Weekly*. *The New York Times*, too, addressed the movement, its tone indicating it was a *fait accompli*. The ongoing presence of the campaign on social media was ubiquitous, and its staying power in mainstream media demonstrated the movement had cachet, charisma, and clutch.

We will not know for a few years what, if any, difference the "We Need Diverse Books" campaign will make—whether publishers will start producing more books by multicultural authors, prizing committees will recognize more such books, consumers will purchase those books, and whether, most critically, *children will be reading more diverse books*. I'm guardedly pessimistic. If the last 50 years are any kind of indication, this campaign may not make much difference. I strongly support the practical tactics of the We Need Diverse Books campaign but fear that practice alone won't result in the desired outcomes. A wholesale change in thinking must occur, and I believe that theory can be the factor that moves practice into cultural change. Specifically, I encourage the children's book prize committee members, especially those on the Newbery Committee, to learn about and become practitioners of the school of theory known as intersectionality, an identity-based approach that enables a greater understanding of what identity is, does, and can do. For intersectionality is a theory that requires demonstrable outcomes. Known primarily for overlapping categories of identity, intersectionality also requires social activism. I believe the members of the Newbery Committee are already positioned to pursue world-bettering through social action.

In 1965, Nancy Larrick published "The All-White World of Children's Books," her well-known article about the lack of diversity in children's book publishing. Having investigated the topic for three years, surveying more than 5,000 trade books published since 1962, Larrick denounces publishers for their "blatant racial bias" and expresses concern about the effect of the "gentle doses of racism" that their books proffered to children of color.[3] She deplores the "almost complete omission of Negroes from books for children." Despite its age, Larrick's article remains relevant and widely circulated, and can be useful for contemporary discussions of diversity, intersectionality, and prizing.

Two comments Larrick makes in the article are especially pertinent. She twice points out that while the country has changed, children's book publishing has not. First, she writes "Integration may be the law of the land, but most of the books children see are all white (63)," and then she expresses disbelief that this situation persists: "Surely the effect of Little Rock, Montgomery, and Birmingham could be seen by this time, I reasoned" (63). Larrick started her study thinking that the progressive social movements that swept through American culture would have impacted what is published, but she concluded that they had not. Larrick also mentions potential loci of change. She discusses book clubs, explaining that hardcover book clubs include no books with black children in them but that paperback book clubs do, presumably because members of paperback books clubs choose what books to receive while those in the more elite hardcover clubs do not. The suggestion is that a revolution could occur from within. One entity that could change things, Larrick hopes, is the newly formed Council for Interracial Books for Children, comprised of such luminaries as Benjamin Spock and Langston Hughes, because it aims to award prizes to manuscripts featuring non-white children. The goal of the Council is to help these prize-winning manuscripts find publishers, with its members negotiating directly with editors. Larrick's article ends on a note of hope for the future.

Twenty-one years later, in a column in *The New York Times*, Walter Dean Myers assessed the current scene, noting the success of the Council for Interracial Books and the emergence of multicultural writing for children in the 1970s. "Things were looking up," he said. "The quality of the books written by blacks in the 70s was so outstanding that I actually thought we would revolutionize the industry, bringing to it a quality and dimension that would raise the standard for all children's books." But the progress was undercut when President Johnson left office, and the new president, Nixon, dismantled Johnson's Great Society program. Myers realized his hopes were "Wrong. Wrong. Wrong." Whereas in 1974, 900 of the over 2,000 books published for children included black characters, by 1984, the number was cut in half. And by the time that Myers was writing his article in 1986, "for every 100 books published this year there will be one published on the black experience." Myers ends the piece with despair. He believes the only way change will come about again is with another revolution such as was seen in the 1960s.

> We can be sure, however, of one thing: if we continue to make black children nonpersons by excluding them from books and by degrading the black experience, and if we continue to neglect white children by not exposing them to any aspect of other racial and ethnic experiences in a meaningful way, we will have a next racial crisis.

What, we should ask, did *not* happen between 1965, when Nancy Larrick called for a more inclusive children's literature, and 1986, when Walter Dean Myers made the same observations and complaints that Larrick made 21 years earlier? Both Larrick and Myers mention the Council for Interracial Books for Children and its award program; Larrick talks about its future potential, and Myers proves that the award program did have some effect, citing various successful authors and books that the award committee cultivated. Soon after Larrick's article was published, identity-based children's book awards began to proliferate. Established in 1968, The Sydney Taylor Book Award, given to authors of Jewish literature for children, was the first identity-based award. The Coretta Scott King Awards, given to African-American authors for books focused on the African-American experience, was established soon after, in 1969. Shortly thereafter, the Stonewall Book Award given to books that portray with excellence the gay/lesbian/bisexual/transgendered experience, was first awarded in 1971. Larrick hoped that the Council for Interracial Books, through its award program, whether or not it facilitated getting books into print, would still "accomplish a great deal [...]. White supremacy in children's literature will be abolished when authors, editors, publishers, and booksellers decide they need not submit to bigots" (85). Clearly, the Council's award program functioned and the identity-based book award programs that quickly developed have been doing important work as they have remained in existence for over 40 years. But why didn't Larrick's prediction come true? Why has white supremacy persisted in children's literature despite the good work of those on the award committees?[4]

The answers to these questions can be found in the contested notion of "identity." Before the Sydney Taylor, Coretta Scott King, and Stonewall Awards were created, before the Council of Interracial Books for Children was invented, the awards for children's literature ostensibly had nothing to do with identity, the primary ones being the Newbery, given since 1922, and the Caldecott, since 1938. Of course, both awards were named after white men, publisher John Newbery and illustrator Randolph Caldecott, but that association was not seen as one of identity. The Newbery and Caldecott awards were created long before people used the word "identity" in relation to race, religion, ethnicity, class, nationality, or sexuality. Before World War II, the term was used in psychology. As Rogers Brubaker and Frederick Cooper explain, in post-war America,

> the notion of identification was pried from its original, specifically psychoanalytic context (where the term had been initially introduced by Freud) and linked to ethnicity on the one hand (through Gordon Allport's influential 1954 book *The Nature of Prejudice*) and to sociological role theory on the other (through figures such as Nelson Foote and Robert Merton).
>
> (3)

Brubaker and Cooper argue that our current usage of the word "identity" rapidly grew with the social change movements of the 1960s:

> For a variety of reasons, the term identity proved highly resonant in the 1960s, diffusing quickly across disciplinary and national boundaries, establishing itself in the journalistic as well as the academic lexicon, and permeating the language of social and political practice as well as that of social and political analysis. [...] And from the late 1960s on, with the rise of the Black Power movement, and subsequently other ethnic movements, [...] concerns with and assertions of individual identity [...] were readily, if facilely, transposed to the group level.
>
> (3)

In other words, the rise of the use of the word "identity" in terms of a person's connection to an ethnic, religious, sexual, national, gender, or any kind of group, was directly associated with the Black Rights movement, as Brubaker and Cooper explicitly state and Myers suggests. Ultimately, the connection is to the Civil Rights Movement itself, as Larrick understood.

One can detect contention in Brubaker and Cooper's explanation of the term "identity"; in describing the historical evolution of the term, they can't avoid making a judgment on its usage. Of course, the purpose of their article is to worry "identity," as their title suggests: "Beyond Identity," hints that the term is insufficient. They announce their problem with the word in their first paragraph: "The argument of this article is that the social sciences and humanities have surrendered to the word 'identity'; that this has both intellectual and political costs; and that we can do better" (2).

Battles rage around and within the topic of identity, and most adults are aware of the term "identity politics." Becoming prominent in social discourse in the 1990s, identity politics divided people into either proponents or opponents of group affiliations. Stances concerning the need for group affiliations and rights loosely fell along liberal or conservative perspectives, with the Right generally against the idea that groups had needs or rights and the Left determined to prove that they did.

A prime example of the public debates surrounding identity politics is Marc Aronson's polemical essay about identity-based children's book awards, published in 2001 in *Horn Book* magazine. In "Slippery Slopes and Proliferating Prizes," Aronson argues against children's book prizes based on identity, rushing headlong into the identity politics debates of the time period that continue today. Using buzzwords and terms like "balkanized," "Culture Wars," and "Affirmative Action," Aronson contends that awards should be based on content and not identity; one of his main arguments is that the Newbery Committee won't give awards to books by black or Latino authors since those identity categories have their own book awards. He also argues that identity-based awards would discourage librarians from buying the winners, thinking they had no use for them if that identity group doesn't use their library. He asks

> if you have to be black to win the award, do you have to be black to appreciate the winning book? The implication that only blacks can write well about blacks sets up the implication that only they can *read* well about them, too.

Aronson's tone, his impassioned stance, and his demand that something be done are all indicative of the argumentative discourse surrounding identity politics in the late twentieth century. *Horn Book* magazine is a trade publication available in bookstores and sent to subscribers, who are mostly librarians and teachers. The article is still available online and very easy to access. Aronson was speaking to "the people." In the more cloistered halls of academia, the arguments about identity politics were also proliferating, with a more intense focus on what identity is and what it does.

Simply, the academic debate about identity can be divided into two sets of claims, the essentialist and the constructivist. Brubaker and Cooper published "Beyond Identity" in 2000, but these terms are still being used fifteen years later. Essentialist approaches to identity see people as being inherently, naturally, who they are. This view would hold that people are born into their identities. Essentialist thinking of this sort can be seen in certain strains of French feminist theory in the early 1970s, as with Hélène Cixous's theory of *l'écriture féminine*, writing derived from the body. On the other hand, constructionist perspectives of identity are associated with post-structuralism and conceptualize identity as produced by one's environment and experiences, as with queer theorist Judith Butler's argument that gender is performative rather than fixed.

Summarizing this debate, Brubaker and Cooper also explain why it is not easily resolved. They describe constructivist approaches as theorizing identity "as multiple, fragmented, and fluid" (footnoting Butler's), and set it against "essentialism," which has been "vigorously criticized" (6). By the time they are writing "Beyond Identity" in 2000, Brubaker and Cooper were claiming that "constructivist gestures now accompany most discussions of 'identity'" (6). But even at this early point in the academic discussion of identity politics, Brubaker and Cooper see that the poles are not as distinct and as far from each other as people believe.

> Yet we often find an uneasy amalgam of constructivist language and essentialist argumentation. This is not a matter of intellectual sloppiness. Rather, it reflects the dual orientation of many academic identitarians as both *analysts* and *protagonists* of identity politics. It reflects the tension between the constructivist language that is required by academic correctness and the foundationalist or essentialist message that is required by academic correctness if appeals to 'identity' are to be effective in practice.
>
> (6)

More recently, theorists have sought such synthesis. In 2011, in his book *Identity Complex*, Michael Hames-García provides homosexuality as an example of how a person could be both essentialist and constructivist. Explaining that

> This debate concerned the status of homosexuality as something that exists or does not exist independently of cultural context or as something that can exist across different cultural contexts. Many readers will recognize this as a debate over "essentialism" versus "social constructionism."
>
> (72)

This debate is critical to the consideration of identity-based children's book awards because some of the awards have criteria that require that authors *be* a certain identity, and others do not. The awards with these criteria include the Coretta Scott King Awards, which requires that authors and illustrators *be* African-American, and the Pura Belpré Medal, which has the requirement that writers and artists *be* Latino/a. The American Indian Youth Literature Award (AIYL) criteria states: "Author and or illustrator must be recognized by the Indian community of which they claim to be a part and be connected to the people."[5] Identity-based awards that do *not* require that people *be* a certain identity include the Sydney Taylor, the Stonewall, and the Schneider Family (for books dealing with disability).

Several identity-based children's book awards are ambiguous or changeable when it comes to identity-based eligibility. The Asian/Pacific American Literature Awards for Youth and Children have this criterion: "Works should be written or illustrated by an Asian/Pacific American, but not limited to [them]."[6] The awards given by the Consortium of Latin-American Studies Program (CLASP) avoid the issue of authors' and illustrators' identities by honoring *books* not *people* with the awards. Perhaps the most controversial identity-based award is the Lambda Literary Award, for the Lambda

Literary Foundation decided in 2009 that authors had to be homosexual to be eligible for the award and then changed that rule in 2011.[7]

The 2009 decision motivated Thomas Crisp to write an article in support of the Lambda committee's decision to limit the awards to LGBQT people. Crisp defends the decision and develops a sensitive, provocative argument about why essentialism must prevail for this award. Fully aware of what essentialism is and called an essentialist by those who disagree with his position, Crisp argues that "For the purposes in inciting social change (in this case, related to the Lambda Literary award), I argue that LGBT-identified people must essentialize ourselves in order to achieve our larger political objectives" (96).

Crisp raises two points in this statement that I need to address. The first is the argument that LGBT-identified people must essentialize themselves. As the Lambda Literary Foundation discovered over the years, the definition of homosexuality is not static and in fact has changed much over the 27 years of the organization's history. Heated discussions have taken place over the inclusion or not of bisexual people, transgender people, and the use of the word "queer." While the organization did not go into detail when it published its decision to return to the practice of not requiring that authors identify as gay, they did explain that the issue has "sharply divided" their community. Sexual identity did remain a criterion for judges and for certain awards that received funding from outside sources (pertaining to stages in authors' careers). One letter written by "Chris M" and published on the LLF website after the 2011 decisions captures the tenor of the debate:

> Sexuality is complex, you can't just group people into gay, lesbian and straight and call it a day, and there are plenty of people who don't identify as male or female. I'm a femromantic asexual neutrois—according to these guidelines, I wouldn't be eligible for any of the LGBT categories despite being incredibly queer with regards to both my gender and relationship preferences. (I can't identify as either heterosexual or homosexual because they rely on the idea that there are only two sexes or genders. I don't date the "opposite" gender and I don't date the "same" gender—I'm interested in women, but I'm not one, nor am I a man.)[8]

Chris M's remarks illustrate the claims of constructivist theorists who view identity as in flux, fluid, and unfixed. If a person refuses existing identity categories, instead opting to define himself or herself (the pronouns are inadequate) across a spectrum or in a way designed individually, then how can a committee assign or deny a particular identity to anyone? From a constructivist point of view, all identity-based awards that require an author *be* something cannot restrict the award from people who claim an identity, whether other people recognize that identity or not. Such reasoning is what makes Brubaker and Cooper throw up their hands and dismiss the notion of identity. Aronson makes the same point when he brings up the subject of Latino/a authors. He uses the Pura Belpré award criteria to make this argument:

> The Spanish requirement is one problem with the Belpré, but the idea of being Latino itself is another. [...] [A]n arch-conservative Miami Cuban could win for writing about being a militant Chicano organizer; an elegant Argentinean émigré could be honored for a novel about being a poor Central American farmer [...] a member of a family that had lived in the Southwest for hundreds of years could be selected for writing about a Puerto Rican shuttling between New York and Ponce. The umbrella definition of being Latino—which has no precise meaning—allows that person total freedom to deal with any Latino topic, while a person who does not use that term to define him or herself, no matter how knowledgeable about the specific subject he or she writes about, is forever banned from winning the prize.

These constructivist arguments help us see that identity definition can easily fail when applied by some people to others. Sometimes a political lens occludes identity altogether. A case in point is the twitter post quoted at the beginning of this article, the one in which Aisha Saeed asserted that there were no diverse children's literature authors originally lined up to speak at BookCon. She describes all four authors, Rick Riordan, Jeff Kinney, James Patterson, and Daniel Handler (Lemony Snicket), as white and male. One of these men, however, has an identity that complicates her claim. Handler is Jewish, and he sees his writing as influenced by his Jewish background. Saeed may not see Handler's diversity, and indeed, many scholars do not think of Judaism as part of multiculturalism, but a majority of Jews often feel they are a minority and that their experiences are not recognized, valued, or understood. Jewish people were not considered white at the turn of the twentieth century, and even today, Jews are stigmatized and victimized.[9] Jewish people do not necessarily benefit from nor are protected by the white, male status when anti-Semitism strikes.[10]

I don't mean to suggest that Crisp is entirely wrong in his call for essentialism. His arguments for the necessity of books with queer characters is convincing. But the LLF's own struggles with identity definition or certification make clear the limit of Crisp's argument. The LLF uses the language of "self-identified," demonstrating the conclusions they have reached about how to "tell" what a person "is." One can see the problems in that approach; people can dishonestly claim identities, or their minds may change about what their identities are, or they have multiple identities that may interfere with each other when people try to fit them into identity categories.

Essentialism is not enough, and constructivism is too much. The arguments within academia regarding identity illuminate for us why identity-based awards are complicated and political. But they do not explain why the awards are not resulting in increased diversity in the publishing and purchasing of children's books.

The second aspect of Crisp's argument significant here is his straightforward claim that he has a political objective. Such a statement is not only specific to his argument but also specific to identity studies in general. In her book *Object Lessons* (2012), Robyn Wiegman claims that at the heart of all identity studies is the goal to have political objectives, to make a difference in society. Identity studies, she asserts, "invest so much in making explicit what other fields do not explicitly name by framing their modes and manners of analysis as world-building engagements aimed at social change" (4). Wiegman believes that the desire for social change animates all of identity studies—no matter which identity they are organized around—and that they all share the goal of seeking social justice. Whether academic departments and programs can actually achieve social justice is one of the major questions of Wiegman's work, and she argues this question often, but one position she consistently maintains is that identity studies has built into it the "demand that an object of study be commensurate with the political desire that it calls it forth and the attendant assumption that critical practice is an act of justice" (27). Clearly, Crisp wrote his article with this assumption, and in fact Aronson did, too. Both of them believe that in discussing identity issues they are calling for improvement in the world, in what Wiegman calls "world-building."

Of course that is the aim of all identity-based book award committees. Indeed, the people who make up these committees are *doing* the work of social justice. They provide one possible answer to Wiegman's question of "on what critical terms, with what cultural materials, methodological priorities, and theoretical discourses has the study of identity been given disciplinary shape, and how has belief in its political agency been produced and sustained?" (5) Book award committees are an institutional, functional, actual practice of identity studies, a place where identity studies come to life and into practice outside of academe.

The people on these committees do important work, and in the terms of the committees themselves, they are successful. The Coretta Scott King, Pura Belpré, Sydney Taylor, Lambda, and other awards all recognize books every year. The winners of the Coretta Scott King Awards, in particular, get much attention, and those awards are probably the best known of the children's literature identity-based awards. But something is still *not* happening: very few books featuring African-American children are published.

Walter Dean Myers was dismayed in 1986. Writing again in *The New York Times* in 2014, he is even more dismayed. Citing the study conducted by the Cooperative Children's Book Center, the newspaper reports that of the 3200 children's books published in 2013, only 93 contained African-American characters. The CCBC *received* 3200 books; they estimate the number published is 5000. The chart the CCBC supplies on its website displays the startling information that the number of books with African-American characters in children's literature has been decreasing precipitately, from a high of 172 in 2008. Since that year, the number has been lower and lower every single year—shockingly so.[11] Myers explains the problem:

> In 1969, when I first entered the world of writing children's literature, the field was nearly empty. Children of color were not represented, nor were children from the lower economic classes. Today, when about 40 percent of public school students nationwide are black and Latino, the disparity of representation is even more egregious. In the middle of the night I ask myself if anyone really cares.
> (*The New York Times*, March 16, 2014)

Myers has to wonder yet again why the nation has become more multicultural but children's literature publishing has become less diverse. In 2014, the U.S. has an African-American president, and still one can hardly find an African-American character in a children's book.

In the same issue of *The New York Times*, Walter Dean Myer's son, Christopher Myers, also published an editorial about the paucity of diversity in children's book publishing titled "The Apartheid of Children's Books." In that piece, Christopher Myers gently places blame on the publishing industry or "The Market" for why children of color remain vastly underrepresented in children's books, explaining there is not one clear reason:

> The mission statements of major publishers are littered with intentions, with their commitments to diversity, to imagination, to multiculturalism, ostensibly to create opportunities for children to learn about and understand their importance in their respective worlds. During my years of making children's books, I've heard editors and publishers bemoan the dismal statistics, and promote this or that program that demonstrates their company's "commitment to diversity." With so much reassurance, it is hard to point fingers, but there are numbers and truths that stand in stark contrast to the reassurances. The business of children's literature enjoys ever more success, sparking multiple movie franchises and crossover readership, even as representations of young people of color are harder and harder to find.

Lee and Low, publishers who specialize in multicultural literature, asked a number of prominent authors, publishers, and educators the question "Why Hasn't The Number of Multicultural Books Increased in Eighteen Years?" and published the responses on their website. Many views are expressed there, most of which focus on marketing although not all necessarily criticizing publishing. Some focus on the lack of access and networking opportunities for authors of color; others discuss funding cuts and an apathetic book-buying public. No one reason arises as prominent, but everyone agrees the problem is overwhelmingly huge.[12]

In no way do I suggest that the essentialism of identity-based children's book awards is to blame here. Obviously, institutions much bigger than awards committees have major impacts on what gets published and bought. But it is worthwhile to ponder whether essentialism—the objective that authors *be* a certain identity—does or doesn't help awards committees do their work. It seems our next step is to look at book awards that *do* result in better sales, in books that *do* reach many children.

Of course the most obvious book award to do that kind of work is the Newbery. As Kenneth Kidd explains, "Although the Medal carries no cash prize, it can more than double the sales of a book, as well as increase sales of the author's other books. More important, the Medal keeps titles and authors in circulation for decades" (168). The Newbery is not consciously an identity-based award although as I have said it is named after a white man, which itself is an identity. White maleness is so hegemonic that it is considered neutral, as Critical Race Studies and other theories explain. But the ALA is seemingly unaware of such, extending the cultural assumption that white maleness is "normal." In the criteria for the Newbery award, no explicit mention of identity is made. Books and authors are given awards for excellence and for being "distinguished,"[13] which is defined as:

- Marked by eminence and distinction; noted for significant achievement
- Marked by excellence in quality
- Marked by conspicuous excellence or eminence
- Individually distinct.[14]

The last part of the definition, individual distinction, does have a subtext of identity. The American Library Association, which created, hosts, and administers the Newbery awards, obviously intends, with the use of the word "individual," that the books be original and unique, and not hackneyed, predictable, or formulaic. But it also suggests that work should not be connected in any way with a specific group. The criterion implies that an award cannot be given because of the connection between a book and an identity group. The judges on the committee might argue with me about what "individually distinct" means. But they cannot contest the fact that they did not award the Newbery Award to a writer of color between 2009 and 2014.

In 2008, Melita Marie Garza excoriated the Newbery for the lack of diversity among the books the committee gives the top prize. She pointed out how although the diversity among American citizens has increased, the number of books with diverse protagonists has decreased, as we well know by now. Trying to find answers for this disturbing trend, Garza asked Pat Scales, the president of the Association for Library Service to Children, the division of the American Library Association that gives out the Newbery award. Scales replied with, "the Newbery is given for literary quality—ethnicity, gender, nothing of that is necessarily taken into consideration." I recently interviewed a new member of the Newbery Committee, who showed me the immense binder judges are given with criteria and instructions. I asked her if there was any mention anywhere in the training materials about sensitivity, multiculturalism, or diversity, and she told me that there was none. It is clear that in the six years since Garza interviewed Scales that nothing changed. In her article, Garza points out that authors of color and other kinds of diversity do win the honor awards. Since 2009, that trend continues to hold. Jacqueline Woodson, Rita Williams-Garcia, and Thanhha Lai, among other authors of color, all have won honor awards. As Kidd notes, however, "very few Honor Books are as widely known as the Medal winners" (177).

How is it possible that year after year writers of color are good enough to win honor awards but not good enough to win the top prize? What factors come into play when judges consider what "distinguished" and "individual" mean and decide they don't mean authors of color? How many hairs are split that result in white winners when authors of color do well in the Honors categories? Marc Aronson was seemingly correct when he opined that with identity-based book awards, those on the Newbery Committee would not bother with books with non-white characters. As he put it,

> The danger in every award that sets limits on the kinds of people, or types of book, that can win it is that it diminishes the pressure on the larger awards, the Newbery and the Caldecott, to live up to their charge to seek the most distinguished children's books of the year.

We have seen how Robyn Wiegman views identity studies as being deeply invested in "world-building." Wiegman devotes *Object Lessons* to specific identity groups and the studies around them, including one chapter on the concept of intersectionality. Intersectionality is a critical method that examines not specific identity groups in isolation but how overlapping categories of identity affect individuals. The term was first used by the legal scholar Kimberlé Crenshaw, who pointed out that looking at the issue of violence against women solely through the lens of gender, as the law had been doing, occludes the way that race, ethnicity, and class intertwine with gender. She argued that one cannot achieve a complete understanding of identity without looking at the intersections of race, class, gender, ethnicity, etc. Crenshaw is a lawyer, not an academic identity theorist, but her arguments have been taken up and embraced by other segments of thinkers. Social scientists are particularly concerned with intersectionality, and those in the humanities also find the theory useful. Through the lens of intersectionality, one can understand how someone can be both an essentialist and a constructivist at once, in the ways that Brubaker and Cooper as well as Hames-García pointed out, as even our own understandings of ourselves overlap and sometimes contradict.

The aspect of intersectionality that I want to emphasize is its focus on praxis. For it is critical to the theory that analysis leads to social justice. *Doing* something about injustice is core to intersectionality. According to Patricia Hill Collins, while the field of intersectionality has evolved since Crenshaw coined the phrase in 1991, its

> focus remained staunchly on engaging in a host of projects that might foster social justice. Thus, from its inception, intersectionality was not a theory of truth, a form of academic currency to be brokered for the next scholarly publication, with the implications of scholarship neatly severed from the lives of the people who were forced to live with its consequences. Instead intersectionality mattered in real people's lives [...].
>
> (ix)

In their anthology *Emerging Intersections: Race, Class, and Gender in Theory, Policy, and Practice*, Bonnie Thornton Dill and Ruth Enid Zambrana maintain the focus within intersectionality on praxis by demonstrating that "in addition to its academic and intellectual concerns, intersectional scholarship matters outside the academy because day-to-day life and lived experience is the primary domain in which the conceptualization and under-standing of these constructs is and has been grounded" (3). Several of the contributed essays address how intersectional analyses can lead to praxis, including the creation of programs and practices to reduce the numbers of high school drop-outs and to recruit and retain faculty of color at the university level. They demonstrate that the knowledge of intersectionality and the analyses provided by it yield more successful outcomes and help more people. Dill and Zambrana explain:

> The major theoretical conclusion is that social change cannot occur without institutions of higher education allocating resources to those alternative initiatives within their institutions that have an intersectional lens, that seek to promote inclusivity in knowledge production, curriculum transformation, mentoring, and pedagogy, and that actively seek to use knowledge to achieve social justice.
>
> (277)

Examples of praxis in the dissemination of diverse children's literature can be seen in two book distribution programs, the P J Library and the Stories for All Project. These entities are both involved with giving out free children's books. As Naomi Lesley explains, the P J Library is a program focusing on Jewish children's literature that has 125,000 active subscribers. It sends out 10,000 to 18,000 copies of each book it chooses. Initiated in 2005, it has become so successful that it has brought out-of-print books back into print and sought out authors to write for it. Some publishers have gone so far as to develop "Jewish-themed imprints in an effort to attract the P J Library's business" (7). A philanthropist donated money to make the P J Library possible, and other philanthropists and foundations joined the program, ensuring its continuation. While big money backs the organization, none of the subscribers pay for the books they receive.

The new Stories For All project, a program within the First Book organization, is operating with a similar objective: it gives free multicultural books to children. As Lesley describes it, "SFA combines elements of both grassroots and bulk purchase strategies. First Book provides low-cost and free books to community organizations—libraries, schools, churches, soup kitchens—that serve predominantly low-income children. Communities can select and request their own books" (10). Both the P J Library and First Book illustrate the point Larrick made about book-of-the-month clubs in 1965: in hardcover book clubs, the publisher chose the books, and in the paperback clubs, the readers selected the books. The number of African-American characters in books selected by readers was much higher than in those selected by publishers. When the choice is in the consumer's hands or the hands choosing on behalf of young readers, diversity is marketable.

To date, First Book has distributed 120 million books. Stories For All, within First Book, is being developed in conjunction with the We Need Diverse Books campaign. Their website describes the project, which includes a book publication campaign for unpublished authors telling stories from underrepresented communities as well as a curated special collection of Latino-focused materials.[15] Both the P J Library and the First Book organization are managing the children's book "market" on their own terms. By bringing in donors and serving large numbers of people, they are able to influence what is published. It is the users, or those acting on behalf of users, that determine these direct-market campaigns, not what publishers think audiences want or what past sales through traditional channels have shown them will sell. These are grass-roots projects that illustrate how social activism can make changes in society, and more specifically, children's literature.

The We Need Diverse Books campaign, of course, is predicated on praxis, creating initiatives and planning strategies. It has grown not just in visibility but also in activity since it was launched last April. Some of its initiatives include a donation drive, a program called Diversity in the Classroom, a Children's Literature Diversity Festival scheduled to take place in the summer of 2016 in Washington, D.C., and of course grants and awards. To this day, the belief in the efficacy in grants and awards holds fast.

On October 16, 2014, the WNDB campaign announced its new grants and awards program, named after Walter Dean Myers (who died in July). The "Walter" will be given to "published authors from diverse backgrounds who celebrate diversity in their writing and '[allow] children to see themselves reflected back.'"[16] The grants are designated for unpublished authors "who are creating diverse works." The amount of the award will be based on how much money is donated through the fundraising campaign.

Based on my investigation of identity-based book awards, I have to wonder how much efficacy the Walter will have. Judges on existing identity-based book award committees are consciously striving for social justice. They believe strongly that the work they do is critically important for the identity groups on whose behalf they do it. They are right, in a theoretical sense, but what we have seen is that they have not been able to do the "world-changing" that Wiegman sees as the goal of identity studies insofar as the publication of books featuring protagonists of color has not changed since Nancy Larrick's call 50 years ago.

It's possible that the We Need Diverse Books campaign and initiatives will make changes, and I am hopeful that the new award and grants in Myers's name will result in the changes he sought and never saw in his lifetime. But I think that what must happen now is that the Newbery committee itself changes, and I am suggesting that education, self-awareness, and understanding of intersectionality can help the ALA become more inclusive and socially active.

Patricia Hills Collins asks, "Can intersectionality make the leap to emerge as a universal way of building knowledge and transforming institutions?" (xiii). I believe that it can, and that the Newbery committee can be transformed by it. The Newbery committee cannot give itself instructions like "make sure the book has an African-American protagonist." Identity-based committees must be overt in directives that are that specific, but the Newbery committee cannot subvert in this way by whispering these rules to each other or keeping them off the record. But the Newbery committee can see itself as a group engaged in social action, in making the world a better place. In fact, that is how the Newbery committee originally conceived of itself, as Kidd explains:

> [it] helped revitalize faith in the idea of the public sphere, very much at issue in the period, the subject of treatises by Walter Lippman and John Dewey among others. [...] Children's Book Week was designed explicitly as an exercise in character building through books, and the Medal, though a more literary project, endorsed the association of literature with character and citizenship. [...] [Anne Carroll] Moore and [Frederic] Melcher clearly saw themselves as participating in and even reshaping public life.
>
> (172)

The goals of the Newbery award were always to serve the public and to improve character and citizenship through literature. Those goals were seen as part of civil uplift and social progress then; today, no one would argue that uplift and progress are *not* the goals of the committee. Today, uplift and progress are not necessarily defined in the same terms as they were in the 1920s. It is incumbent upon members of the award committee to understand the history of the award and to interpret its original goals for today.

My friend who is on the Newbery Committee this year has read Kidd's article and shared it with the other judges. Reading about the history and institutionalization of the award may make the judges more aware of what the award set out to do and what they can now do. It would be a step toward the committee members increasing their education and self-awareness.

Intersectionality, with its two emphases on overlapping, non-essentialist identities, and on social activism, can be a guide for Newbery Committee members. They can look for books that exhibit excellence and distinctiveness and *also* reflect the world around us today, in its infinite categories of identity, thereby promoting excellence through diversity. They can create criteria that don't spell out any specific identities but that commit the committee to an awareness of the diversity of the world around them.[17]

My goal is not to eradicate the identity-based awards. We are a long way from not needing them. We need to honor and celebrate the different identity categories that people inhabit. But we cannot continue not to give the biggest prizes to authors of color, and the Newbery Committee cannot continue to ignore identity. If the members take an intersectionalist approach, prioritizing social action and asserting that identity of any sort is important, then we might see change. One day we might see characters of all sorts of colors and connected to many various identity groups in the books that win the top Newbery prize. It is my hope that this change comes about sometime in the twenty-first century, long before we reach the centennial anniversary of Nancy Larrick's *cri de coeur* 50 years ago.

Notes

1. https://twitter.com/aishacs/status/459341841352372224 December 28, 2015.
2. http://weneeddiversebooks.tumblr.com/FAQ, December 28, 2015.
3. Larrick explains:

   Of the 5,206 children's trade books launched by the sixty-three publishers in the three-year period, only 349 include one or more Negroes—an average of 6.7 percent. Among the four publishers with the largest lists of children's books, the percentage of books with Negroes is one-third lower than this average. These four firms (Doubleday, Franklin Watts, Macmillan, and Harper & Row) published 866 books in the three-year period, and only 4.2 percent have a Negro in text or illustration. Eight publishers produced only all-white books.

   (64)

4. In 1998, Bonnie Miller, in her "What Color is Gold? Twenty-One Years of Same-Race Authors and Protagonists in the Newbery Medal," explained that no author of color had won the top award since Mildred Taylor had for *Roll of Thunder, Hear My Cry* in 1977.
5. http://ailanet.org/docs/AIYLA_Criteria_5_09.pdf December 28, 2015.
6. www.apalaweb.org/2013-asianpacific-american-award-for-literature-winners/ December 28, 2015.

7. www.lambdaliterary.org/reviews/08/29/lambda-literary-foundation-announces-new-guidelines-for-lambda-literary-awards-submissions/ December 28, 2015.
8. www.lambdaliterary.org/reviews/08/29/lambda-literary-foundation-announces-new-guidelines-for-lambda-literary-awards-submissions/ December 28, 2015.
9. Cf. Karen Brodkin, *How Jews Became White Folks and What That Says About Race in America.*
10. As the coeditors of this book mention in the introduction, in 2014 Handler made an "ill-conceived" (his word) joke about Jacqueline Woodson's allergy to watermelons at the National Book Awards ceremony. Handler came under intense and justified criticism. I note here that in the wake of Handler's comment, his whiteness and maleness were even more emphasized and no one mentioned Handler's Jewishness and possible positionality as an outsider. Handler discusses his Jewish heritage and its influences on his writing at http://bwog.com/2014/09/03/the-kids-arent-all-right-a-conversation-with-daniel-handler/.
11. http://ccbc.education.wisc.edu/books/pcstats.asp December 28, 2015.
12. http://blog.leeandlow.com/2013/06/17/why-hasnt-the-number-of-multicultural-books-increased-in-eighteen-years/ December 28, 2015.
13. Miller aptly points out the problem with the word "distinguished":

    If the implicit definition of "distinguished" is "marked by excellence," "distinct," and "marked by distinction," then the Newbery definition of distinction is inarguably self-characterized. The vagueness of this definition certainly is a cause for concern. It is a definition whose meaning is completely dependent upon an individual's standards for what should be considered excellent—i.e. an individual's opinion.

14. www.ala.org/alsc/awardsgrants/bookmedia/newberymedal/newberyterms/newberyterms December 28, 2015.
15. www.firstbook.org/first-book-story/index.php?option=com_content&view=article&id=297.
16. http://publishersweekly.com/pw/by-topic/childrens/childrens-industry-news/article/64420-diversity-group-announces-walter-dean-myers-award-and-grants.html December 28, 2015.
17. In 2015, the Newbery Committee did award an African-American author, Kwame Alexander, the Newbery Medal for his book *The Crossover*. The selection of Alexander heartens me, but I do not think we'll see the kind of change in the choice of winners that is necessary. I am reminded of the situation with the Academy Awards. In 2014, the film *Twelve Years a Slave* won the "Best Picture" award, and three African-Americans or of African descent were nominated in all acting categories, but in 2015, no African-American actors, directors, or writers were nominated, in "the most racially uniform group of acting nominees since 1998." This lack of diversity prompted the host Neil Patrick Harris to say, "Today we honor Hollywood's best and whitest. Sorry ... brightest" (www.huffingtonpost.com/2015/02/22/neil-patrick-harris-mocks-white-oscars_n_6707250.html). December 28, 2015.

7 The Pura Belpré Medal
The Latino/a Child in America, the "Need" for Diversity, and Name-branding Latinidad

Marilisa Jiménez García

> [P]resented to a Latino/Latina writer and illustrator whose work best portrays, affirms, and celebrates the Latino cultural experience in an outstanding work of literature for children and youth.
>
> —Pura Belpré Medal criteria

The American Library Association (ALA) marks the twentieth anniversary of the Pura Belpré Medal for Best Latino Children's Literature in 2016, making this a key moment in which scholars might reflect on the Medal's mission and legacy. Since 1996, the Belpré Medal has ostensibly raised the visibility of Latino/a children's and young adult (YA) authors and illustrators. Established by two Mexican-American librarians, Oralia Garza de Cortés and Sandra Rios Balderrama, the Medal honors the legacy of the first Latina librarian in the New York Public Library and the first published Latina children's author who sought to provide Latino/a youth with culturally relevant literature. The Medal named in her honor strives to ensure that Latino/a authors and illustrators endure in a literary field and market prone to racial erasure. Countless reports and calls for diversity in children's literature, however, frame Latino/a children's and YA literature as almost non-existent. How do we explain this disconnect or seeming lack of effectiveness? Has the Medal failed to make a significant difference? Or do commentators fail to see Latino/a children's literature *despite* its presence and *despite* the positive effects of the Belpré Medal?

Such questions must be pursued in light of the broader racial segregation of American children's literature, reflected and confirmed in its prizing activities. Unfortunately, American children's literature scholarship has largely shied away from examining that segregation and how it can be reinforced and reproduced in scholarship itself. The 2014 Children's Literature Association (ChLA) conference in South Carolina represented a long-overdue call for engaged critical attention to race and diversity in the study and analysis of children's literature—even to activism.[1] As she has done in her earlier work, keynote speaker Katherine Capshaw proposed that scholars consider and adopt the socio-cultural tools offered by fields such as ethnic studies. I would add that there remains an all-too-persistent field-wide and unspoken consensus that "children's literature" refers to

Anglo-normative traditions, with anything else requiring an "ethnic" tag or lens.

Despite their positive effects, book prizes based on race and ethnicity such as the Belpré have done little to rupture the racial politics of the children's literary world. As the social media campaign-turned-nonprofit organization demands: #WeNeedDiverseBooks.[2] Yet, the current conversation on diversity in children's literature only rehearses a century-old predicament. In this essay, I want to emphasize this message instead: #WeNeedMoreThanLibros. We need more than diverse books and even more than diverse book prizes. We need a field of children's literature—English departments, educators, libraries, and publishers—that includes people of color. And we need antiracist mechanisms that push past the narrow affirmations of literary distinction. This chapter analyzes perceptions of the Latino/a child in the U.S. in the diversity conversation, while also examining the Belpré Medal as both a kind of remedy for, and problem with, name-branding *latinidad*[3] on the children's bookshelf.

Perhaps stemming from public awareness of the growing Latino/a population in the U.S. classroom, the Latino/a child historically appears in academic and popular discourse as a source of anxiety. Latino/a children embody notions of an ever-changing America with an ambiguous racial, national, and linguistic heritage. They also challenge, both legally and practically, our general idealizations about the privileges of U.S. citizenship. For example, consider the plight of undocumented Mexican and Central American youth protesting for legal status while Puerto Rican youth, citizens from birth, demand full rights of citizenship, including educational equity. Even the much discussed #WeNeedDiverseBooks campaign positions the Latino/a child as a problem and object for intervention (Lewis 1966; Nieto 1995; Rich 2012; Diaz 2013). Latino/a children are depicted as a "needy" bunch. They "need" more stories representing Latino/a heritage, parents "need" to read to Latino/a children, and, by extension, society "needs" more books representing Latino/a and other ethnic minorities. The Latino/a child, it seems, requires literature about his/her heritage, a heritage often interpreted as cultures and traditions derived from a Latin American/ Caribbean homeland and home language of Spanish, regardless of birthplace. Yet, without denying the importance of cultural pride, my analysis of the Belpré Medal suggests that the sustained emphasis from publishers and authors on immigration and migration narratives rehearses an overwhelming message for Latino/a children: You are not from here, meaning the U.S. That message determines what "need" means in problematic ways.

In this chapter, I move beyond the conversations about the lack of Latino/a children's literature and need for culturally relevant books, and also beyond the celebrations of folk culture (food, music, sports heroes, festivals, etc.). I examine how the Medal tracks a course for Latino/a children's literature, what it rewards, and how it speaks to the place of the Latino/a child as an established U.S. identity. How, I ask, did the establishment of the Belpré

Medal and its particular set of winning titles represent a critical agenda for Latino/a children's literature? My discussion also considers the function of prizing and canon formation in general. I reflect on prizing and canon formation as a means of underlining how difference, particularly racial, linguistic, and national difference, fares in children's book prizing history. Medals such as the Belpré address and also constitute a "need," thereby propagating a kind of specialized segregation. This function is especially apparent when we compare the Belpré Medal to the alleged top prize in American children's literature, the ALA's John Newbery Medal, given for the "most distinguished contribution to American literature for children published by an American publisher in the United States in English."[4] How do such prizes define what is and is not American literature for children? What is absorbed by and/or left out in the criteria of "English"? Was the Belpré Medal merely intended to fill a Latino/a gap? If it has not changed the larger landscape of children's literature, has it created a canon of Latino/a children's literature, and if so, is that a good thing or not? Ultimately, I read the "success" of the Belpré Medal as also a failure of the larger children's literature field to incorporate Latino/a children's literature, and to learn from the broader cultural conversation about what it might mean to be an "American" child.

"Separate is Never Equal": The Belpré Medal, the "Needy" Latino/a Child, and the Organization of Children's Literature

Duncan Tonatiuh, a two-time Belpré winner for illustration and narrative, receives much-deserved merit and attention for his work in Latino/a children's literature. As with other Medal winners, Tonatiuh's honors give him a certain amount of credibility when engaging parents, teachers, and students during his classroom, library, and bookstore visits.[5] Tonatiuh's combination of pre-Colombian art and tough political issues, such as border crossing (*Pancho Rabbit and the Coyote, A Migrant's Tale*) signals the new wave of Belpré-winning titles. His latest *Separate is Never Equal: Sylvia Mendez and Her Family's Fight for Desegregation* (2014) takes on the issue of school desegregation. The story of Sylvia Mendez's struggle to receive an equal education and attend the same school as white children, almost fifteen years before *Brown v. Board of Education* (1964), revisits this historic, though often forgotten, court decision. In the book's foreword, Tonatiuh's comments on how he sees *Separate is Never Equal* as a way of reminding children, and society as a whole, of this important moment in U.S. Latino/a history. Tonatiuh's title suggests the propensity in U.S. culture to exclude people of color from mainstream narratives of schooling, history, and children's literature.

Separate is Never Equal has been extensively promoted during the #WeNeedDiverseBooks campaign. That campaign rehearses the complaints and problems that have plagued American children's literature with regard to diversity for almost 100 years, signaling the need for field-wide revolution rather than simply more or better books. Since around the 1920s, the model for systematizing the children's bookshelf has simultaneously nurtured a sense of global child citizenship and a specialized segregation. The rise of children's librarianship and children's reading rooms, as Jacquelyn Eddy has shown, developed during a time when pioneering children's librarians such as the New York Public Library's Anne Carroll Moore were interested in internationalizing American children's reading habits. This meant an emphasis on collecting international folklore and fairytales as representative of each nation's heritage (Eddy 2006).[6] The New York Public Library (NYPL), as a landmark cultural institution, and Moore, through her leadership and training of librarians of color such as Augusta Baker and Pura Belpré, made a lasting impression on the child's literary world, both through the organization of children's reading rooms and the influence on publishers. Indeed, Baker and Belpré remain central figures in African-American and Latino/a children's literature, respectively. Further, Belpré became the namesake for the Latino/a children's prize. These women did more than systematize and catalog "ethnic" traditions. Because of the NYPL's training and emphasis on performing story hours, something again which was highly professionalized, Wilson and Belpré also participated in a literary and cultural project. In Belpré's case, her story hours led to her own published books which by 1931 created a foundation for a Latino/a children's literature in the U.S. in English, and to an extent Latino/a literature as a whole (Jiménez García 2014).

Yet, when it comes to Latino/a children's literature, as with the Latino/a child and Latino/a culture, the American mainstream seems to perpetually discover it, perhaps inspired by each decade's census numbers. In each decade, the conversation re-hatches: Who are Latino/as? Is it best to use the term Latino/a or Hispanic? How did Latino/as arrive in the U.S.? Is it a matter of immigration, migration, diaspora? What about the use of Spanish? Keep it? Take it away? What about Spanglish? The redundancy of these anxieties, though critical, continually frames the Latino/a child as a foreigner as opposed to a historical, complex U.S. identity. Indeed, when it comes to the Puerto Rican child, though legal citizenship is a non-issue, the denial of his/her position as inside U.S. culture still prevails. In children's literature, scholars usually trace the diversity conversation to the civil rights era and Nancy Larrick's 1965 study on "The All White World of Children's Books" or the work of the Council on Interracial Children's Books,[7] who published guides on racial bias and the scarcity of Latino/a materials for children (Serrato 2014). However, Belpré argued for the need to recognize Latino/a children in children's books as early as the 1930s. Throughout her sixty-year career, she commented on everything from stereotypical characters to the lack of books to unsupportive school systems to the importance of parent interaction (Sánchez González, *The Stories I Read*, 2013).[8] Sound familiar? Reflecting on children's librarianship and publishing history, we see that minority cultures were part of the formation and development of these areas, and their subsequent practices. Yet attempts to integrate these cultures into the mainstream conversation on children's books persistently fail.[9]

With a short hiatus during her marriage to Clarence Cameron White, Belpré labored for 60 years, in New York City's densely Spanish-speaking neighborhoods, including Spanish Harlem and the South Bronx. She trained other Spanish-specialist librarians such as Lillian Lopes and helped found the South Bronx Project, an intensive outreach strategy in one of the U.S.'s most disadvantaged neighborhoods. Belpré held that the Puerto Rican child in particular needed to learn her heritage through storybooks and story-telling, since thanks to the U.S. colonial project, the dominant belief was that Puerto Ricans had no history (Jiménez García, "Pura Belpré" 2014). As with Moore's sort of mini-United Nations of fairytales and folklore, Belpré re-told and re-wrote folkloric traditions which she believed gave this child access to an empowering historical purview, built a sense of community, and ignited opportunities for learning.

Unfortunately, we have memorialized and/or forgotten Belpré in telling ways. Her work remains available in selected public libraries in the U.S., mainly areas with dense Latino/a populations. But her books have largely been out of print for over 40 years. Clearly, a rich group of writers has emerged since that time, but the diminishment of Belpré's achievements is a serious problem for the history of U.S. Latino/a writing and American children's literature. Shelley Diaz and Phillip Serrato both underline a lack of awareness of Latino/a titles as the root of the diversity problem, as opposed to a lack of Latino/a books (Diaz 2013; Serrato 2014). That is, we have the books, yet parents, teachers, and readers don't know enough about them. The challenge is two-fold: Latino/a titles require support from the publishing industry, and also support from the wider public, including scholars.

One reason why Latino/a pioneers such as Belpré and Chicano writer and labor organizer Ernesto Galarza ("mini-libros") fall off the literary radar is because they are often coded as activists rather than as artists and writers. That coding hinders the construction of Latino/a children's literature as a literary tradition.[10] For example, before Lisa Sánchez González's important work on Belpré, few knew about Belpré's writing and published work (2001, 2013). The relationship between writing and activism in Latino/a communities arguably confuses the mainstream literary market, contributing to Belpré and Galarza's titles remaining out of print, and to the sense of Latino/a children's literature as a sudden, pressing need rather than an ongoing tradition. Latino/a children's literature needs to confront this notion that it is a sudden need and that its generators are well-meaning activists but not authors. It is certainly true that Latino/a authorship in children's literature, especially in the 1920–40s and late 1960s, has functioned as a form of activism. But one function does not cancel out others. As Sánchez González has shown, Belpré was a brilliant, fantastical, and feminist writer. The Belpré Medal's logical mission to reward an author who "best portrays, affirms, and celebrates the Latino cultural experience in an outstanding work of literature for children and youth" underlines activism and literary achievement as productive counterparts, though public circulation of Belpré's titles is limited.

As the case of Belpré makes clear, children's book prizing is a segregated institution in more than one way. For better and for worse, the Belpré Medal exists because the Newbery Medal exists. As Kenneth Kidd has specified, "the Newbery Medal helped establish the modern awards system of children's literature" making the ALA and librarians the "tastemakers" in children's literature, although arguments exist for other children's book tastemakers, such as *The New York Times Bestseller List* and *Notable Children's Books of the Year*, which, I would add, often leave out Latino/a writers (Kidd, 2007, 168; Fitzsimmons 2012). Librarians formed the Newbery mission by emphasizing both literariness and a utilitarian and pedagogical approach to children's books (echoed in the "we need" rhetoric of today). Given its founding in 1921 and, again, given the contributions of people of color for children's literature at the time—including Baker, Belpré, and W.E.B. Dubois—the Newbery Medal's history repeats the pattern of excluding people of color from the conversation on what it means to be an American child and have an "American *literature* for children" (emphasis mine). This exclusion is built into the mission. Certainly, when you claim to represent the totality of literature for American children, generations will question how you shift according to that nation's population.

Realistically, the Newbery has done little to shift in terms of diverse representation, awarding only seven Medals in its 92-year history to authors of color: Virginia Hamilton for *M.C. Higgins, the Great* (1974), Mildred D. Taylor for *Roll of Thunder, Hear My Cry* (1977), Christopher Paul Curtis for *Budd, Not Buddy* (1999), Linda Sue Park for *A Single Shard* (2001), Cynthia Kadohata for *Kira-Kira* (2004), and Kwame Alexander for *The Crossover* (2014), and Matt de la Peña for *Last Stop on Market Street* (2015). In terms of Latino/a history, the closest the Medal comes prior to de la Peña's recent win is in its 1965 and 1966 winners, *Shadow of a Bull* by Maia Wojciechowska and *I, Juan De Pareja* by Elizabeth Borton de Treviño respectively. Both reward Spanish, European heritage, as Wojciechowska focuses on the life of a Spanish bullfighter, while Treviño centers on the life of the slave, painter, and apprentice of Spanish artist Diego Velásquez. Juan De Pareja, interestingly enough, has been claimed by those interested in Afro-Latino/a history; Pareja notably makes an appearance in Afro-Boricua writer and painter, Eric Velasquez's *Grandma's Gift* (2010), a Belpré Medal winner. Through Pareja, Velasquez presents the reality of mixed racial heritage to child readers. Pareja is an empowering figure as young Eric, the child protagonist, sees a painting of Pareja by Diego Veláquez in the Metropolitan Museum of Art and dreams of becoming an artist.

Dominican-born writer and Belpré Medal winner Julia Alvarez has said that perhaps the ALA should describe the Newbery Medal as "awarded to the writer of the best book about white, two parent households" (Garza, "Blacks, Hispanics" 2008). Newbery Medal committees have not recognized Latino/a writers or books with Latino/a protagonists in the scheme of American literature for children, which helps to justify the Belpré Medal.

One way that the Newbery Medal criteria perhaps excludes Latino/a representations is that literature must be in English, although authors may use foreign language words where "appropriate in context." In such a case, Spanglish would qualify. Even so, most Latino/a children's literature is English-dominant, reflecting the Latino/a diaspora community's identification with English. REFORMA (the National Association for Promoting Library Services to Latinos and the Spanish Speaking) librarians Garza de Cortés and Rios Balderrama began planning the Belpré Medal in 1985 for the purposes of cultivating Latino/a writers and illustrators. In Rose Z. Treviño's *The Pura Belpré Awards: Celebrating Latino Author and Illustrators* (2006), Rios Balderrama writes that when patrons in Texas and California asked for bilingual books and "asked for books that pictured Latino children," librarians were at a loss (xiii). Again, the alleged paucity of materials calls into question the availability of titles by Belpré, Galarza, Nicholasa Mohr, established by the 1980s. Balderrama underlines that the Medal's purpose was to undergird existing Latino/a authors and "affirm the diverse experiences of Latino/a children."

Resisting invisibility seems ingrained in the Belpré Medal's mission. Garza de Cortés and Balderrama modeled the award after the ALA's Coretta Scott King Award, a prize they admired mostly for the visibility it gave authors and illustrators of color. This desire to bring Latino/a authors and illustrators to the forefront led founders to seek a stronger network of alliances in the children's book industry beyond REFORMA. Balderrama writes that "the Belpré Award also needed the recognition and visibility that the Caldecott Medal, Newbery Medal, and Coretta Scott King Award enjoyed" (xv). REFORMA joined forces with ALA to promote the award. In this case, we see the Belpré Medal was imagined as more than as a means of supporting and publicly rewarding Latino/a writers and illustrators, but as a safeguard against the age-old problem of forgetting Latino/a children's literature. This amnesia by the children's book industry and children's literature field as a whole has ironically contributed to the scarcity of materials available for circulation, even when a rich if smallish tradition of materials was indeed available. Indeed, the Belpré Medal serves as a kind of memorial to Latino/a writers: it carries the burden less of creating a tradition of Latino/a children's literature, but of assuring that the existing tradition remains in view. This is a different sort of canon formation, as we often think of canons as containing a host of titles set off (for relative reasons) from the common many. Here, we have a very few set off from the few, so that in the future, at least some may remain in circulation, in-print, and on store shelves.

The Pipeline and the Bottom Line: The Belpré Medal and the Commodification and Study of Latino/a Children's Literature

The Belpré Medal, then, resists the narrative of the mainstream children's literature business that there are no Latino/a books and/or authors. The

Medal affirms a mission which differs from that of the Newbery mission. As Kidd has argued, the Newbery Medal's creation meant that children's books were elevated to a level of art as opposed to books as strictly utilitarian— that children's books served more than a "practical" need, but also "aesthetic and cultural needs" (167). Drawing on Pierre Bourdieu's categories of "highbrow" and "lowbrow," he argues that the Newbery Medal cultivates an "edubrow" culture, a kind of middle-class prestige culture invested in education "an edubrow project with literary tendencies and aspirations" (175). The Belpré Medal, by contrast, functions as a form of activism, maintaining the existing canon while responding to (if not necessarily interrogating) the rhetoric of need.

In today's diversity conversation, what is meant by "needing" diverse children's books? Who "needs"? Minorities or society as a whole? Even in the #WeNeedDiverseBooks campaign, the focus has been on Latino/a children needing to see themselves in books, and indeed, this is important. Latino/a characters should play an important role in the imaginary landscape of the American child's world. However, this sense of Latino/a children needing Latino/a books, African-American children needing African-American books, and so on, evokes the kind of institutional segregation in public education which courts ruled unconstitutional in the 1960s. Such logic of specialized segregation reaches back to Belpré's early career and the professionalization of children's librarianship. For example, as Baker and Belpré gained training and specialization, they were sent to neighborhoods which were characterized as having the greatest need for African-American and Latino/a (mostly seen as bilingual) services. This meant that librarians were sent to neighborhoods with dense populations of African-American/Latino/a families. I have argued elsewhere that while this approach emphasizes the importance of specialized services as a means of reaching and affirming young people of color, it also means that these systems of specialization were segregated by class and race (Jiménez García 2014).

To illustrate the pervasiveness of this segregation, consider the recent NYPL exhibit *The ABC of It: Why Children's Books Matter* by children's literature historian Leonard Marcus, which focuses on the history of children's literature and children's reading rooms.[11] When we come to the exhibit pictures of the old NYPL main reading rooms, we see that it was a space for white children. Belpré's memory is preserved in (only) one of the exhibit stalls, showing puppets made for *Perez and Martina* along with a picture of Belpré conducting story hours at La Casita Maria, a Puerto Rican religious and cultural center (Marcus). The U.S. approach to the children's literary world, pedagogically, creatively, culturally, and socially, for the most part, has affirmed specialized segregation. The prizing system replicates this segregation. In so doing it replicates racialized ideologies of utilitarian "need" and aesthetic distinction. The marginalization of children's books for and about people of color responds to and intensifies this logic of need, making it hard if not impossible for these books to rise beyond the merely or evidently utilitarian. The added responsibility of preserving a marginalized tradition makes matters worse.

When it comes to Latino/a children's literature, from Belpré forward, we have a tendency to absorb this material as didactic and ethnographic—invaluable for its cultural content—rather than seeing it as artistic, experimental, and intellectually challenging. Latino/a children's writers have fared similarly in the scholarship. The problem of segregation extends beyond publishing and the library and educational scene to the scene of literary and cultural criticism. The tradition of Latino/a children's literature, and scholarship on that literature, has been championed by education and library scholars.[12] However, because of disciplinary differences, some understandable, the literary and education fields rarely build from each other's work. The current conversation on diversity suggests that interdisciplinary collaboration is imperative. Tagging Latino/a children's literature as part of multicultural education and/or bilingual education has helped pave a trail for education scholarship, however, as Serrato notes, the multicultural tag may have alternative effects, particularly in the classroom:

> [...] [I]f teachers and parents only see, approach, or present Latino/a children's texts under the auspices of "multicultural literature," which is to say anthropological samplings of what it is like to "be Latino," or as books that allow Latino/a children to "[see] themselves reflected in their reading," they are seriously shortchanging and pigeonholing these texts. Such a perspective effectively reduces/restricts the utility or worth of these texts to token encounters with "diversity" (which is to say, otherness). Ultimately, as "multicultural literature," Latino/a children's literature becomes/remains for many consumers a potentially intimidating or estranged "other" kind of literature (which is to say, literature by, about, and for "others").
>
> (5)

In addition to the multicultural classification, the slow development of Latino/a children's literature in the academy as *literature* plays a part in how these works have been categorized and reviewed. Latino/a literature courses, let alone courses focusing on Latino/a children's literature, are rare to non-existent in English departments nationally.[13] In children's literature programs in the humanities, very few full-time faculty specialize in Latino/a children's literature, and the overall numbers of faculty of color are very shamefully low. Of the ChLA's referred journals, the *Children's Literature Quarterly* has perhaps published more critical articles on Latino/a children's literature with a particular focus on the portrayals of Mexican-American farmworkers.[14] If literature departments do not contribute to the advancement of Latino/a children's literature, indeed to the advancement of other ethnic children's literature in general, through the hiring of faculty and creation of courses, how can the field gain more representation and critical inquiry? Academic studies that do focus on the complexity of Latino/a children's literature often place the roots of these texts in the ethnic studies movements of the 1970s, such as the Galarza in the Chicano movement. However, it is clear that ethnic cultural and literary laborers such as Belpré, Baker, and Langston Hughes were present from the beginning of the rise of American children's literature as a popular industry worthy of prizing (Sánchez González 2001; Capshaw-Smith 2004; Serrato 2014).

The Belpré Medal strives to lift Latino/a children's literature into a realm where these texts form part of a grand literary tradition as well as market. This aspiration is all the more interesting since the general consensus in the publishing world has been that Latino/as literature is basically a non-commodity (i.e. Latino books don't sell). Whatever its failings, the Belpré Medal affirmed the existence of a market for Latino/a children's books. The Medal places a seal of approval that makes "Latino/a" books desirable to booksellers, parents, and schools. Booksellers and publishers hold Belpré Medal celebrations, reminding parents and children about Belpré's mission to Latino/a children—celebrations usually culminate in the selling of books. Belpré award winners such as Tonatiuh and Matt de la Peña participate at conferences such as ALA, sign books and take pictures with supporters—which also usually culminates in the selling of books.[15] Ironically, a woman whose books are out of print helps sell books. "Pura Belpré" is now a category on Amazon.com.[16]

The Face on the Medal: The Changing Phases of *Latinidad* in Children's Literature or What the Medal Rewards

In *Keywords for Children's Literature* (2011), editors Philip Nel and Lissa Paul justify the inclusion of the term "Latino/a" over "Native American" in the collection by saying that the term has developed "a richer and more complex critical discourse [...] there is a debate about the term's meaning, and its gets used in conflicting ways" (3). As I conclude this chapter, I want to focus on how the Belpré Medal defines "Latino/a": "people whose heritage emanates from any of the Spanish-speaking cultures of the Western Hemisphere" (ALA). When I presented this definition at a recent lecture on the Belpré Medal in Spanish Harlem, some educators and parents felt it was inappropriate for children who arrived recently from a Latin American country. Those kids, it was felt, may still identify as Latin American, as opposed to Latino/a. "Latino/a," most felt, refers to those living and identifying in the U.S. Others felt the term left out representative languages such as Portuguese and Ladino.[17] The Belpré Medal's creation also represents an attempt by the children's librarians and the book industry to codify, indeed name-brand, Latino/a culture, something that is near impossible for a group of distinctive nations and languages. A Puerto Rican woman standing in as the face of *latinidad* in children's literature, both its prestige and its commodification, introduces some productive complexities, more than I am able to address here.[18] Belpré's mixed-race heritage as an Afro-Boricua, and her position as a trilingual librarian and storyteller (she also spoke French) points us to the complicated nuances of *latinidad*, even if the Medal criteria fall short.

Belpré once wrote on how composing what she called "multi-ethnic literature" meant that an author was responsible for "the interpretation of a group of human beings to a reader who will form, from his idea ... [an] image, true or distorted" (n.d.). Distorted or not, the images of Latino/a culture in Latino/a children's literature have changed since the Medal's start in 1996. Early winners tended to be poetry collections, or stories emphasizing the dynamics of family, or biographies of cultural heroes such as Diego Rivera and Cesar Chavez. An emphasis on positive, normative portrayals of *latinidad*, some say, functioned as a way of countering the negative stereotypes of drugs, crime, and violence present in earlier narratives by non-Latino writers (Brady 2013). Lately, particularly post-September 11, Belpré Medal and Honor winners have tended to take on riskier issues. One book in particular, *Before We Were Free* (2002) by Julia Alvarez, also a well-known adult author, examines the difficult era of the Trujillo dictatorship in the Dominican Republic. The story plays homage to *The Diary of a Young Girl* (1955) by Anne Frank. In her acceptance speech for the Medal, Alvarez said she had searched for children's and young adult literature that dealt with "the holocausts on our [Latin America and the Caribbean] side of the Atlantic" (2004, 14). Alvarez's use of the term "holocaust" coincides with a trend in children's literature to address historical traumas and their consequences. *Before We Were Free* is a response to Alvarez's fruitless search for material with the historical traumas in Latino/a history. Other authors have followed the trend of re-visiting the holocausts, such as Sonia Manzano in *The Revolution of Evelyn Serrano*, about the Young Lords revolt, and Margarita Engle in *The Lightning Dreamer* (2013), about Cuban abolition. Recent Belpé Medal winners also make strong political statements with regard to what it means to be Latino/a, questioning the complexities of gender and race. For example, 2012 winner *Aristotle and Dante Discover the Secrets of the Universe* by Benjamin Alire Sáenz deals with sexual orientation, and 2014 winner *Yaqui Delgado Wants to Kick Your Ass* by Meg Medina deals with colorism, specifically where the light-skinned protagonist gets bullied at school for not "looking" Latina. The question of what is Latino/a enough in children's books has also come into question. For example, in *The Living* by Matt de la Peña, a 2014 Honor winner, readers only know the characters are Latino/a from references in the novel to border towns and proper names.

The Belpré Medal helps us track a progression of writers and illustrators challenging the norms of what it means to be Latino/a, which constitutes a literary and political project. The Belpré Medal seems inseparable from political activism, even agitation. Yet, would we want such a separation? In a time when the lack of diversity in children's books has been called an "apartheid," and President Barack Obama and former-Secretary of State Hillary Clinton have called attention to the educational disparities of Latino/a children, the Medal suggests to the field of children's literature that we can no longer keep the term "children's literature" in an Anglo-normative vacuum.[19] The Medal also reminds us that studying ethnic traditions should encompass the broader field of literary study. Otherwise, as the history of the Medal's history shows, we have a tendency to forget the labor and presence of people of color. Thanks to the Belpré Medal, Latino/a texts for children have a better chance at staying in print, on shelves, and on syllabi.

Despite the diversification of themes and concerns in Medal-winning titles, the immigration and/or migration experience persists as a popular and arguably problematic theme. Writers have portrayed the experiences of crossing the border, confronting English, and other forms of culture shock to young readers. As Serrato also notes, scholars focusing on Latino/a have likewise "tend[ed] toward matters of immigration and immigrant experiences … Such matters are certainly important and worthy of attention, but there is more to Latino/a children's literature than immigration" (2014, 6). Serrato argues that scholars should work toward "the formulation of new terms for understanding … that transcend the confines instituted and maintained by the tag 'multicultural literature'" (2014, 6). I would add that the emphasis on immigration and migration perpetuates the idea of the Latino/a child as homeless, such that characters are forever coming and going without a place to stand. Considering that U.S. Latino/a children's literature goes back at least 94 years, one has to wonder when the children's literature industry will realize that such literature is here to stay—and that such literature, like the Latino/a child, is actually from the United States and has long been at home, despite claims to the contrary.

Notes

1. Katherine Capshaw Smith, "Ethnic Studies and Children's Literature Studies, A Conversation Between Fields," Keynote Address, 2014 Children's Literature Association Annual Conference, Columbia, South Carolina, June 21, 2014. https://storify.com/ericahateley/kate-capshaw-chla-2014?utm_source=t.co& utm_content=storify-pingback&awesm=sfy.co_rYeq&utm_campaign=&utm_medium=sfy.co-twitter accessed December 14, 2015.
2. The "We Need Diverse Books" hashtag campaign began through a grass-roots organization by the same name in early 2014 and quickly gained support from authors of color such as Jacqueline Woodson, Meg Medina, and Matt de la Peña. Publishers such as Lee and Low also joined the examination of kid lit diversity by publishing "diversity gap" studies: www.leeandlow.com/curriculum-corner/diversity-gap-studies. Accessed December 14, 2015.

    Academics such as Phil Nel, Debbie Reese, and Ebony Elizabeth Thomas have also been active in terms of lending support. By late July 2014, "We Need Diverse Books" had incorporated into a non-profit organization. For more info see: http://weneeddiversebooks.tumblr.com/ accessed December 14, 2015.

3. *Latinidad* is a phrase referring to a kind of pan-Latino/a identity and culture in the U.S.; it carries the idea of *identidad* or identity.

4. Newbery Medal terms and definitions, http://www.ala.org/alsc/awardsgrants/bookmedia/newberymedal/newberyterms/newberyterms accessed December 14, 2015.

5. "Duncan Tonatiuh Wants Latino Children to See Themselves in Books" by Monica Olivera. *NBC Latino*. www.nbcnews.com/news/latino/duncan-tonatiuh-wants-latino-children-see-themselves-books-n136901 accessed December 14, 2015.

6. This can go back to the nineteenth century in terms of folklore and nationalism.

7. The Council on Interracial Children's Books published a series of newsletters and guidebooks identifying what they called "anti-human" values in children's books and textbooks, namely racism, sexism, and ageism. One such volume is the *Human and Anti-human Values in Children's Books* (1976), which included a rating system for educators and parents. A distinction should be made between pointing out racial bias and refuting stereotypes in children's texts and arguing for literary study and quality of children's and young adult books. These are not always the same thing, though, as with the relationship to writing and activism, they should not exclude each other.

8. *Too Small to Fail*, part of the Clinton Global Initiative, http://toosmall.org/. accessed December 14, 2015.
   Key phrases in this initiative include the "word gap," or that children need to hear more words for proper development, including talk and read-aloud.

9. My use of the NYPL, Anne Carroll Moore, and the training held at this institution is not meant to totalize the NYPL as the only influential agent in creating an approach to librarianship. However, I do believe the NYPL's prominence make it an important example in terms of researching the ideology of organizing and systematizing children's literature and children's libraries. More research should be done in terms of critical race theory and the foundations of the U.S. library system.

10. For more information on Galarza's mini-libros, see Roberto M. deAnda's "Ernesto Galarza and Mexican American Children's Literature in the United States" (2012).

11. *The ABC and Why of It: Why Children's Books Matter*, curated by Leonard S. Marcus. New York Public Library, Stephen A. Schwarzman Building, Gottesman Exhibition Hall, http://www.nypl.org/events/exhibitions/abc-it. accessed December 14, 2015.
    Exhibit through 9/7/14.

12. In particular, I underline the work of Sonia Nieto, Carmen Martinez-Roldan, and Carmen Medina.

13. At my own institution, the City University of New York, a historically Latino/a, public, open-access institution which saw the advent of Puerto Rican Studies, along with other ethnic studies programs, and houses Belpré's archival collection, there are a handful of faculty dedicated to teaching Latino/a literature over the 18 schools (colleges and junior colleges).

14. Perhaps, the most current article is Scott A. Beck's "Children of Mexican Farmworkers in Picture Storybooks: Reality, Romanticism, and Representation."

15. La Casa Azul Bookstore, "Pura Belpré Celebration," February 6–8, 2014.

16. Interestingly, Amazon.com categorizes the award for "Latino Literature" not just children's literature, The Pura Belpré Award for Latino Literature, www.amazon.com/s/ref=lp_6285431011_nr_n_8?rh=n%3A283155%2Cn%3A%21233408 8011%2Cn%3A%212334119011%2Cn%3A6285431011%2Cn%3A62888 41011&bbn=6285431011&ie=UTF8&qid=1404245813&rnid=6285431011 accessed December 14, 2015.
17. Part of La Casa Azul's "Pura Belpré Celebration" including a Teachers Development Workshop directed by myself and Galia Sandy, the store's schools program coordinator. The title of my talk was: "The Pura Belpré Medal: Why Latino/a Children's Books Matter," February 6, 2014.
18. Arlene Davila goes much further into the complexities of commodifying Latino/a culture in her book *Latinos, Inc.: The Marketing and Making of a People* (2001).
19. Christopher Myers, "The Apartheid of Children's Literature." *The New York Times.* www.nytimes.com/2014/03/16/opinion/sunday/the-apartheid-of-childrens-literature.html accessed December 14, 2015.

8 Peter's Legacy
The Ezra Jack Keats Book Award

Ramona Caponegro

Established in 1985 and now given to both new picture book authors and illustrators, the Ezra Jack Keats (EJK) Book Award[1] honors "picture books written [and illustrated] in the tradition of Keats—that is, with original, well-told stories that reflect the universal qualities of childhood and the multicultural nature of our world" ("FAQ" n.p.). While "the tradition of Keats" evokes his many lauded picture books ("FAQ" n.p.), it is the image of Peter from *The Snowy Day* (1962) that graces the EJK Book Award's seal. *The Snowy Day* is a milestone in multicultural children's literature, sparking both praise and criticism for its portrayal of an African-American child enjoying the commonplace wonder of a new snowfall. It is also the first book that Keats both wrote and illustrated on his own, so it is even more fitting that Peter appears on an award seal that recognizes the work of emerging picture book authors and illustrators.

The EJK Book Award stands out not only because of its recognition of authors and illustrators who are in the early stages of their careers but also because of its dual focus on universality and diversity, two seemingly contradictory emphases for one award. Although a New Writer Award and a New Illustrator Award have both been given out annually since 2001, these two awards are "known collectively as the Ezra Jack Keats Book *Award*" ("Ezra Jack Keats" web, 2014, n.p.; emphasis mine), uniting two essential—but essentially different—parts of the picture book under one award. Likewise, the EJK Book Award attempts to unite different approaches to multicultural children's literature, such as "issues" books and "melting pot" books, under the auspices of one award. Moreover, while the prize celebrates authors and illustrators who write and draw characters and events from within their own cultures, the award also honors books by authors and illustrators who create works "outside" of their own cultures, again following in the tradition of Keats. Rather than choosing sides amidst such divisive controversies within multicultural children's literature, the award tries to be as inclusive as possible on all fronts. Admittedly, problems with this all-inclusive approach arise: a universal childhood is far more of an idea than a reality, and unfair power dynamics, as well as potentially inauthentic representations, can result when authors from more dominant cultures publish stories featuring characters from other, traditionally marginalized cultures. Nevertheless, there can be political and social advantages to focusing on the diverse identities of characters rather than their creators and to highlighting common, if not universal, moments of childhood, as evidenced by the example of Peter in *The Snowy Day*. The EJK Book Award also brings greater attention to a diverse array of authors, illustrators, and characters, uniting their stories under one tradition and one prize. Finally, for the purposes of this essay, the award's ambitions make it a unique case study within the larger debates and goals of multicultural children's literature.

Like its namesake, the EJK Book Award frequently champions what Rudine Sims Bishop calls "melting pot" books, those that emphasize the similarities between, and shared everyday experiences of, people from different cultures. While these books may feature diverse child characters, their contents "are not only about Any Child, they are written for Any Reader" (Sims 41). Many scholars and critics, including Bishop,[2] are wary of "melting pot" books because "the refusal to acknowledge cultural differences may be a hint that such differences are undesirable, or, at best, to be ignored" (Bishop 7). But "melting pot" books, or as Corinne Duyvis describes them, works of "incidental diversity," are quickly gaining in popularity because they fulfill the desire for multicultural books to have storylines that do not revolve entirely around characters' diverse identities, as well as social and personal problems that are related to these identities. *The Snowy Day* and Keats's six other picture books with African-American protagonists[3] may be among the most well-known and beloved "melting pot" books, but the EJK Book Award recipients themselves reflect a diversity of experiences, ranging from seasonal changes to social justice issues, and reveal varying depictions of cultural similarities *and* differences. Since the 1960s, multicultural children's literature has expanded to encompass different understandings of itself—as literature about different races and ethnicities, as literature about any and all underrepresented or disempowered groups, and as literature about people of all cultures. While all three of these understandings of multicultural children's literature are still accepted and employed by different scholars and practitioners, the EJK Book Award embraces the broadest possible understanding of diversity, one that includes different ways of thinking and being in the world, as well as different cultures. In short, the award honors a diverse array of works deemed to be broadly relevant and valuable with the only strict caveat being that these works must come from newly established authors and illustrators.

Like the picture book creators it celebrates, the EJK Book Award is still fairly new, and very little has been written about it. Much of the information in this essay about the prize's history and developing criteria comes from the records held at the Ezra Jack Keats Foundation in Brooklyn, New York. The EJK Book Award was proposed in 1983 by Hannah Nuba, the founder and first director of the New York Public Library's Early Childhood Resource and Information Center (ECRIC), and was supported by the Ezra Jack Keats Foundation, then under the auspices of Martin and Lillie Pope.[4]

A Holocaust survivor, Nuba's "sense of dislocation as an immigrant child trying to adjust to a new country helped shape her desire to help other children and their parents" ("Hannah Nuba" n.p.). After witnessing how the children in the ECRIC responded to Keats's picture books, Nuba saw the establishment of the EJK Book Award as another way of helping children and their caregivers (Pope). Through the joint efforts of Nuba and the Popes, the first EJK New Writer Award was given in 1986 to Valerie Flournoy for *The Patchwork Quilt* (1985), an intergenerational story about preserving family memories.

The prize for new picture book writers was bestowed biennially until 1999 when it became an annual award. Then Julie Cummins, the Coordinator of Children's Services at the New York Public Library, made a formal request to Deborah Pope, the Executive Director of the EJK Foundation, for the establishment of the Ezra Jack Keats New Illustrator Award, urging, "With the annualization of the EJK New Writer Award, it is appropriate now to advance fully the spirit of Keats' work by recognizing new illustrators" (Cummins n.p.). Her request was based in part on a letter that Leo Dillon wrote when he declined to serve on the EJK Book Award Committee partially because of the award's emphasis on picture book texts rather than illustrations. Dillon observes,

> Knowing Ezra and sharing the difficulties of surviving as an illustrator in conversations with him, we [Leo and Diane Dillon] can't help feel[ing] he would be disappointed that the focus of his talent is on his writing, not including his graphic contribution.
>
> (Dillon 2000 n.p.)

Following the urging of Cummins and the Dillons, the EJK New Illustrator Award was created and first awarded in 2001 to Bryan Collier for his cityscape collages in *Uptown* (2000), a love song to Harlem.

Two awards, one for authorship and one for illustration, continue to be awarded each year, and, in 2012, the first EJK Honor Book Awards were given out in each category. In 2012, the EJK Foundation also formed a new partnership with the de Grummond Children's Literature Collection, housed at the University of Southern Mississippi, to administer the EJK Book Award and to host the annual award ceremony as part of the Fay B. Kaigler Children's Book Festival. In a press release announcing the change in partnership from the New York Public Library to the de Grummond Collection, Deborah Pope notes, "As the major repository for Ezra's work and a leader in the world of children's literature, the de Grummond is a natural partner for us to further Ezra's legacy through the Book Award" ("The Ezra Jack Keats New Writer" 2014 press release, n.p.). Moreover, the de Grummond Collection's experience with administrating its own award, the University of Southern Mississippi Medallion, which Emily Murphy analyzes in her chapter in this volume, enhances the partnership between the de Grummond Collection and the EJK Foundation. Both of these changes—the addition of the Honor Book Awards and the prize's new co-sponsoring organization—coincided with the fiftieth anniversary of the publication of Keats's *The Snowy Day*.

Even as the number of titles recognized by the EJK Book Award has grown, the criteria for the award have also evolved throughout the award's history. The current guidelines and criteria for the EJK New Writer Award are as follows:

> The EJK New Writer Award is given to a new writer for a picture book written in the tradition of EJK that:
>
> • Highlights the universal qualities of childhood and the strength of the family
> • Reflects the multicultural nature of our world
> • Has an original text and original story (no folk tales or retelling of folk tales)
> • Unifies illustrations and text
> • Avoids stereotypes
> • Is respectful of the child's intelligence, sensitivity, curiosity, and love of learning
> • Displays freshness and originality of language and literary expression.
>
> This award is given for distinguished writing and text, not for illustration.
>
> The intent of the New Writer Award is to identify and encourage early talent. *To be eligible the author will have no more than three children's picture books previously published.*
>
> Books that have *not* already received awards will be given preference.
> ("Ezra Jack Keats New Writer Award and the Ezra Jack Keats New Illustrator Award" 2–3; emphasis in original)

The first six criteria for the EJK New Illustrator Award, as well as the guidelines regarding the illustrator's previous number of publications and the preference for books that have not won other awards, are identical to the criteria for the EJK New Writer Award. Additionally, the seventh criterion for the EJK New Illustrator Award is that "The illustrations should [d]emonstrate excellent command of the chosen medium [and] [d]isplay freshness and originality in style and/or form of artistic expression" ("Ezra Jack Keats New Writer Award and the Ezra Jack Keats New Illustrator Award" 3).

Though the criteria for the EJK Book Award are unique, particularly in regard to the emphasis on universality, it is hardly the only book award to declare itself a multicultural prize. As Kenneth Kidd affirms, "To be sure, civil rights and other progressive social movements have helped to diversify prizing, through the creation of new awards and through critique of the [Newbery] Medal" ("Prizing" 182). As the Civil Rights Movement was ending, the Shirley Kravitz Children's Book Award (later renamed the Sydney Taylor Book Award), created to honor works of Jewish children's literature, and the Coretta Scott King Award, established to celebrate works of African-American children's literature, were launched in 1968 and 1969 respectively. Then, from the late 1980s onwards, other multicultural awards followed, including the Lambda Literary Award for LGBT children's literature (1990),[5] the Pura Belpré Award for Latino/a children's literature (1996),[6] and the Schneider Family Book Award for representations of disability in children's literature (2004), among other prizes.

All of the aforementioned awards have much more specific criteria than the EJK Book Award in terms of the cultures that must be represented in order for books to be eligible for these awards. Despite the variety of cultures being honored by different children's book prizes, the focus of discussions about multicultural awards is frequently on the cultural identities of the authors and illustrators, a complicated issue that both June Cummins and Marilisa Jiménez García unpack in their respective essays in this collection. As Thomas Crisp observes in his article about the changing eligibility requirements for the Lambda Literary Award,[7]

> In recent years, these disagreements [about literature] have sometimes centered around issues of identity politics and representation: Who has the right to tell particular stories and who gets to decide which books are "authentic" depictions of members of a population? These debates often locate their nexus in awards for representations of traditionally marginalized people, with invested parties (i.e. authors, scholars, librarians, and publishers) disagreeing as to whether or not it's "fair" for some of these awards to limit eligibility to those people who self-identify as members of the population being depicted.
>
> (93)

Focusing her discussion on the Coretta Scott King Award and the Pura Belpré Award, Andrea Davis Pinkney defends identity-based awards that "limit eligibility to those people who self-identify as members of the population being depicted" (Crisp 93), calling these awards "a gateway to progress" (Pinkney Awards, n.p.) since they honor books whose characters and creators are frequently overlooked by other prizes, such as the Newbery and Caldecott Awards. Marc Aronson, on the other hand, opposes identity-based prizes, arguing, "These awards cause both white writers and writers of color to suffer the imposition of non-literary criteria on their craft" (n.p.). Not surprisingly, given the criticism that Keats, a White, Jewish author/illustrator, received for depicting characters of color, the EJK Book Award does not include any mention of the cultural identities of potential winners in its criteria. It has honored both authors and illustrators who have written about characters within and "outside" of their own cultural experiences, even as it has celebrated authors, illustrators, and characters from "inside" many different cultures.

The primary identity concern of the EJK Book Award is the newcomer status of potential recipients, admittedly also a "nonliterary criteri[on]" (Aronson n.p.). In fact, as the EJK Foundation's records show, the guidelines regarding the number of potential recipients' previously published books have become more stringent over time, decreasing from six books ("The 1997 Ezra Jack Keats New Writer Award" n.p.) to five ("5/01 Draft" 3) to three (Auerbach n.p.), the award's current limit for defining emerging status in the field. The Coretta Scott King/John Steptoe[8] New Talent Award also uses three previously published books as its standard for determining newness. Established in 1995 as the Genesis Award, the now retitled Coretta Scott King/John Steptoe New Talent Award "recognizes a writer or illustrator whose early potential speaks of things to come" (Henrietta Smith 2009, xii), while also meeting the other criteria established for the Coretta Scott King Award. Although the Steptoe Award and the EJK Book Award employ different parameters of multiculturalism, both awards strive to recognize and promote new authors and illustrators who are creating diverse books.

Yet, in contrast to the Coretta Scott King Award, the Pura Belpré Award, and the Schneider Family Book Award, which are sponsored by the American Library Association, the organization responsible for the largest number of children's book prizes in the United States, the EJK Book Award is supported by two much smaller organizations within the field of children's literature, the EJK Foundation and, more recently, the de Grummond Children's Literature Collection. As a way of compensating for its size and commensurately fewer channels of promotion within the field of children's literature, the EJK Foundation has developed strong links between its literary prize and the literary heritage of Keats. In discussing the Newbery Medal, Kidd remarks,

> Like the Book-of-the-Month Club, if at a different pace, the Medal responded to what Radway calls the "problem of singularity" (163) attendant to the idea of literature—how to market and sell new books without undermining ideals of distinction and talent. Like both the Club and the Great Books plan, the Medal linked texts to a tradition of merit while responding to the pressures of the day.
>
> ("Prizing" 169)

Similarly, the EJK Book Award connects the respect and acclaim awarded to Keats and his books with the new authors and illustrators that it celebrates annually. As Keats's most well-known (albeit most publicly controversial) character, *The Snowy Day*'s Peter has been particularly associated with the award. Claudia J. Nahson observes, "Peter, that endearing little boy with a red-hooded outfit, has acquired an almost iconic quality" (vii), and the EJK Book Award capitalizes on the affection and familiarity invoked by the figure of Peter in his red snowsuit by prominently featuring him on its seal. In this way, the EJK Book Award is able to promote the works of Keats and the works of new picture book creators determined to be following in the tradition of Keats simultaneously.[9]

As previously noted, Keats received both praise and pushback for his efforts at promoting diversity and universality in *The Snowy Day*. Reflecting on Keats's importance within multicultural children's literature, Anita Silvey comments, "As someone who had experienced both poverty and anti-Semitism, Ezra Jack Keats found himself sympathetic to city children from different races and backgrounds who had suffered as he had. These children mattered to him" (7). Consequently, in *The Snowy Day*, Peter, an African-American child in a city, appears on nearly each page, though experiences of poverty and discrimination do not surface at all. As the 1963 Caldecott winner and "the first major full-color picture book to portray a black child" (Silvey 8), *The Snowy Day* already merited a great deal of attention, but Maurice Berger asserts that the book's

> positive reception owed much to the state of race relations in the early 1960s. As the modern civil rights movement was in full swing—the federal courts were systematically dismantling *de jure* segregation, and historical protests and boycotts were foregrounding the problem of racism in America—Keats's book was received with enthusiasm by many progressive educators, librarians, and parents, black and white.
>
> (30)

This enthusiasm was dampened, though not destroyed, by challenges to Keats's right and ability, as a White, Jewish author/illustrator, to depict an authentic child of color, as well as his decision to feature this child in a culturally generic situation. As M. Tyler Sasser notes, "In addition to problems with Keats's race, disconcerted readers also voiced concern over *The Snowy Day*'s not privileging, or even considering, any aspect of Black culture or Black identities" (366). The book's "melting pot" qualities, which were so celebrated by some teachers, librarians, and parents, were also perceived by others as a drawback rather than as an appeal.

Nevertheless, Peter's quiet romp through the snow inspired Harlem Renaissance leaders such as Langston Hughes, Ellen Tarry, Grace Nail Johnson, and Charlemae Hill Rollins (Sasser 360) and paved the way for "issues books" to be among the winners of the EJK Book Award. Sasser argues,

> Beginning with *Brown v. Board of Education* and Emmett Till's murder (1955), both civil rights activists and those who staunchly opposed integration routinely employed the idea of a natural, innocent child. Thus, far from being apolitical, Peter instead participates in civil rights discourse through his perceived innocence.
>
> (360)

The Snowy Day, with its portrayal of Peter as "Any Child" (Sims 41), "buttresses a discourse within the civil rights movement that sought to use both interracial collaboration and the innocent child to attain its goals" (Sasser 361). Intentionally or not, Keats provided a character around which integrationists could rally, suggesting that "melting pot" books or works of "incidental diversity" can engage with political and social issues as readily as other children's books that present seemingly more overt agendas. Therefore, it is not surprising that the EJK Book Award has been presented to multiple "issues" books, works that engage with social justice concerns, since these books can also be seen as following in the tradition of Keats, right alongside the "melting pot" books.

Of course, *The Snowy Day* and, by extension, the EJK Book Award and its recipients are more commonly associated with "melting pot" books, and the importance of "melting pot" books or works of "incidental diversity" has been reasserted in the most recent clamor for a greater number of multicultural children's books, particularly in the face of claims about an overabundance of "issues" books. For example, Laretta Henderson observes, "[F]or the most part African American children's and young adult literature is just as issues driven as is the adult literature, e.g. stories about slavery, the Civil Rights Movement, and biographies of important figures in African American history" (300). In response to such observations, Roger Sutton argues that more "everyday" books about nonwhites rather than "books whose social worthiness is the first—and sometimes last—thing you notice" need to be created in order to increase the number of children's books being published about people of color ("Editorial" n.p.). Likewise, Christopher Myers calls for a greater diversity of genres that feature children of color, asserting that

> [t]his apartheid of literature—in which characters of color are limited to the townships of occasional historical books that concern themselves with the legacies of civil rights and slavery but are never given a pass card to traverse the lands of adventure, curiosity, imagination or personal growth

sets dangerous limitations on how child readers see themselves and their options, both in the present and the future (Myers "Apartheid" n.p.). Myers also insists that as a picture book creator he has a responsibility, as well as a desire, "to depict whole human beings, to allow the children in my [his] books to have the childhoods they ought to have, where surely there are lessons and context and history, but there is also fantasy and giggling and play" (Myers "Young Dreamers" 14).

Certain EJK Book Award recipients provide this outlet for play and imagination for child characters of color, as well as for all potential readers. For example, *Silly Chicken* (2005), by Rukhsana Khan, for which Yunmee Kyong received the 2006 New Illustrator Award, features a Pakistani girl who is jealous of her mother's affection for the family's chicken, at least until she falls in love with a chick of her own. In *Tell Me a Story, Mama* (1990), Angela Johnson, the recipient of the 1991 EJK New Writer Award, introduces a young African-American girl who asks her mother for family stories before proceeding to tell the stories herself. And, in Linda Ashman's *Rain!* (2013), for which Christian Robinson was awarded the 2014 EJK New Illustrator Award, a young African-American boy in a frog hat convinces other city dwellers that bad weather has its upsides. Besides honoring books in which child characters of color playfully interact with their families and neighbors, the EJK Book Award, in the tradition of Keats, also celebrates "everyday" books in which characters from diverse cultures overcome common challenges, such as choosing good friends (*My Best Friend*, 2005), finding ways to stop a baby from crying (*Cinnamon Baby*, 2011), and facing the start of a new school year (*Mom, It's My First Day of Kindergarten!* 2012).

Such works of "incidental diversity" frequently go unacknowledged by other multicultural awards, but the "melting pot" picture books' techniques of quietly identifying similarities among people carry political and social power that should not be underestimated. Just as the figure of Peter resonated with Harlem Renaissance leaders, as well as progressive teachers, librarians, and parents, during the Civil Rights Movement, Christopher Myers sees an ongoing need to add the image of Peter playing in the snow to people's "image libraries" of African-American youth ("Young Dreamers" 13). In an editorial written the day after George Zimmerman was acquitted of the 2012 killing of Trayvon Martin, an unarmed African-American teenager, Myers reflects,

> I wondered: if the man who killed Trayvon Martin had read *The Snowy Day* as a kid, would it have been as easy for him to see a seventeen-year-old in a hoodie, pockets full of rainbow candies and sweet tea, as a threat? What might have been different if images of round-headed Peter and his red hood and his snow angels were already dancing in his head.
>
> ("Young Dreamers" 13)

Clearly, more "melting pot" books are needed not only because there should be a wider variety of multicultural children's literature but also because books about our common humanity may make cultural differences seem less threatening.

Yet, precisely because cultural differences are still often feared, we also need "issues" books. As Duyvis notes,

> It's a fact that ableism, homophobia, and racism influence countless aspects of people's everyday lives. Micro-aggression, stereotypes, internalized prejudice, flagrant bigotry, institutionalised [sic] discrimination [...]. There are also other matters to consider: accessibility, hair or skin care, limited dating pools, communities, culture, etc.
>
> (n.p.)

Just as Christopher Myers connects Trayvon Martin with Peter, Andrea Davis Pinkney connects Martin with Emmett Till, a fourteen-year-old African-American boy who was lynched for allegedly whistling at a White woman in 1955, in her 2014 May Hill Arbuthnot Lecture.[10] Lamenting the senseless deaths of these two young men, she advocates for the essential need for books that teach children and adolescents about the Civil Rights Movement, history, and resisting oppression.

Books about issues of discrimination and injustice frequently win multicultural awards, such as the Coretta Scott King Award, the Pura Belpré Award, and the Lambda Literary Award, as well as other progressive awards, such as the Jane Addams Children's Book Award, but they have been the recipients of the EJK Book Award too. For example, Deborah Wiles and Jerome Lagarrigue received the 2002 EJK New Writer Award and New Illustrator Award respectively for their picture book, *Freedom Summer* (2001), which portrays an interracial friendship in a town that would rather destroy its swimming pool than integrate it. Set in the same time period as *Freedom Summer*, *Going North* (2004) depicts one African-American family's northward pilgrimage in search of higher wages and more equitable treatment, while *Most Loved in All the World* (2009) reveals an African-American mother's preparations to send her daughter out of slavery via the Underground Railroad. In *The Stamp Collector* (2012), a prison guard and an incarcerated dissident writer share stamps, letters, and eventually a story in an unspecified country (presumably China) in which freedom of expression is outlawed. And in *Bird* (2008), an African-American boy narrates the ways in which his older brother's drug addiction and resultant death have devastated his family. These award-winning "issues" books explore historical injustices, as well as ongoing struggles.

The EJK Book Award responds to the needs for both "issues" books and works of "incidental diversity," offering a wide variety of diverse books, while also interpreting multiculturalism in the broadest possible terms. The award has gone to books that feature characters from many different cultures, including non-marginalized cultures, both domestically and internationally, as well as to authors and illustrators from a variety of different cultural backgrounds. The award has also recognized diversity through different ways of thinking and responding to the world as the two friends do in choosing alternative routes to Boston in *Henry Hikes to Fitchburg* (2000) and as Lester and the troupe of clowns do in their decidedly different reactions to Aunt Clara's knitting in *Lester's Dreadful Sweaters* (2012). The range of books that have been honored by this award highlights the subjectivity of the terms "multicultural" and "universal," as well as the term "excellent," a vague but recurring standard for prizing that Robert Bittner and Michelle Superle address in their chapter in this collection. Yet while there can be problems inherent in an understanding of multicultural children's literature that does not consider the shift in power dynamics when "multicultural" no longer only refers to cultures that have traditionally been marginalized, there are also benefits to having so many different picture books and their creators united under the auspices of the EJK Book Award.

Looking back on his adolescent reading practices, Walter Dean Myers asserts, "I didn't want to become the 'black' representative, or some shining example of diversity. What I wanted, needed really, was to become an integral and valued part of the mosaic that I saw around me" ("Where Are" n.p.). The EJK Book Award creates its own mosaic of award recipients, while also helping its winners to launch careers that establish them within the larger mosaic of children's literature. Many of the award winners, such as Angela Johnson, Deborah Wiles, Ana Juan, Bryan Collier, Meg Medina, and K.G. Campbell, have gone on to create other great—and diverse—books, but there remains a need for characters like Peter who are able to spark decades' worth of conversation and change.[11]

Notes

1. The EJK Book Award is entirely separate from the biennial International Award for Excellence in Children's Book Illustration, which the Ezra Jack Keats Foundation, the United Nations International Emergency Fund (UNICEF), and the United States Board on Books for Young People (USBBY) sponsored between 1984 and 1994. The last of these awards was bestowed in 1992 ("A History" n.p.).
2. Rudine Sims Bishop has published scholarship under both of her last names: Sims and Bishop.
3. Keats wrote and illustrated seven books with African-American protagonists: *The Snowy Day* (1962), *Whistle for Willie* (1964), *Peter's Chair* (1967), *A Letter to Amy* (1968), *Goggles!* (1969), *Hi, Cat!* (1970), and *Pet Show!* (1972).
4. The EJK Foundation was founded by Ezra Jack Keats and Martin Pope in 1964. In his will, Keats bequeathed the royalties from his books to the Foundation, which operates as "both a charitable organization and the legal representative for Ezra's books" ("A History" n.p.). In addition to the EJK Book Award, some of the Foundation's other notable projects include the Ezra Jack Keats Bookmaking Competition for third through twelfth grade students and the Ezra Jack Keats Mini-Grants, which support arts and literacy programs in public schools and libraries. For more information about the Foundation's activities, visit its website (www.ezra-jack-keats.org/).
5. The Lambda Literary Awards were first presented in 1989, but the first award within the children's/young adult category was not given out until 1990.
6. Marilisa Jiménez García's chapter in this collection focuses on the Pura Belpré Award and its recipients.
7. In his article, "It's Not the Book, It's Not the Author, It's the Award: The Lambda Literary Award and the Case for Strategic Essentialism" (2011), Thomas Crisp supports the Lambda Literary Foundation's 2009 decision to require authors to identify as members of the LGBT community in order to be eligible for its awards. In 2011, however, the Lambda Literary Foundation reversed its previous position, stating that its awards "are open to all authors regardless of their sexual orientation or gender identity unless otherwise noted" (Awards guidelines n.p.).

8. John Steptoe was an award-winning African-American author/illustrator whose picture books depicted various aspects of the African-American experience. His first book, *Stevie*, was published in 1969, only seven years after *The Snowy Day*, perhaps inevitably leading to comparisons between the two author/illustrators and their works. For example, Rudine Sims writes,

> Ray Anthony Shepard (1971), in a controversial article in the *Interracial Books for Children Bulletin*, compares Ezra Jack Keats's books unfavorably to those of John Steptoe, a young Black artist. Shepard asserts that Keats creates kids who only *look* Black, while Steptoe's kids "know what's happening."
>
> (45; italics in original)

9. The EJK New Writer and New Illustrator Award Selection Committee is tasked with determining which picture books by new authors and illustrators best fit within the tradition of Keats and the criteria of the prize. Since 1999, the committee members have served three-year terms, with an optional consecutive second term ("5/01 Draft Procedures" n.p.). The committee consists of nine people

> selected to represent fields such as illustrators, authors, librarians, early childhood educators, book reviewers, literary critics, and members of such professional organizations as IRA [International Reading Association], NCTE [National Council of Teachers of English], ALA [American Library Association], NAEYC [National Association for the Education of Young Children], and the Children's Book Council.
>
> ("Ezra Jack Keats New Writer Award and the Ezra Jack Keats New Illustrator Award" 1)

10. As part of her 2014 May Hill Arbuthnot Lecture, Pinkney describes her deep desire to publish a book about lynching for a young audience, which led to her editing Marilyn Nelson's *A Wreath for Emmett Till* (2005), which was awarded a Printz Honor Award for excellence in young adult literature and a Coretta Scott King Author Honor Award. Pinkney remarks, "I noticed an uptick, last year, in *A Wreath for Emmett Till* fan mail immediately following the case of Trayvon Martin." Pinkney then visually imagines a fictionalized encounter between Till and Martin with both of them as students at Morehouse College. She dons a hoodie to evoke Martin, asking, "What does one wear to deliver the May Hill Arbuthnot Lecture? Perceptions are important, for better or for worse, for hoodie [Martin] or for hat [Till]. How many of us judge a book or a kid by its cover?" Then she discusses her need to write and publish books that depict people fighting and overcoming injustices (Pinkney "2014 May Hill").

11. I would like to thank Deborah Pope for her assistance in arranging my visit to the Ezra Jack Keats Foundation, for making its papers about the development and changing criteria of the EJK Book Award available to me during my stay, and for her insights into many matters related to the award. I am also grateful for the support of the Children's Literature Association's Diversity Research Grant and the Department of English Language and Literature's Research Fund Initiative at Eastern Michigan University for supporting this project.

9 Race and the Prizing of Children's Literature in Canada
Spotlighting Canada's Governor General's Literary Awards

Barbara McNeil

Introduction

Schooled in the professions of librarianship and teaching, I have been social-ized to pay attention to, and to validate the prizing of children's literature. In the discussion that follows, I employ critical race theory (CRT) (Aylward 1999; Delgado and Stefancic 2000; Gillborn 2005, 2006; Goldberg 2009; Ladson-Billings 2005, Ladson-Billings and Tate 1995) and post-colonial thought (Battiste 2009; Yazzie 2009; Bradford 2007) to critically examine how racialization in the context of colonial/post-colonial domination and subordination has influenced the prizing of children's literature in Canada.

I commence with a general discussion about prizing, and then zoom in on the impact of race on prizing children's literature. This is followed by prob-lematizing winners of Canada's pre-eminent literary prize: The Governor General's Literary Award for children's literature in English and in French. To do so, I critically analyze and trouble two pieces of literature that won this award using the theoretical frameworks identified above. The chapter concludes with a summary and recommendations.

The Meaning of Prizing

The prizing of children's literature is a process that assigns both meaning and value. Expressing a related perspective, Kidd submits that to "prize a book ostensibly is to value it, to mark it out as distinguished ..." (2009, 197). Underscoring and extending the notion of valuing, scholars such as Terry Eagleton historicize the phenomenon of literary valuing by pointing out that the "very definition of literature is indissociable from the nurtur-ing and transmission of certain highly specific ideological values" (1983, 76). According to Eagleton, literary valuing is related to aesthetics and the "effectivity of art and the ideological struggle over evaluation" that is at once perennial and unavoidable—it cannot be elided (76). Eagleton argues that "value is always 'transitive'—that is to say, value for somebody in a particular situation—and that it is always culturally and historically spe-cific" (1983, 77). From such perspective we can conclude that valuing and prizing are context-based and subjective social processes and practices. Fur-thermore, such social processes and practices like children's literature itself are not neutral; rather, they take place in and are reflective of the wider ideological, social, and political context from which they spring and that gives them meaning. Citing George Eliot Eagleton reminds us that "there is no personal life that is not determined by a wider public one, and the way we deal with each other in our smallest interpersonal encounters is not finally separable from the destiny of nations" (1985–6, 104). Therefore, the prizing of children's literature is an act of political interpretation.

In alignment with the foregoing, post-colonial scholar Huggan convincingly asserts that "literary texts, like other cultural forms, have no intrinsic meaning or value: meaning and value are contingent, rather on changing sets of historical circumstance" (1997, 76). From such a sociological perspective, prizing—that is to say valuing—is never neutral. It is not innocent; it is subjective, context, and socio-historically dependent. An aesthetic as well as materialist process, prizing/valuing includes and excludes, affirms, and denies, refuses, as well as represses. It is done by some people, for and on behalf of themselves and others who have particular interests.

In view of the complex and contested nature of literary prizing, it behooves critics, scholars, and consumers of such texts to operationalize "constant vigilance" to the "regimes of value" in which children's literary productions are "produced, distributed, and consumed" (Huggan 1997, 412). To enact such vigilance, an understanding and radical critique of the institutions and agents involved in prizing children's literature in Canada is needed and it is to this I turn.

Prizing Children's Literature in Canada

An appropriate, ethical and realistic discussion of prizing of children's literature in Canada acknowledges that the nation itself is a site of contestation and struggle given the unavoidable truth that it is terrain characterized by "postcolonial colonialism" (Yazzie 2009, 39). Colonization involved, and involves, an extremely harsh process of domination and subordination of all aspects of economic, cultural, social, and political life by the dominant European groups that is being valiantly resisted by Indigenous peoples who have "survived colonization and cognitive imperialism" (Battiste 2009, xvi).

Non-white settlers (e.g. African-Canadians, those of Chinese, Japanese, East Asian descent, and others) have also experienced a similar plight under a regime of white supremacy dominated by Anglo and French Canadians (in that order) in a society where racial, ethnic, and linguistic ordering thrived, and still thrives. These groups, similar to Indigenous ones, have over the course of time, acted resiliently and boldly for literary recognition and to establish their literary presence in Canada.

The preceding discussion is useful for underscoring that Canada and its major institutions are marked by colonization, racial ordering, and are under the hegemonic control of European—white settlers, of whom the most powerful are of British and French ancestry. Examples of such institutions include those involved with publishing and prizing children's literature. As concerns children's literature prizing, the Governor General Literary Awards (commonly known as the GGs), administered by the Canada Council for the Arts, is among the most prestigious and lucrative prizes in the nation. Each winner receives an award of $25,000. Information from the Canada Council for the Arts explains that

> The Governor General's Literary Awards are given annually to the best English-language and the best French-language book in each of the seven categories of Fiction, Literary Non-fiction, Poetry, Drama, Children's Literature (text), Children's Literature (illustration) and Translation (from French to English).

The Council's website lists the following set of "fundamental values" that guide its work. It states:

> As an organization, we:

- maintain an *arm's length relationship* from government, which allows the Council to develop policies and programs and make decisions without undue political pressure or influence.
- support *freedom of artistic expression* from control or dominance by external forces such as governments and markets, a value reinforced by the arm's length relationship.
- believe *in government investment in the arts as a public good* enabling the arts to contribute to peoples' lives, encouraging arts development across Canada, and freeing art from complete reliance on the marketplace.
- seek to *develop excellent art in* Canada by focusing *on professional artistic activity by individuals and organizations*, respecting *artistic excellence* as the primary criterion in providing grants, and relying on peer assessment as the best method for determining comparative merit in a national context.
- believe *in the value of a national perspective of the arts*, to enrich knowledge within the Council and the arts community, foster attitudes inclusive of all art forms and artistic traditions, and provide national and international leadership.
- respect Canada's *official languages* and recognize the need to support professional artistic activity by both French- and English-speaking Canadians.
- respect the *regional diversity* of Canada and recognize the need to support professional artistic activity in all parts of the country.
- respect the histories, traditions, languages, and contemporary practices of *Aboriginal Peoples* and seek to foster the development of Aboriginal artists and organizations.

- respect artists and arts organizations from *diverse cultural and racial backgrounds* and traditions and seek to develop the work of these artists and organizations.

I draw attention to the Canada Council for the Arts' expressed valuation of the two "official languages," respect for "regional diversity" and the last two items on the list that pertain to Aboriginal peoples—respect [their] histories, traditions, languages etc., and the commitment to "respect artists and arts organizations from diverse cultural and racial backgrounds and traditions and seek to develop the work of these artists and organizations." An equity framework was subsequently developed in 2012 to also guide prizing done on behalf of Canadian citizens and their vision of the country.

The Equity Framework of Canada Council is an extensive document that is available online. Noteworthy for my purposes are the Framework's "commitment to institutional values and an adherence to the *Canadian Charter of Rights and Freedoms, the Canadian Human Rights Act, the Employment Equity Act, the Canadian Multiculturalism Act, and the Official Languages Act*" (italics in the original) (Canada Council for the Arts 2014). Although the preceding are heartening as well as intellectually and ideologically important declarations, what is even more important is evidence that attests that the Canada Council lives and manifests the values embedded in its framework through what and whom it chooses to validate in its prizing.

The Equity Framework of the Canada Council makes no reference to the United Nations (UN) Conventions on the Rights of the Child, which specifically addresses the rights of children (Convention" May 28, 2014). I argue in the discussion that follows that inclusion of the UN Convention on the Rights of the Child in the Canada Council's Equity Framework is important—especially since 1988 when the Canada Council added categories that specially relate to literature for children and after 1989 when the UN Convention on the Rights of the Child was adopted.

Race and Prizing of Children's Literature in Canada

In this section I use two specific pieces of literature to problematize, critique and trouble works that have been recipients of Canada's premier prize for children's literature: The Governor General's Literary Awards. The online Canadian Encyclopedia points out that "like any prize, the Governor General's Awards are controversial from time to time; contemporary judgments do not always stand the test of time. There is a general complaint that writers have not always won for their best work [...]" (Governor General's Awards 2014).

Such statements resonate with my perspectives on two works that have won Canada's premier prize for children's literature. I begin with Anne Villeneuve's *The Red Scarf/Écharpe Rouge*, winner of the Governor

General's Prize for children's literature—illustration (in French) in 2000, and later published in English in 2009.

Winning the prize for illustration, the *Red Scarf* is primarily a wordless picture book; it has eight precious words of text—words that introduce the main character. He is Turpin, an anthropomorphized, white, male dog who is a taxi driver. His surprise adventure ensues after issuing these words of lament, "Another gray day, says Turpin, the taxi driver." In brief, the book employs an ink and crayon-fashioned cartoon to tell the story of a bored Turpin, who after dropping off one customer, picks up another. This time the customer is a human male dressed in top/fancy hat and black coat. In dizzying haste, the distinguished looking customer accidentally leaves his red scarf on the back seat of the taxi. Seeing the scarf, the bored but honest Turpin, rushes after the customer to return it.

Unaware of the pursuing Turpin, the fancy coat-and-hat-wearing man enters a "red top," a circus tent—a space of performance, where the audience is encouraged to mock, laugh at, and have fun at the expense of the performers. The images used by Villeneuve illustrate a stereotypical world allusive of the nineteenth-century circus, inclusive of menageries characterized by unusual animals. Villeneuve clearly shows us a world of exoticism, orientalism (Said, 1978/2006), the unusual, the unexpected, freak shows/side shows (reliant on displaying so-called "human oddities" such as a male fakir (an elephant trainer dressed à la oriental) and a female fakir (lion trainer)).

Arriving at the entrance of such a world, Turpin encounters a member of the exotic menagerie: a green lizard on a unicycle that guards the entrance that leads to the performers. At first unwilling to allow passage to the frenzied Turpin, the lizard is eventually persuaded by the taxi driver and his evidence—the red scarf, and ultimately lets him through. With the dazzling red scarf in hand, Turpin moves further and further into the zany world of playful and curious circus characters. He meets a polar bear on roller skates from whom he flees only to find himself facing a lion that is equally curious about the taxi driver and the red scarf. The lion eventually snatches it from the terrified but determined Turpin, and swallows them both. The female fakir arrives in the nick of time, sees the lion with the red scarf, and with whip and chair in hand, saves Turpin and the red scarf. Once again, an explanation is needed and is granted by the mission-oriented dog.

Hearing Turpin's story, the lion trainer provides the direction needed to locate the owner of the scarlet scarf. Dedicated to reuniting scarf and owner, Turpin eventually catches the man but the latter is still in a hurry. Turpin follows and finds himself in the spotlight on a stage where the reader sees a simian—a circus monkey hanging on a pole and curiously as well as whimsically looking at the unexpected visitor. This page marks the beginning of my unease, disquiet and disbelief and this is because of Villeneuve's rendition of the monkey: he wears a North African fez, his eyes are bulging, nostrils are flared, lips are painted red, and the exaggeratedly thick lips appear to run from ear to ear. A page later, a thick-lipped monkey appears, this time in

top/fancy hat, and can be seen on two subsequent pages. On the penulti-
mate page of the story, Turpin is in the company of two similarly depicted
monkeys, the female lion tamer, and the owner of the red scarf who wave
good-bye to him. The monkeys are anthropomorphized in blackface minstrelsy. According to Décoste,

> Blackface, a practice whereby a white actor painted his face black
> before mocking African slaves and their descendants, is a formula
> ingrained in the history of North America. Blackface minstrelsy was
> a lucrative and easy form of entertainment for whites from the 1800s
> onwards. Caricaturing African-American patois, song, and dance cre-
> ated and reinforced racist stereotypes in an era where Blacks were con-
> sidered subhuman. In time, Black comedians would adopt self-derision
> as entertainment, as it was often the only alternative to menial, miser-
> able employment reserved for these second-class citizens. Stereotypes
> embodied in the "Jim Crow" characters of blackface minstrels played
> a significant role in cementing and proliferating racist images, atti-
> tudes and perceptions worldwide.
>
> (Para. 2)

As an African-Canadian, mother, teacher, scholar, and citizen advocate
for social justice, I feel compelled to trouble Villeneuve's recuperation and
reproduction of racist discourses through the use of questionable simian
imagery that are evocative of blackface minstrelsy of the nineteenth century in a work for children. Furthermore, I am deeply dissatisfied that a
work that draws on such reprehensible and offensive discourses and that
employs deeply racist images of blackface minstrelsy was awarded Canada's
premier prize for children's illustration in the year 2000. For whose edifi-
cation and pleasure is this work intended? It is certainly not the Black or
African-Canadian child and I believe enough in positive humanity to be
convinced that it is not in the best interests of white and other children to
experience Villeneuve's monkey in blackface that blends and merges monkeys with Black people.

I assert that the racist imagery of the exaggerated, thick, red lips of the
monkeys is demeaning to African-Canadians/Blacks, and all others committed to the affirmation of the dignity of all people—especially children.
For example, "in the Universal Declaration of Human Rights, the United
Nations has proclaimed that childhood is entitled to special care and assistance" (United Nations) and it is my contention that the monkeys depicted
in Villeneuve's book, (whether consciously or not) allude to the images of
racial ridicule directed at Blacks. Imagery such as those of the anthropomorphized monkeys in Villeneuve's award-winning book have the strong
potential of derogating the self-image of African-Canadian and Black children everywhere. Yet, there has been a disturbing silence about the racist
iconology summoned by Villeneuve.

There is nothing harmless about the reproduction of blackface minstrelsy in Villeneuve's book. The racist discourse and biological racism (Harding 2006) illustrated in *The Red Scarf* are not traditions that should be resurrected or reproduced in children's literature. There is no space in such literature for the discourse of a minstrelized, "cute" grinning monkey explicitly coded in North African fez and the kind of exaggerated lips—the overall stereotypical representation of Blacks in minstrel shows. A question that must be asked is this: at whose expense are the monkeys cute?

It is at the expense of all children, since racism hurts us all, but it is primarily at the expense of Black/African-Canadian children who should not be exposed to such imagery in primary schools (since that is the principal audience for *The Red Scarf*). Indeed, it may be possible for teachers, parents, and teacher-librarians to use the book without provoking strong reactions from children (of all races) but there is the rub. The book may be absorbed and/or interpreted as one of pure, good fun about Turpin and his exciting day under the red top of a circus and this is exactly why the situation is troubling and exasperating. Children rely on adults to make reasonable book choices that are identity and dignity enhancing for all. *The Red Scarf* is not such a book; yet the Canada Council's Governor General's Literary Award has prized it in a manner that lends credibility, acceptability, and trustworthiness to the book. This is a pity.

Why did the author depict the monkeys in the fashion she did? What occluded the vision and heart of the author from foreseeing, imagining, and feeling the potential hurt her depictions would cause? What caused the malfunction of peer assessment on which the Canada Council relies for evaluating the book's suitability for a Governor General's Literary Award? What made this work acceptable to them? What caused the failure to consider the book's potential to perpetuate toxic racism? Also, why has the presence of these particular monkeys not elicited questioning and/or critique from reviewers? Why was/is this book acceptable to them, to us as tax-paying Canadian citizens who constantly claim strong commitments to a fair, just, and anti-racist society? To find answers, I turn to CRT.

A primary insight of CRT is that "racism is normal, not aberrant, in American [and Canadian] society" (Delgado and Stefancic 2000, xvi). These scholars point out that "[b]ecause racism is an ingrained feature of our landscape, it looks ordinary and natural to persons in the culture." This perspective on racism can be deployed to explain the conflation of monkeys with Black people in a work of literature for children, the subsequent prizing of such literature by the dominant literary prizing agency in Canada, and the general silence about it by reviewers in white controlled presses. Therefore, CRT is useful for uncovering the continuing dynamics of racialized power and its embeddedness in practices that may appear to be stripped of any explicit, formal manifestations of racism (Crenshaw et al. 1996).

The bestowing of a Governor General's Literary Award on *The Red Scarf*, validates CRT's view that racism is indeed "endemic" and "'normal' not aberrant nor rare" but rather "deeply ingrained [...] culturally" (Delgado and Stefancic xvi). The granting of the award to *The Red Scarf* speaks to the myopia and indifference of prevailing white supremacy that appears blinded to the oppressive nature of its domination of the prizing of children's literature and points to insensitivity to the histories and social locations of marginalized racial groups such as African-Canadians. Furthermore, the prizing of Villeneuve's award-winning work, speaks to the pertinence of one of the defining elements of CRT: the call to context and a challenge to ahistoricism.

The prizing of the book reveals a regrettable ahistoricism—failure to consider the historical hurtful association between Blacks and monkeys as well as blackface minstrelsy—and thus a lack of knowledge on the part of the mostly state-funded Canada Council, the awards administrator, as well as on the part of the Governor General who sanctioned the award by presenting it. Their failure to closely examine the illustrations and to consecrate the book highlights the importance of adopting critical social consciousness (Freire 1970)—"an on-going interaction of reflection, dialogue, and action" as praxis in the world (Darder, Baltodano and Torres 2009, 13).

Reflection, dialogue, and critical action are essential when evaluating children's literature in multiracial, multiethnic, multicultural, and multilingual societies such as Canada. In the interest of social justice for all groups, it must be incumbent on award givers such as the Canada Council to reject ahistoricism in favor of historicism/New historicism, which calls for the inclusion of context—social and political circumstances (Myers 1988–9) in the (re)construction, interpretation, and use of literature.

The Canada Council's publication of an Equity Framework in 2012 (and updated in 2014) represents a movement (at least on paper) toward being more responsive, sensitive, respectful, and inclusive of the histories and diversities of Canadians. However, I assert that the Equity Framework, though well-intentioned, remains rooted in white supremacy and illustrates a disappointing and an attenuated criticality on the part of that institution because it is silent on the issue of race and the role it has played in the construction of Canadian society. There does not yet appear to be sensitivity and understanding that utilizing a critical racial lens or using the lens of CRT to analyze narratives and images about racialized Canadians is a necessary though "hot potato" issue in the prizing of children's and other literature. Consider, for example, *Northwest Passage* (Rogers and James 2013) the picture book that won a Governor General's Literary Award for illustration—of a children's text in English in 2013.

The book is an illustrated narration of a well-known Canadian "road" song of the same name, *Northwest Passage*, by folklorist Stan Rogers. It tells the story of Roger's overland mimetic journey of the Franklin expedition and is James' contemporary recounting of the voyage. The song, together with James' non-fiction commentary are projects of praise, expressing admiration for European colonial enterprises such as that of explorer John Franklin (1786–1847) and his men who unsuccessfully sailed the Beaufort

Sea in search of a northwest passage to the Orient/Pacific Sea. A white settler anthem to imperialism/colonialism, the refrain of the song is as follows:

> Ah, for just one time
> I would take the Northwest Passage,
> To find the hand of Franklin reaching for the Beaufort Sea,
> Tracing one warm line through a land so wide and Savage,
> And make a Northwest Passage to the sea.

Lyrics such as the foregoing, indicate Roger's affection and strong identification with the white colonial/imperial project, and the illustrator's valorization of the song through art and commentary, and the retelling of the Franklin expedition represents a contemporary reification of colonial conquest of Indigenous lands and silences, through exclusion, the brutal experience, and legacy of colonization on Aboriginal Canadians.

Given the colonial content and context of the song, I employ post-colonial Indigenous thought (Battiste 2009) and theory (Bradford 2007) to examine *Northwest Passage*. Post-colonial Indigenous thought enables us to understand that Aboriginal Canadians still lament the loss of their lands, and are "still undergoing trauma and stress from genocide and the destruction of their lives by colonization" (Battiste xxii). Therefore, the prizing of a book whose text (the song lyrics) and illustrations valorize colonization and white triumphalism illustrates the ongoing existence of colonial mentalities and structures and "neocolonial tendencies that resist decolonization."

If we are to take the Canada Council at its word that,

> [i]n accordance with the *Canadian Charter of Rights and Freedoms* and the *Canadian Human Rights Act*, the Council recognizes the individual worth and dignity of all people. Canadians concerned about equity, fairness and social justice must ask how the lyrics that accompany James' illustrations affirm the individual worth and dignity of all people.
>
> (Canada Council for the Arts 2)

Ironically, the prize was awarded in a year (2013) that saw widespread protests across Canada via the Idle No More Movement which "calls on all people" to "honor Indigenous sovereignty and to protect the land & water" as explained on its webpage.

The most egregious aspects of the lyrics is the use of a stereotypical Euro-colonial trope via the phrase, "through a land so wide and savage [...]" in the song's refrain. It is found in the first pages of the book. My question is this, what makes a land "savage?" Especially, since, to the illustrator's credit, the image that accompanies the text shows a dodger-blue sea, flanked on one side by gorgeous green and on the other, a gray and black rock on which stands a polar bear overlooking the explorer's ships. The beauty of the double-page spread stands in sharp contrast to any notion of a "savage" land, thus it is unclear as to why James has mobilized such lyrics to tell the story of Franklin's expedition. Therein lies the problem.

Similar to Villeneuve in *The Red Scarf*, the illustrator's mobilization of Roger's anthem to colonialism and European colonialist explorers in *Northwest Passage*, center stages the word "savage." When used in the context of colonial exploration and colonized spaces in reference to Indigenous/Aboriginal lands, the word "savage" is historically heavily freighted and is the source of considerable suffering for colonized peoples. James, the illustrator, bears full responsibility for using his art—his canvas, as a platform to reinvoke, recast the land of Indigenous peoples as "savage"—a space not civilized according to European epistemology. James grievously reconstructs Aboriginal spaces such as the arctic as unproblematically available for taming, for civilizing, for domesticating, for coming under the full control (read exploitation) of Europeans—a land ready for taking.

Additionally, savage is a word that is replete with symbolic emotional, psychological, and spiritual violence for Indigenous and other colonized peoples in Canada and elsewhere. It is the word the colonizers used to refer to Indigenous/Aboriginal North Americans (Ablavsky 2014; Harding 2006; Mitchell and Hearn, 1999; Raibmon 2000) and it provided the justification for exploitation, dispossession of lands, schools of pain and shame such as residential schools, cultural and linguistic denigration, and decimation.

Along with the above, I draw attention to the phrase "wide and savage" from the refrain of the song. It is used as a cultural vehicle to tell the story of the Northwest Passage and re-affirm Eurocentric colonialist ideologies about Indigenous lands and people. I maintain that the word "wide" is a metonym for "wild" because "wild and savage" was a standard stock phrase in colonialist discourse to describe Indigenous peoples that were subjected to Euro-imperialism. Robinson (2006) for instance, explains the English colonial perspective this way,

> Since local law went unrecognized, the law of England became the law of the Australian colony. Neither civilized nor in legal possession of the land, "wild" and "savage" natives were conflated with the natural artefact of the bush. Like the wild-erness, they were destined to fade away or, like the land, to be domesticated and civilized as the only route for co-existence.
>
> (885)

Such colonialist perspectives and ideologies were equally applied to Indigenous people elsewhere in the English empire—Canada and the United States for example, and are captured by Cave who cites colonialist writing that represents Indigenous Americans as "wild men in need of civilizing" and who were "no less savage, wild, and noisome than the very beasts themselves" (1988, 278). These examples serve to document the frequency with which the word "wild" was linked with "savage" in white colonial self-serving imaginings of Indigenous people under English colonial rule and lends credibility to the contention that Roger's use of the word "wide" is a metonym for "wild."

Such a metonymic strategy may be interpreted as an attempt to tone down racist colonialist imagery but it is so closely linked to the word for which it stands, that both the songwriter (Rogers) and the illustrator (James) are complicit in producing and reproducing demeaning colonialist imagery about Indigenous lands and people. As prize-giver, the Canada Council bears considerable responsibility for sanctioning a work for children that flaunts racist and disrespectful imagery about Aboriginal/Indigenous Canadians.

I note with perturbation that the harshness of colonialism, its racism, domination, subordination, and marginalization are silenced in both Rogers' and James' discourses; the Indigenous/Aboriginal people in the book are represented as passive, benign people, ancillary to the main thrust of the colonialist narrative and relatively indifferent to colonial occupation.

Therefore, *Northwest Passage* is a picture book that perpetuates white supremacy and white triumphalism in literature for children and is most likely to validate and affirm white children's construction of history. The book is a performance of Whiteness (Gillborn 2005) and through its winning of a Governor General's Literary Award for illustration; we see the prizing of white supremacy.

I assert that the book is prized primarily for its recuperation of dominant settler narratives and is an example of literary prizing of, and on behalf of, white supremacy and its interests. Where is the concern for equity if tax-payer, citizen-generated, state funds are being used to prize literature that is only in the interest of some Canadian children? This is a question the Canada Council needs to ponder in light of its development of an Equity Framework and announced commitments to Canadian Human Rights laws and vision.

Opportunities for Improving Prizing

Analysis of the prizing of *The Red Scarf* and *Northwest Passage* suggest that the system of white supremacy, its silencing of racism and its presumption of racial reconciliation between whites and oppressed non-white groups such as Aboriginal/Indigenous Canadians and African-Canadian/Blacks have led to reactivation/reproduction of racist imagery and language in children's literature and the prizing of such literature. I share Bonnie Miller's view that "such discriminatory writing [and imagery] about minorities" is "no longer acceptable" or tolerable (1998, 36). The presence of offensive racial imagery and language in the picture books examined point to the need for greater historical literacy and critical consciousness (Freire 1970) on the part of prize-givers (funders) and assessors. Moreover, in the case of state-funded prizes in societies marked by colonialism and racial ordering, there is an unequivocal need for fairness, equity, and social justice that are nuanced to consider the equality of all groups and in particular, the audience of the cultural artifacts for which the prize is given (e.g. children's books whose primary audience is children). On whose behalf is the prizing of children's literature with disturbing racist content made?

I call for a more critical, and radical application of the Canada Council's own Equity Framework, to bring greater scrutiny, vigilance, and vision to the prizing of children's literature. I believe key "Canadian values" such as those found in the *Bill of Rights*, the *Charter of Rights and Freedoms*, the *Canadian Human Rights Act* as well as the *United Nations Conventions on the Rights of the Child* need to explicitly and actively inform, undergird, and surround the prizing of children's literature in Canada given its role and use in processes of socialization and identity formation. This means that literary prizing needs to be ethically conceptualized and articulated and in ways that are overtly (but not only) conscious of race, racialization, and our collective history of racial domination and exclusion. There is no better time to start than right now. Excellence in literary prizing invites the use of multiple intersecting and competing lenses. Children's literary prizing in Canada needs to be anti-racist, anti-colonial, and anti-oppressive if it is to serve the interests of humanization and social justice. With regard to the *UN Conventions on the Rights of the Child*, I signal the importance of respecting the following articles: 3(1), 17(E), 19 and 29(D) as a place to start. With regard to children's rights, I contend that award givers and those making the selection, need to, in the words of the UN, "consider the best interests of the child."

The best interests of children in post-colonial societies calls for what Décoste (2013) describes as, "intercultural awakening, social awareness and cultural maturity," and socio-historical awareness. With this, Canadian authors and illustrators are called upon to "find more innovative ways to educate and entertain their plural audiences, and help build a country where all citizens benefit from a minimum of respect and civility" in their literature (Décoste).

I also submit that the unhappy instances I discussed can be ameliorated and overturned through the presence of identity-focused, culturally as well as racially responsive awards for prizing children's literature. Canada needs awards analogous to the American Indian Youth Literature Book Awards (American Indian Library Association [AILA]), The Coretta Scott King Book Awards (American Library Association) and the Pura Belpré Awards (American Library Association and REFORMA). These awards are proactive and progressive and are overtly intended to, in the case of AILA, "identify and honor the very best writing and illustrations by and about American Indians," in the case of The Coretta Scott King, to reward "outstanding African-American authors and illustrators of books for children and young adults that demonstrate an appreciation of culture and universal human values" and in the case of the Pura Belpré, to reward "a Latino/Latina writer and illustrator whose work best portrays, affirms, and celebrates the Latino cultural experience in an outstanding work of literature for children and youth" (ALA).

With reference to Canada, the situation of literary prizing in relation to racial and cultural minorities shares some similarities with that of the United States but has a marked difference, in that the major Canadian prizes for children's literature receive substantial funding from the state and therefore must meet a high standard of equity. In Canada today, agency, advocacy, recognition, and heightened sensitivity toward social diversity and pluralism have begun to engender change in literary prizing for children.

An encouraging example is the recently announced Burt Award sponsored by the Canadian Organization for Development through Education (CODE). Agentic in its purpose, The Burt Award seeks to intervene in the "shortage of relevant, quality books" by nurturing literary production by and about First Nations, Inuit, and Métis people (Burt Award 2016) as well as linking "firmly to ideals of education and uplift" (Kidd 2007, 178). Along with the preceding, I argue that the Burt Award contributes to opportunities for Aboriginal writers in Canada to actualize one of the conceptual tools of CRT—that of story-telling and the production of counter-stories (Delgado and Stefancic 2000) from racial and cultural insiders.

Such stories are much desired since they are liable to engender affirming identity development among Aboriginal children and youth and are also apt to counter white supremacist notions and negative colonial representations of Aboriginal Canadians. Additionally, the strong participation of Aboriginal people in the writing and evaluation of the literature bodes well for the prizing of literature that is affirming of the positive identity formation of First Nations, Métis, and Inuit children, their human worth and dignity.

Equally meritorious and deserving of a specific, identity and race-focused prize are African-Canadians and other racialized people, such as East and South Asian Canadians, in order to diversify and pluralize prizing in white dominant spaces. I restrict the discussion to African-Canadians here because of the earlier discussion about Villeneuve's disturbing book.

The existence of a taxpayer and/or privately funded prize for African-Canadian children's literature would help to explicitly acknowledge that literary prizing is, and has always been a raced, not a neutral social construct. Such a prize would create space for even greater diversification in children's literary prizing—an institution that has been identitarian from the outset. The prizing of African-Canadian children's literature has a reliable potential to stimulate literary production from an emic—insider—perspective. The dream is that the literature generated would critically, accurately, artistically, and creatively document the group's historical and contemporary experiences, as well as its questions, visions, and dreams. Such literary prizing would enhance literary equity and social justice and would enrich the nation's literary soil. The time for an African-Canadian literary prize is now.

Conclusion

My analysis of the prizing of *The Red Scarf* and *Northwest Passage* with social justice-oriented theories and discourses revealed that the prizing of children's literature in post-colonial Canada is not neutral; it takes place in a context of Whiteness, and acts on behalf of specific interests—white supremacy, and its ongoing use of colonial representations that are injurious to children from equity-seeking groups such Aboriginal people and African-Canadians. As a mode of resistance, I highlighted the inequity, and questioned the ethics of such literary prizing.

In order to interrupt further entrenchment of hegemonic prizing I signaled the need for critical consciousness, and socio-historical awareness on the part of prize funders/givers and evaluators. I conclude by proposing that all children—the consumers and recipients of literary messages in children's literature—deserve literary prizing that is critical as well as self-reflexive and founded on, and articulated through, ethics and shared values congruous to national and local Human Rights laws as well as the *UN Conventions on the Rights of the Child*.

10 Finding Nominations

Children's Films at the Academy Awards

Peter C. Kunze

In 2002, the Academy of Motion Pictures Arts and Sciences (AMPAS) presented the first Academy Award for Best Animated Feature to *Shrek* (Adamson and Jenson, 2001), a computer-animated film that offered a revisionist take on fairy tales. Loosely based on William Steig's picture book, DreamWorks's *Shrek* demonstrates a new strain of animated film that envisions children's cinema as an entertainment experience aimed at the whole family. Broad humor targets the children, while innuendo and allusions speak to the presumed adult audience. Pixar's John Lasseter explained these films' appeal to *The New York Times*: "Great story, great characters—we make movies that we want to see" (qtd. in Holson, "As Animation" col. C-6). Add to that toe-tapping song-and-dance numbers lifted from the musical genre, and it is no wonder the animated feature has earned the "kind of returns that have made the Academy take respectful notice, at last, of animation" (Strassel col. A-26).

Despite their commercial and even critical success, animated films like *The Little Mermaid* (Clements and Musker, 1989) and *The Lion King* (Allers and Minkoff, 1994) have garnered very little attention from film scholars and (until more recently) from prizing institutions.[1] The academic field of children's literature studies has been more attentive to film and media, including animation, with scholars such as Jack Zipes, Ian Wojcik-Andrews, Terry Staples, and Noel Brown writing foundational articles and monographs. The 2010 Children's Literature Association conference featured children's literature and media as its theme, and in the past five years, nine articles across *Children's Literature*, *Children's Literature Association Quarterly*, and *The Lion and the Unicorn* have taken film and/or television as their primary focus—a small, but noticeable number. While important research in children's film understandably focuses on the text, scholarship into the children's culture industry has proven a fruitful area of inquiry and one that offers rich new possibilities for future work by scholars of both children's literature and media, especially in light of rising critical interest in media industry studies.[2] This chapter continues in that vein. Through a discussion of the children's animated film and the Academy Award, I argue two key points. First, the Academy Award for Best Animated Feature may be seen as a *de facto* prize for children's media narratives, covering feature-length film entertainment primarily produced for children and adapted from genres associated with children's literature, including fairy tales and myths. Second, including this award among children's literary prizes expands upon our understanding of prizes and what they do, culturally, economically, and professionally.[3] Approaching the Academy Award for Best Animated Feature in this way spotlights a highly influential yet often underappreciated body of texts within children's culture while also examining the relationship between the culture industry and the professional institutions that organize and support it.

The Politics of Film Prizing

Prizing the so-called family film at the Academy Awards has been a sporadic and sometimes odd affair. *The Sound of Music* (Wise, 1965) and *Oliver!* (Reed, 1968) won Best Picture against relatively unimpressive competition, while acting awards have gone to Anne Revere in *National Velvet* (Brown, 1944), Edmund Gwenn in *Miracle on 34th Street* (Seaton, 1947), Yul Brynner in *The King and I* (Lang, 1956), and Julie Andrews in *Mary Poppins* (Stevenson, 1964). As James F. English notes, awarding prizes legitimates an institution's reputation and their roles as "facilitators of decision making [rather] than as decision makers in their own right" (154); therefore, bestowing an Oscar on films for children symbolically erodes the Academy's authority to recognize the best films that its members have produced, since the "best" must adhere to middlebrow impressions of what constitutes artistic achievement and sophistication. Family entertainment surely remains Hollywood's most enduring and most lucrative source of revenue, but the Oscars aim to endow the Academy and the recipients with what Pierre Bourdieu has called "symbolic capital," that is "a reputation for competence and an image of respectability and honorability" (285). In its accessibility to a wide audience, breadth of visual and aural pleasures, and fantastic nature compared to traditional "Oscar caliber" fare, children's entertainment fails to satisfy the unclear yet pervasive standards of distinction articulated by the dominant taste interests in the film industry and culture-at-large.

Generally speaking, one profession (librarians) awards the Newbery Medal to another (writers), but the Academy Award emphasizes recognition among peers.[4] Voters in each branch decide the nominees (directors in the Academy vote for director nominees, for example), but all voters vote on the final winner. The Academy, comprised of a select group of Hollywood talent now exceeding 6,000 members, recognizes both its fellow members and colleagues with its annual awards. The Academy Awards remains its most visible activity, but its founding was more a matter of controlling than extolling. Fearing further unionization, MGM head Louis B. Mayer called a meeting of producers that resulted in the Academy's founding in 1927. Its initial purpose was to act "more or less as a company union" (Sklar 84), though its public purpose was to promote the industry through its commitment to "improve the artistic quality of the film medium" (qtd. in Schatz 100). Like the Newbery Medal, which was established earlier in the decade, the Academy Award provides an opportunity to recognize "distinguished contributions" to the field. What should also be noted is how both awards—the original American prizes in their fields and by most accounts still the most prestigious—also initially served to legitimize their respective artistic practices as serious art forms. Cultural taste, informed by a class-based elitism, initially perceived film and children's literature as inferior art forms to grand opera or literary fiction, for example. The Academy Award actively sought to elevate the general cultural perception of their respective art forms through the identification of superior "performances" or "contributions," as determined by a knowing body of peers. We can see that mission even in the iconography of the awards, with the Academy Award featuring a sword-wielding figure standing upon a film reel, and the Newbery Medal an open book surrounded by a torch and laurel.

As the first, longest-lasting, and the most esteemed American film prize, the Academy Award quickly developed prestige within the industry and a nickname, "Oscar." In his autobiography, Frank Capra reports early membership was comprised "mainly of important Brahmins under contract to the major studios" (105). As a filmmaker starting out in the smaller studios, nicknamed "Poverty Row," Capra saw the Oscar as a symbol of professional mobility. An Oscar meant not only recognition, but a chance to advance professionally to the major studios, so the Academy Awards quickly became a powerful career builder as well. Consequently, Capra decided at the time "I would have an Oscar on *my* mantelpiece, or bust" (105).

With time, however, a backlash against the Academy Awards and the implications of cinematic prizing began to develop, particularly among actors, who arguably stood to gain but also lose the most from winning. In 1971, Best Actor nominee (and eventual winner) George C. Scott dismissed the ceremony as "a two-hour meat parade, a public display with contrived suspense for economic reasons" (qtd. in Wiley and Bona 447).[5] Three years later, Dustin Hoffman angrily called the ceremony "obscene, dirty and no better than a beauty contest" (qtd. in Wiley and Bona 501). Hoffman would later accept his Best Actor Oscar for *Kramer v. Kramer* (Benton, 1979), but not without challenging the competitive rhetoric of the ceremony: "I refuse to believe I beat Jack Lemmon, that I beat Al Pacino, that I beat Peter Sellers [...]. We are part of an artistic family" (qtd. in Wiley and Bona 581). James F. English rightly observes that criticizing, even refusing, such awards "has become a recognized device for raising visibility and leveraging success" (222). Taken together, these comments raise a variety of valid concerns about prizing: the commercial nature of the ceremony itself, which both promotes the industry and raises considerable revenue through advertisements; the unavoidable subjectivity (and perhaps futility) of evaluating art through competition; the celebration of individual achievement in an inherently collaborative art form. Yet one cannot deny the financial boost and cultural prestige the Oscar brings, both in the immediate and distant future. In 2012, Marc Shmuger, vice chairman of Universal Pictures, remarked that winning on Oscar provides a film with "a permanent place in popular culture" (qtd. in Holson, "The Gold").[6]

The Academy Awards not only illustrate the interests of the Academy and the U.S. film industry; as Emanuel Levy contends, they "embody such basic American values as democracy, equality, individualism, competition, upward mobility, hard work, occupational achievement, and monetary success" (362). Concealed under claims of prestige and the humbling honor of recognition from one's peers, the Academy Awards reward films that feature its finest production values as demonstrated by their "grand visual styles and pseudo-epic vision" (Levy 376), even though Hollywood's greatest profits still come from the popular entertainment undeserving of Oscar's prestige, including comedies, action films, and, of course, family entertainment. Children's films have been ignored, in part, because the Academy's snubs do not impact revenues; Thomas M. Leitch observes that *Aladdin* (Clements and Musker, 1992) and *The Lion King* were "Oscar-poor but cash-rich films whose relative neglect [...] didn't hurt their drawing power on videotape, lunchboxes, and fast-food franchises" (7). Ignoring these films, despite their innovative stories and high production values, uncovers the true cultural work being done here: promoting the industry by prizing its most indulgent, most sophisticated, and (sometimes) least profitable narratives that satisfy middlebrow sensibilities, even though the lifeblood of the industry remains formulaic genre films. For a long time, children's films, with their wide appeal and merchandising capabilities, seemed too commercial and too successful to be taken seriously as art.

Censorship and Prizing

As librarians began to turn away from censorship as a professional practice in the late 1930s, they placed increasing emphasis on patrons' rights to read what they choose, which became a "core professional as well as cultural value" in the 1950s (Kidd "Not Censorship" 200). This gradual transition does not really occur in the film industry, however, because censorship and prizing have always been relatively synchronous practices. Academy President Douglas Fairbanks Sr. presented the first Academy Awards on May 16, 1929, and a year later, Daniel Lord, a Jesuit priest, and Martin Quigley, publisher of the *Motion Picture Herald*, drafted the rigid guidelines that became the Production Code in the belief that "No picture should lower the moral standards of those who see it" (qtd. in Weinberger 380). Hollywood generally disregarded the Code until the 1934 hiring of Joseph Breen, who, as head of the Production Code Administration (PCA), strictly enforced it beginning on July 15, 1934—a Sunday, no less (Doherty 70). For over 20 years, a film's release required the approval of his office, and Breen himself often worked with directors and producers to tidy up scenes, plot points, or characters that his office found to be unsavory. So the AMPAS worked to ensure a positive public perception of the film industry and the Motion Picture Producers and Distributors of America (MPPDA) worked to protect its members' business interests; these initiatives, of course, are not mutually exclusive endeavors. While one made a concerted effort to recognize the finest the industry has produced, the other worked to ensure a moral standard that persisted into the 1960s until it largely disintegrated from creative backlash and the eventual introduction of the ratings system.[7]

Joseph Breen's censoring power over Hollywood cinema from 1934 to 1954 came from Hollywood itself, and here film diverges from the model in children's books, where censorship often comes from school boards, special interest groups, parents, and sometimes even librarians. Hollywood's censorship, though managed by a specific division, was fundamentally internal so as to avoid government regulation. Book censorship results from external entities imposing their curricular aims, ideologies, and purchasing power onto authors, libraries, schools, and, by extension, the publishing world. Although the assault on books may come from various people and perspectives, it almost never escalates to the point that publication stops or the federal government intervenes. The uproar over a book, therefore, can impose its own kind of distinction and boost sales. As Kenneth Kidd observes, "being a censored writer is cause for celebration because it means that your books are having a social effect, are being taken seriously" ("Not Censorship" 209). This situation is not the case for Hollywood cinema, at least not during Breen's tenure; failing to obtain the PCA approval could keep a film out of theaters, trigger religious condemnation, and represent financial suicide for a studio. Internal censorship, therefore, often proved to be even more limiting and devastating than the threat of external censorship. Yet Steven Weinberger argues some filmmakers found evading censors led to clever cinematography or editing that the filmmakers believed improved the final film (390).

Hollywood censorship ultimately failed whereas prizing continued and flourished with the creation of, among others, the National Board of Review Awards (1930), the Golden Globes (1944), the People's Choice Awards (1975), and the Screen Actors Guild Awards (1995). Each award clearly represents a separate group's values and approach to cinema aesthetics, but more importantly, these awards assert each group's right—as critics, filmmakers, Hollywood personnel, reporters, or simply members of the viewing public—to determine the "best" in cinema (English 51). Since the Academy Award was the initial award and remains both the most publicized and most watched of ceremonies, it serves as the benchmark for professional success in the film industry in spite of its numerous (and rather obvious) shortcomings.[8] Nevertheless, the symbolic capital the Academy Award carries within the industry and among the viewing public makes the recognition of family entertainment an important industrial, aesthetic, and cultural victory.

An Award of Their Own

While children's films are neither recognized with their own award nor generally included among the major prizes, the most-nominated and winningest individual in Hollywood history is ironically Walt Disney, who received 22 Oscars in his lifetime, including eight consecutive wins in the Best Animated Short category, which has been awarded, in various permutations, since 1932. The conservative politics of Disney's films have led to a generally unfavorable reputation among academics, yet Beverly Lyon Clark notes that Walt Disney's work, especially his short films, was well-regarded among artists and intellectuals in the 1930s, including Mark Van Doren, H.G. Wells, and Sergei Eisenstein (169). In another irony, Disney's turn to animating humans in the feature-length *Snow White and the Seven Dwarfs* (Hand, 1937) marked the decline of Disney's reputation among many academics and even some fellow animators,[9] but it also earned him a special Academy Award for "a significant screen innovation which has charmed millions and pioneered a great new entertainment field for motion picture cartoon" (qtd. in Osborne 61). Recreating Disney's trademark cloying style,[10] the Academy had Shirley Temple present him with the Oscar—along with seven miniature Oscars.

Despite Walt Disney's undeniable and international influence, the Academy avoided creating an award for feature-length animation or children's film. This oversight, in part, may reflect a sense that animated films would not increase the film industry's prestige amount the larger arts and culture scene. Since children's films aim to entertain without offending, they often skirt the pressing social concerns at the heart of more prestigious film productions. The animated features of Walt Disney offered a lavish spectacle comparable to that of film musicals, but such films do not easily fit into the categories the Academy established for honoring films, most obviously acting and directing.[11]

Another reason, which A.O. Scott offers, argues that genres make for poor categories because they ebb and flow; this explanation, though sensible for children's movies, falters in its comparison of animated films to comedies and action films. The latter are defined by plot conventions, iconography, and mode, whereas the former is strictly formal. Scott's stronger point is that Walt Disney Studios would have dominated the category for much of the 1940s and 1950s, but the number of feature-length animated films released during the 1960s and 1980s waned, even at Disney (B4). Nevertheless, they were largely responsible for the revitalization of the form in the 1980s with the release of *The Little Mermaid. Beauty and the Beast* (Trousdale and Wise, 1991) received an impressive Best Picture nomination in 1992, cementing the renewed financial viability and critical acclaim of feature-length animation. Whereas contemporary Oscar-winning animated short films were often prizeworthy feats of technology and storytelling, they were rarely seen by the public, especially when compared to their feature-length counterparts. An oversight of feature animation not only ignored increasingly impressive efforts in a foundational film practice, but also seemed to downplay the monumental box-office success attained by these works. In addition to Disney's renewed investment in feature animation in the 1980s, visual storytelling in general—including graphic narratives and primetime animation—experienced a boom that radically reimagined and updated underappreciated or even stagnated genres like comic books or animated television series. Including a range of texts from Art Spiegelman's *Maus* through the burgeoning Fox network's *The Simpsons*, this artistic renaissance earned critics' respect and new generations of fans. In turn, these revisionist texts, which fused a reverence for their respective genre with postmodernist sensibility based in play, garnered critical attention and awards.[12] As a cultural and industrial venture, prizing recognizes and reinforces technical achievement as well as commercial success.

In the 1990s, Disney films simply made too much money to ignore, though the subsequent Oscar nominations were generally for music. Calls for an animation Oscar began, fueled in part by the remarkable innovation *Toy Story* (Lasseter, 1995) brought to animation and filmmaking in general. A completely computer-generated movie, *Toy Story* inaugurated a cinema where films were not actually filmed. At the time, hand-drawn animation seemed doomed, and by 2000, the financial failure of *Quest for Camelot* (Du Chau, 1998), *The Iron Giant* (Bird, 1999), and *Titan A.E.* (Bluth and Goldman, 2000) led studios to scale back or even shut down their animation divisions, and some animators, most notably Don Bluth, to leave the film industry altogether (Lyman, "Animators"). Although digital animation did not end hand-drawn animation completely, the lack of viable contenders for an animated feature Oscar stalled the award until 2000. The first new Oscar added since Makeup in 1981, the Best Animated Feature Oscar requires at least eight acceptable contenders to be theatrically released in Los Angeles County in the calendar year to activate the category and give the award. Subsequent criteria include a running time of 70 minutes (later changed to 40), a "significant number" of major animated characters, and animation for at least 75% of that running time ("Rule Seven"). Feature-length animation had to prove itself within its own industry to warrant separate prizing. Who actually wins the statuette, of course, poses a range of other difficulties.

Some industry leaders, including Jeffrey Katzenberg, who led Walt Disney Studios through its animation revival in the late 1980s and eventually left to co-found DreamWorks, feared such an award would lead to "the ghettoization of animation" (qtd. in Solomon). Notably, the Academy still allows the Best Animated Feature to be nominated for the Best Picture Oscar.[13] Since Best Director is its own category, the Best Picture Academy Award goes to the film's producer(s). Best Animated Feature, however, can effectively go to the producer, the director, or both. Initially, the Academy allowed the nominee to designate the recipient upon submitting the film for consideration, a person referred to as the "key creative individual." The first winner, Aron Warner for *Shrek*, was the head of the animation division at DreamWorks.

Thereafter, the film's director received the award until the 2014 ceremony, where a team of three individuals—producer and director(s)—could be recognized and were when producer Peter Del Vecho and directors Chris Buck and Jennifer Lee won for *Frozen* (Buck and Lee, 2013). This caveat underscores the collaborative nature of filmmaking as well as the fraught issue of film authorship. Furthermore, it represents an implicit understanding of the Oscar's symbolic capital. While an Oscar win for actors often means more money, it provides directors with greater discretion over their future projects (Emanuel Levy 306). Prizing, therefore, empowers the winner going forward rather than simply recognizing his or her accomplishments.

Since its earliest days, the Academy Award served to affirm technical developments. The Oscars "set up a state-of-the-art standard" by recognizing "the quality film with acceptable innovations" (Bordwell, Staiger, and Thompson 313). In this way, prizing becomes a litmus test for where the industry (or the prize-giving industry) wants the craft to go, by legitimating certain innovations but not others. The establishment of the Best Animated Feature Award correlates with, and helps to promote, the rise of digital cinema, despite some high-profile detractors.[14]

More critically for the purposes of this chapter, the acknowledgment of animated feature films allows for something ordinary categories rarely afford: ongoing acknowledgment, recognition, and celebration of children's cinema.[15] As mentioned earlier, the Academy Awards do not reward content-based genres but rather formal ones. An award for children's film does not exist because no content-based film Academy Award exists, save perhaps the Best Foreign Language Film. By recognizing animated features, the Academy de facto prizes children's entertainment. And in fact, the vast majority of the nominated films—all of the winners to date—have been either rated G or PG. It is worth noting, however, that anti-smoking advocates wanted *Rango* (Verbinski, 2011), the 2011 Best Animated Feature winner, rated R for nearly 60 instances of characters smoking. Dr. Stanton Glantz of the Center for Tobacco Control Research and Education at the University of California-San Francisco went so far as to claim, "A lot of kids are going to start smoking because of this movie" (qtd. in Rubin). Such opposition testifies not only to our ongoing social investment in the media images consumed by children, but also the roles censorship and prizing play in navigating "good" and "bad" culture for the public as well as the highly subjective nature of such assessments.

Though the prizing efforts of the AMPAS are noticeably capricious, the Oscars remain too firmly entrenched in American culture to fade away any time soon. Nevertheless, such initiatives deserve increased and continuing critical scrutiny because they reveal the preferences and prejudices of the creators and consumers of Hollywood cinema. The Oscars are too easily dismissed as mindless entertainment, but the ideological implications of the awards resonate socially, culturally, industrially, and economically. What does it mean to be of "Oscar caliber"? What does it mean that acting winners are predominantly white, while the few African-American recipients tend to win for playing slaves, domestic workers, and drug addicts? And, for our purposes here, what does the reception of children's cinema mean for our understanding of children, childhood, and children's culture?

Conclusion

Attention to children's films—films directed primarily toward children, and/or films focused on the lives of children—is on the rise. Since the Academy Awards have broadened the Best Picture nominations to include up to ten films, the nominated films have included children's films like *Up* (Docter, 2009), *Toy Story 3* (Unkrich, 2010), and *Hugo* (Scorsese, 2011) as well as dramas for an implied adult audience that seriously attempt to take the complex emotional lives of children as their focus, including *Extremely Loud and Incredibly Close* (Daldry, 2011) and *Beasts of the Southern Wild* (Zeitlin, 2012). Of course, increased inclusion in the award categories does not necessarily correlate with progressive representation, as some of these films evoke problematic stereotypes and tropes.[16] Criticism can meet these challenges by addressing the ideology, politics, and consequences of an institutionalized appreciation that simultaneously celebrates and silences pieces of our culture. Of course, one could follow the logic of English's thesis to argue that criticizing the cultural practice of prizing itself serves as a form of prizing—prizing in the form of selective interpretation. This possibility is unavoidable, but as long as the critic proceeds with this concern in mind and in collaboration with others sharing in this healthy skepticism, surely we can avoid defeatist resignation and/or mere reproduction of the cultural status quo, finding a productive balance of appreciation and interpretation.

Notes

1. That is not to say there has not been some excellent work, including monographs by Sean P. Griffin, Chris Pallant, Tom Sito, and J.P. Telotte, that discuss, in part or in whole, the resurgence of feature animation since the 1980s.
2. Media industry studies often serves as an umbrella term for a range of approaches to studying media production, distribution, and consumption, including, but not limited to, production studies, political economy, cultural industries, creative industries, and critical cultural policy studies. For valuable introductions to this area of inquiry, consult Jennifer Holt and Alisa Perren as well as Timothy Havens and Amanda Lotz. To date, Sarah Banet-Weiser, Heather Hendershot, Ellen Seiter, Janet Wasko, and Jack Zipes have produced important works on the children's culture industry.
3. In *The Economy of Prestige*, James F. English draws attention to how the Nobel Prize and the Academy Award forge different models for cultural prizing. For instance, the Nobel Prize is decided by a small panel of judges, whereas Academy members decided the Academy Awards (69–70). Furthermore, the

Nobel Prize offers a monetary award, but by televising its ceremony, the Academy actually profits from its award-giving (81). Although the Academy Award functions differently financially than the Newbery Medal, its industrial function warrants comparison, especially since both are crucial marketing devices (i.e. placing stickers on films or books as winners or nominees as a marker of quality, identifying an author or filmmaker as a winner or nominee when advertising their latest project, drawing positive attention to their respective fields).

4. Kenneth Kidd has previously noted the similarities between the two awards, especially their "traditions of celebrity, ceremony, and even scandal" ("Prizing" 186n). Of course, some Newbery Medalists, including Eleanor Estes, Beverly Cleary, Susan Patron, Laura Amy Schlitz, had trained and worked (at some point) as children's librarians. (Thanks to Monica Edinger for drawing my attention to additional writer/librarian winners.).

5. Though the ceremony itself is ostensibly a three-hour commercial for the film industry and its "products," the Academy goes to great lengths to maintain the prestige of its award, including preventing winners or their heirs from selling the Award. Before doing so, one has to give the Academy the chance to buy the Award back first—for $10. As James F. English notes, the Academy makes implied "claims to be conferring 'medals of honor' so pure that any brush with commerce will irreparably soil them" (180). Of course, the award, like all awards, is inherently commercial.

6. This remark, of course, is up for debate. Plenty of Oscar-winning films are best known only among film scholars and cinephiles. A more accurate statement may be that winning an Oscar solidifies how the film will be marketed for years to come. DVD cases for early winners like *The Broadway Melody* (Beaumont, 1929), *Cavalcade* (Lloyd, 1933), and *The Great Ziegfeld* (Leonard, 1936) prominently feature the Oscar statuette as a symbolic marker of quality.

7. In 1945, new MPPDA president Eric Johnston renamed the organization the Motion Picture Association of America.

8. Clearly, "best" is a loaded term that nevertheless goes undefined. While sometimes the award goes to one who has demonstrated a clear innovation or considerable aesthetic or technical achievement, there are numerous instances where the award rewards a promising young star or a seasoned as-yet-unrewarded veteran (regardless of performance in said film). Another deviation from the award as the year's "best" achievement is when the Academy, in the words of Emanuel Levy, "tends to compensate the losers, usually in the near future, with belated honors" (264). For example, Levy notes, Bette Davis's Academy Award for *Dangerous* (Green, 1935) was most likely a delayed award for her stronger performance in *Of Human Bondage* (Cromwell, 1934) a year earlier (265).

9. German art historian Erwin Panofsky believed *Snow White* violated the basic principle of animation. According to Panofsky, "the very virtue of the animated cartoon is to animate, that is to say endow lifeless things with life, or living things with a different kind of life" (qtd. in Clark 172). Bill Kroyer and Barry Weiss note an unnamed animator believed Disney "corrupted" animation with "realism" (qtd. in 15).

10. Nicholas Sammond notes, "For over seventy years Walt Disney Productions has made a name for itself by offering products that are ostensibly an alternative to unsavory popular media and a prophylactic against their negative effects" (2).

Sammond's use of "prophylactic" is particularly appropriate, underscoring the sterility of the films' content.

11. Of course, films have one director, who is often perceived as the genius of the film. Such a paradigm inevitably falters in discussing film animation, where sequences may have different directors. (For example, on *Snow White and the Seven Dwarfs*, the Internet Movie Database lists one supervising director and five sequence directors under the director credit.) Consequently, animated films deeply complicate film authorship, especially as understood by the auteur theory, which gained currency in the United States in the 1960s and has remained remarkably pervasive.

12. In 1990, *The Simpsons* won the Primetime Emmy for Outstanding Animated Program; in 1992, *Maus* won a special Pulitzer Prize. Beyond these texts, one might also credit Frank Miller's *The Dark Knight Returns* (1986) and Alan Moore and Dave Gibbons's *Watchmen* (1986–7) for bringing renewed respect to comic books, while *The Land Before Time* (Bluth, 1988), *Who Framed Roger Rabbit?* (Zemeckis, 1988), and *The Little Mermaid* helped revive film animation.

13. This policy echoes the Academy's approach to foreign language films. For example, *Life is Beautiful* (Benigni, 1997), *Crouching Tiger, Hidden Dragon* (Lee, 2000), and *Amour* (Haneke, 2012) were nominated for both Best Foreign Language Film and Best Picture; each won the former and lost the latter. A key difference is that Best Animated Feature elects its recipient(s), whereas the Best Foreign Language Film is accepted by the film's director but awarded to its country of origin.

14. At the 2014 Cannes Film Festival, Quentin Tarantino railed against digital filmmaking: "I'm hopeful that we're going through a woozy, romantic period for the case of digital. I'm hoping the next generation will have more sense and realize what they've lost" (qtd. in Barnes).

15. Past nominee *Chico & Rita* (Mariscal, Trueba, and Errando, 2011), for example, features thematic elements many would consider to be adult-oriented. Nevertheless, only films many would consider to be decidedly child-oriented have won, as of 2014.

16. See hooks's critique of *Beasts of the Southern Wild*.

11 Prizing Popularity

How the Blockbuster Book Has Reshaped Children's Literature

Rebekah Fitzsimmons

Children's literature has always had a distinctly uncomfortable relationship with the effects of popularity and sales on its canon formation.[1] Others scholars in this collection, including Kenneth Kidd, have remarked on the ability of children's literature prizes, like the Caldecott and Newbery, to provide children's books with a distinct financial reward and a likelihood of remaining in print far longer than other children's books (168). However, most mainstream readers view children's literature as a specialized field and are most likely to recognize the titles of bestselling children's books over prize-winning children's books. The next time you encounter a news story about the cultural impact of children's literature or trends in young adult literature (YA), pay close attention to the texts the author cites; most likely, they will be bestsellers and not prize-winners. Most often, the children's books referenced in mainstream popular culture will be drawn from an elite category of bestselling books: blockbusters. To the mainstream reader and cultural critic alike, it appears that blockbuster status is usurping the authority and cultural relevance of traditional book prizes. The blockbuster book phenomenon is rapidly coming to define a hyper-canon within children's and YA books, which in turn is influencing the mainstream conceptualization of children's literature as a whole.

The blockbuster book phenomenon arose out of bestseller book culture. The category of bestseller and, in turn, blockbuster, came to take on a cultural significance similar to a literary prize, while challenging the cultural authority and hierarchy traditionally associated with prizing. As changes in the book industry allowed publishers to actively pursue blockbuster marketing strategies, those strategies also began to subvert and force changes in existing prize and bestseller infrastructures. Children's literature has especially been affected by the emergence of the blockbuster book: some of the largest blockbusters of the last 25 years have been YA series titles like *Harry Potter*, *Twilight*, and *The Hunger Games*. In fact, many critics and non-experts use these blockbuster titles as shorthand for the contemporary children's literature market. In our contemporary moment, blockbuster status indicates an elite category of bestselling books, far more selective than the proliferate number of prizes.

To understand the history of the blockbuster, we must start with the best-seller. The bestseller list is an American invention. Harry Thurston Peck, editor of the monthly literary magazine *The Bookman*, introduced a regional list of "New books, in order of demand, as sold between January 1 and February 1" in 1895 (Hackett 2; Mott 6). The term "bestseller" came into use "to describe what were not necessarily the best books but the books that people liked best" (Hackett ix). Bestseller lists became a popular feature in book-minded publications and it was not long before the term "bestseller" entered the vernacular and bestseller lists crossed over into mainstream culture (Hackett 2). Two of the most significant bestseller lists include *The New York Times Book Review* list, which debuted in 1896 and *Publishers Weekly* list, which debuted in 1912 (Korda xxvii).[2]

A book list based on sales figures not only keeps publishers honest while writing royalty checks but also helps better advertise titles already reaching an audience. In theory, *The Bookman* was attempting to report a factual, measurable metric of popularity. In practice, however, publishing bestseller lists also influences which books will sell well, creating what Anita Elberse describes as "'path dependencies' or 'positive feedback effects'" (130). For example, a bookstore owner might read a list of books selling well in his area and decide to stock a few extra copies of each of the top sellers. The books that appear on the bestseller list receive extra publicity and a boost in sales, creating a feedback loop; in other words, the books on the bestseller list this week are the most likely to appear on the list next week. Most brick and mortar stores dedicate a prominent shelf or display case to bestsellers. Online booksellers likewise feature bestsellers: according to its website, Amazon's Best Sellers contains "our most popular products based on sales. Updated hourly" and is an excellent starting point to "find, discover, and buy." Bestseller lists, then, are not only a record of sales, but also a guide to induce book shoppers to purchase bestselling books.

In the American cultural imagination, the term "bestseller" operates within a specific economy of prestige and carries with it financial and cultural rewards for the titles, authors, and publishers associated with it. Culturally powerful institutions, like *The New York Times Book Review*, carry a great deal of cultural capital and tastemaker status, and so books that appear on those bestseller lists will proudly proclaim this as an accomplishment, or even as a prize. Stickers (which often resemble prize medals) are placed on the front cover of the next book printing, declaring it to be a "#1 *New York Times* bestseller!" Once an author has achieved this status, he or she can be referred to as a "*New York Times* best-selling author" in press releases and biographies in perpetuity. Contemporary book contracts often award bonuses to authors who achieve this status: these escalator clauses increase according to where the book ranks and its duration spent on the list (Miller "Best-Seller List" 296).

In order to maintain the tastemaker status of the list-making institution, however, each bestseller list is highly regulated, though the mechanics behind the list are usually well concealed. Bestseller lists self-select categories of texts that qualify for consideration, eliminating the lowest-brow categories and "useful" texts.[3] Today, newspapers, magazines, bookstores, and online retailers maintain their own bestseller lists, each based on distinct measuring procedures to determine which books are most popular. *The New York Times* uses a distinct formula which weighs sales weekly from chain booksellers, independent booksellers, Internet venues, and other book sale sites, but refuses to disclose that formula "because the *Times* considers its formula proprietary information" (Miller "Best-Seller List" 4).[4] So, while the bestseller list presents itself as a record of sales figures, it is in fact an editorial product, carefully regulated by the periodical or corporation responsible for calculating and publishing it. Variation between the lists can be wide, but perennial bestsellers by authors like John Grisham or Danielle Steel usually appear on all of the lists, although the exact order may fluctuate (Korda xxvi). Further, editors of the lists are empowered to make adjustments to the formula, to change the list's categories, or to make exceptions to the types of books typically included or excluded from the list's preliminary pool.

The term "bestseller" is tied to a specific metric, most commonly the number of books sold over the course of a week. Based on the scope of this metric, bestseller lists can vary widely. Robert Escarpit makes a distinction between "fast sellers" which sell lots of copies rapidly, then disappear; the "steady sellers" which may never appear on a weekly bestseller list but maintain a strong level of sales over an extended period of time; and the "bestseller" which combines the best of both categories, selling a great many copies immediately after its release, then maintaining steady sales thereafter (qtd. in Miller, "Best-Seller List" 2). In comparison, a blockbuster book may appear at the top of weekly, monthly, and yearly lists for a period of time far beyond the average bestseller. Some blockbusters have even altered the mechanics of well-known bestseller lists.

When it comes to prestige and financial success, the blockbuster book reaches well beyond a mere bestseller. A blockbuster book sells more copies than any other book in a given amount of time, often with a lot of commercial buzz and publicity surrounding it. A blockbuster is considered to be a certain kind of bestselling book, specially designed for the mass market, and this designation "often carries with it a down-market whiff" (Dargis). This negative connotation might be in some way tied to the term's origins. The term "blockbuster" was first used in the 1940s to describe "the powerful bombs that the British Royal Air Force used to decimate German cities during World War II, the so-called blockbusters" (Dargis). It was appropriated by the media toward the end of the war to describe anything that had a strong impact on the public: a headline in the *Chicago Tribune* from February 20, 1945 reads "Midnight Edict is Blockbuster to Manhattan: Expect Curfew to Kill Supper Clubs." After the war, "the term was taken up and used by Hollywood from the early 1950s on to refer on the one hand to large-scale productions and on the other to large-scale box-office hits" (Neale 47).

According to *New York Times* critic Manohla Dargis, blockbuster

> soon entered the vernacular, appearing in advertisements before the
> end of the war, and as a clue in a 1950 crossword puzzle in this paper
> (46 across) [...] the word blockbuster routinely appeared in articles
> about the Hollywood vogue for super-size entertainments.

Some claim the phrase also derived from popular theater productions
that caused queues to form around the block (Brier 114). Finally, the term
shifted to its contemporary meaning of "products sold in enormous quan-
tities, like movies, but also theater productions, museum shows, hit songs,
books, and even pharmaceuticals" and is thought to describe a specific
type of product within each specific marketplace (Dargis). Critics often
use the term as a pejorative, or "shorthand for overinflated production[s]
that rely more on special effects than words and characters" (Dargis).
Stereotypically, a blockbuster movie is an action/adventure film with a high
budget for special effects and a low focus on artistic expression, while a
blockbuster song contains three chords, a catchy hook, and overly simplis-
tic lyrics.

While bestseller lists have been around for over a century, blockbuster
books are a much more recent phenomenon. Changes in the publishing
industry, such as the introduction of the mass-market paperback in the
1960s, allowed new audiences to purchase books in larger numbers; own-
ing hard-cover books is cost prohibitive for a majority of people in America.
According to Kenneth Davis in *Two Bit Culture*, before the Paperback
Revolution

> only the rarest of books sold more than a hundred thousand copies;
> a million-seller was a real phenomenon [...]. Suddenly, a book could
> reach not hundreds or thousands of readers but millions, many of
> whom had never owned a book before.
>
> (xii)

The popularity of paperbacks expanded the general book audience, which
caused changes in business practices, marketing techniques, and even the
physical shapes and locations of bookstores. For example, auctions for a
book's paperback rights can help create a pre-release buzz: publisher confi-
dence can actually help launch a book onto the bestseller lists (Whiteside 3).

The children's literature market was a large beneficiary of the shift to
paperback editions of mainstream literature; with paperbacks, parents could
afford to purchase a wider variety of texts and children old enough to have
pocket money could afford to buy books of their very own. The inexpen-
sive format also allowed publishers to address controversial topics and put
"books that addressed the issues of race and poverty into the hands of more
of America's young people" (Leonard Marcus 244). Children's librarians,

who were regularly strapped for funds, turned to paperbacks as a means of filling shelves for less: by 1969 "three quarters of the nation's schools were now purchasing paperbacks for library or classroom use" (Marcus 249). As paperbacks were gradually accepted to be a legitimate form of transmission for quality literature, the number of titles increased. Despite concerns that the availability of paperbacks would decrease the profit margins of hard-covers, the market results ultimately proved there were unique audiences for both types of book, and issuing a book in both formats would increase the overall sales of a well-performing title (Davis 42).

The Paperback Revolution led to changes in the bookselling industry as well as the publishing industry. Paperbacks meant that books could be sold in venues other than dedicated bookstores: book racks appeared at news-stands and trains stations. In the 1960s, the rise of the suburban shopping mall led to additional changes in the industry:

> As retail dollars moved out of major cities [...] [s]uburban populations increasingly looked to the mall for a new kind of community center— consumption-oriented, tightly controlled, and aimed at purchasers as citizens who preferably were white and middle class.
>
> (Cohen 274)

This further increased the pressure on publishers to target the white, upper-middle-class family as the ideal audience for the vast majority of children's literature.

This shift toward suburban markets caused bookstores, like B. Dalton, Walden Books, Borders, and Barnes & Noble, to consolidate into large cor-porations, which changed the way books were ordered, sold, and displayed. Small independent booksellers decided individually which books to stock based on taste and customer base: corporate stores often made deals with different publishing houses to purchase a certain number of books. Chain stores stock many of the same titles throughout all their stores and receive bulk-ordering discounts in return, resulting in lower retail prices that inde-pendent stores often cannot compete with. As these corporate bookstores relocated into the "community center" of the suburban mall, they estab-lished a new ethos and aesthetic.

Eschewing the dark, crowded shelves, and elitist attitudes of the tradi-tional bookstore, the chains instead created large spaces in which customers could browse, read, and linger.

> Each of the major chains soon [...] emphasized a distinctly modern, casual look. They did this by using bright colors, contemporary mate-rials for shelving and counters, bold signage, and above all, good lighting. Aisles were wide and shelves were low to create an open, uncluttered feel.
>
> (Miller *Reluctant Capitalists* 93)

Most corporate stores feature bestselling or prize-winning titles on prominently placed tables or shelves at the front of the store, fueling Elberse's path dependencies. These innovative designs, starting in malls in the 1960s and continuing into the big box stores opening in the 1980s and 1990s, also allowed the chains to sub-divide each store into family friendly sections. However, these specialized sections sometimes had the potential to limit or pre-select the audience for a given book.

> While one title could conceivably be classified as either 'self-help' or 'religion,' the corresponding sections will be browsed by different groups of people (with some overlap, of course), and thus the simple act of classification may predetermine a book's audience.
>
> (Miller *Reluctant Capitalists* 97)

In the 1980s and 1990s, this sectioning further entrenched the separation between children's books and adult literature.

The last 25 years, however, have seen a shift in this separation, as some of the largest blockbuster books have been drawn from children's literature, specifically from the YA category. The rise of the children's literature "franchise" based around either a series of books, like *Harry Potter*, *Twilight*, and *The Hunger Games*, or more recently around authors like John Green, echo earlier developments in adult culture, where Stephen King and John Grisham were perennial members of the bestsellers' club. However, the crossover appeal of YA books, or the ability to build an enormous audience around texts accessible by both young and old, makes these properties even more appealing to publishers. The blockbuster prize appears to be upstaging the more traditional establishment prizes and making the recommendations of children's literature experts, like librarians and critics, obsolete when compared to the bestseller list and the book recommendation algorithms of popular online bookstores like Amazon.com. As YA books begin to reach blockbuster status, those titles are moved to a display at the front of the store. Thus, *Twilight* and *The Hunger Games* escaped from the ghettoized children's section in the back and were made available and attractive to a much wider range of book browsers. Recommended reading displays with YA titles similar to these series helped transfer the popularity and high sales figures of blockbuster books to other YA titles.

In terms of cultural success, the blockbuster exceeds the worth of the bestseller. James English argues in *The Economy of Prestige* that literary prizes are a significant metric for transferring cultural prestige onto artistic products, and of converting economic capital into cultural capital. As I have argued elsewhere, the bestseller operates as a form of prize, which grants its "winner" a specific kind of cultural capital within a mass-market economy of prestige, based on evidence of significant financial success and audience saturation.[5] In our contemporary book culture, the blockbuster explodes the taste management apparatus of bestseller lists, which normally limit success to a specific taste culture and cultural marketplace. Blockbusters, however, erode the boundary between popular and literary culture by demanding the attention of critics, academics, and reviewers who usually absent themselves from conversations about "non-literary" texts. The high culture critics who fail to at least acknowledge blockbuster titles (even if only to deride them) risk losing touch with their audience and thus their tastemaker status. In this way, blockbuster books become almost hyper-canonical, forcing individuals outside of the typical bestseller taste culture to recognize and engage with these highly proliferative texts.

The rhetoric of the bestseller greatly resembles that of literary prizes and creates its own cross-genre category. However, while the rhetoric is similar between the bestseller and the literary prize, there is one very important difference: prizes are awarded by the select few, while bestseller status derives from the many. Despite being a measure of popularity, most mainstream bestseller lists preempt many of the genres of literature considered too lowbrow or too popular. The bestseller list acts as a canon maker for the "majority" class and attempts to balance the highbrow standards of literary culture against the lowbrow value of popularity. The very nature of bestseller popularity often means that a book is eliminated from the consideration of the elite. There are many highbrow critics who believe that if a book is popular, it cannot possibly be any good and if a book is truly of high quality, it will never find mass appeal. While this formulation certainly remains true for blockbuster books, these texts, by virtue of their explosive popularity, often find an entrance into elite literary culture discussions, either as objects of curiosity, of derision, or of study. Harold Bloom wrote in a *Wall Street Journal* article that "The Harry Potter epiphenomenon" demonstrated the downfall of literate society, deriding the "ideological cheerleaders" who admired Rowling's work. He quipped: "The cultural critics will, soon enough, introduce Harry Potter into their college curriculum, and *The New York Times* will go on celebrating another confirmation of the dumbing-down it leads and exemplifies." While it is not surprising that Bloom, a purveyor of high culture and a staunch champion of the canon, objects to Harry Potter, it is surprising that he took the time to say as much publicly, rather than simply ignoring Harry Potter "mania." By achieving blockbuster status, the Harry Potter series, doubly excluded from elite literary culture by virtue of its popularity and target children's audience, garnered attention from the normally uninterested elite.

In addition to exploding the taste management and cultural boundaries of traditional bestseller lists, blockbuster books have redefined the importance of the bestseller status as a prize. English argues that the proliferation of prizes in our culture is caused when the system of awards produces gaps or voids, which will "justify and indeed *produce* another prize" (67). If we can accept the concept of bestsellerdom as a type of cultural prize, then it is fair to argue that bestseller lists likewise proliferate in order to meet perceived gaps in coverage. Since the invention of the list, which featured only a single category, the term "bestseller" has become somewhat omnipresent. When *The New York Times* removed children's literature to its own separate category in 2001, the total number of categories was 8.[6] A decade later, in 2010, that list had grown to thirteen categories.[7] As of this writing in December 2015, the list contains 21 weekly categories and 22 monthly categories.[8] This means, every week, at least 25 different books can claim to be a "#1 *New York Times* Best Seller": the proliferation of categories has diluted the authority and cultural capital of that prize. It also makes analysis of the lists and comparison of the status of bestselling books published even a decade apart extremely difficult.[9] The bestseller, then, behaves like a prize, one which has steadily proliferated to reflect a widening array of popular book categories.

The blockbuster book has become the new standard of excellence for major publishing firms, who must pursue "blockbuster strategies" in order to remain financially viable and culturally relevant. According to Elberse, most entertainment companies, including movie studios, television networks, music labels, and book publishers, pursue a marketing strategy in which a select number of products receive the majority of promotional backing. These companies are "making huge investments to acquire, develop, and market concepts with strong hit potential, and they bank on the sales of those to make up for the middling performance of their other content" (3–4). She explains that instead of marketing all products in its portfolio equally, an entertainment company following this strategy "allocates a disproportionately large share of its production and marketing dollars to a small subset of products in the hope that they will bring in the lion's share of revenues and profits" (19). Elberse notes these companies often see the majority of their income (80 percent) come from a small number of their products (20 percent) when those few products (hopefully) achieve high levels of success. She acknowledges that this 80/20 strategy seems extremely risky, given how fickle consumers can be: "Even amid considerable uncertainty, the studio bets heavily on the most likely hits. It makes 'blockbuster bets': big-budget productions aimed at mass audiences" (19). While some companies have made bad bets and suffered for it, Elberse argues that this strategy is necessary because "it mirrors the way consumers make choices among a wealth of competing entertainment offerings. Because people are inherently social, they generally find value in reading the same books and watching the same television shows and movies that others do" (41). The blockbuster strategy relies on the same logic as the bestseller list, since people are more likely to buy books that appear to be popular with others. Elberse continues:

> Compounding this tendency is the fact that media products are what economists call 'experience goods,' that is, audiences have trouble evaluating them before having consumed or experienced them. Unable to judge a book by its cover, readers look for cues as to its suitability for them.
>
> (41)

Those cues might include well-placed advertising, but in the case of books, it might also be placement in the bookstore or an appearance on a best-seller list.

A blockbuster book receives a huge commitment from publishers in terms of marketing and promotion. However, just like films or music, word of mouth also plays an important role. Elberse quotes executives who claim that no amount of marketing can overcome bad word-of-mouth reviews from a film's opening weekend (80). *The Hunger Games* provides an ideal example of the power of word of mouth in a blockbuster strategy. According to Laura Miller's *Salon* article, *The Hunger Games* started off with "in-house enthusiasm" or excitement from the professionals within Scholastic. "Scholastic employees began eagerly passing the manuscript around the office. It was the first stirring of what would become a tidal wave of word of mouth." Scholastic then turned to its network of "booksellers who have exceptional influence with co-workers and peers." These so-called "Big Mouths" act as twenty-first-century children's literature gatekeepers: they "run regional associations, organize book fairs and set up school events. Teachers and librarians come to them for hot tips on new kids' titles." Scholastic reportedly sent the "Big Mouths" photocopied versions of *The Hunger Games* manuscript rather than wait for more polished Advanced Reader Copies (ARCs) in order to build early buzz (Miller, "Making of a Blockbuster"). The early enthusiasm from children's literature specialists helped to create Elberse's suitability cues, which is key to converting word-of-mouth buzz into purchase path dependencies.

The Hunger Games also benefited from the pre-release determination of blockbuster potential from its publisher. Prior to the book's release, industry publications like *Publisher's Weekly* noted "how Scholastic had twice doubled the book's print run in response to 'early raves, particularly online, where commentary has lit up blogs and listservs.' The book was well on its way to bestseller status" (Miller, "Making of a Blockbuster"). By increasing the size of the initial printing twice based on "buzz," Scholastic was able to solicit free publicity, making it more likely that *The Hunger Games* would continue to be talked about. As the release date grew closer, additional articles cited both the online buzz and the size of the first printing as evidence that the book would be a hit (Sellers).

Blockbuster books have blurred genre and age-group definitions. As YA titles are moved to prominent bookstore displays, they appeal to the cross-over market of both children and adults. YA books make excellent cross-over books, which historically can be seen as a return to nineteenth-century reading habits when adults and children read the same texts. A crossover audience also makes for a wider potential sales pool, helping the books reach blockbuster status. This crossover appeal for YA has made marketable YA manuscripts a powerful and highly sought after commodity. *The Hunger Games* debuted on September 28, 2008 on *The New York Times* Children's Chapter Book list at number 9. However, a review from Stephen King in

Entertainment Weekly and an endorsement from *Twilight* author Stephanie Meyer on her blog helped propel the novel into crossover territory, tapping an established fan-base of adults who had already discovered YA books made for good reading (Miller "Making of a Blockbuster").

The interlocking of hugely popular books with blockbuster films, television series, video games, transmedia advertising campaigns, and product endorsements is another proven element of the blockbuster strategy, allowing texts to reach higher levels of sales and cultural saturation (Elberse 223–5). While *The Hunger Games*, much like Harry Potter before it, behaved as a steady seller, the second novel in the trilogy, *Catching Fire*, debuted on September 20, 2009 at number 1 on *The New York Times* Children's Chapter Books list (with *The Hunger Games* right behind at number 2 after 52 consecutive weeks on the list). Since a blockbuster book receives so much of a publisher's marketing budget, the buzz for a book often builds to a high level before the book has even been released. These book releases often cross into the realms of entertainment: the later novels in the Harry Potter series were released in the midst of giant bookstore-hosted parties, where children came in their pajamas or Harry Potter costumes and counted down the hours to midnight (Rich, "Muggle Soirees"; Miller, *Reluctant Capitalists* 128). Other marketing campaigns feature author appearances on talk shows, at book signings, at book readings, or at schools, or public libraries. Sales can also be driven by news of film adaptations in the works or other transmedia adaptations (video games, computer games, commercials). The release of *Catching Fire* was preceded by news of a film adaptation deal, which helped push the entire series into blockbuster status. All this marketing not only sells books but also creates publicity about the release (a record number of copies sold; most copies sold in 24 hours), which in turn reinforces the positive feedback effect on sales.

While this shift toward YA properties has financial implications for children's literature publishing imprints and media corporations that are too complex to analyze in this particular essay, there are also implications for the field of children's literature that must be considered. This more powerful, financially relevant category has driven new genre distinctions, such as "new adult," and increased sales, visibility, and power for YA imprints at large publishing houses. An increased number of YA books are being adapted into films, especially series books which can form a franchise. The select group of texts that achieve blockbuster status quickly create a representative canon that becomes the go-to texts for non-experts to reference when thinking about children's literature. This means, in order for experts within the field of children's literature to reach these non-experts, they must couch reviews, analysis, and other theoretical criticisms around these hyper-canonical texts. This hyper-canon pervades the boardrooms of media conglomerates who seek to find and purchase media properties that represent the next *Hunger Games* or the next *Harry Potter*.

Predictably, there is a growing cultural backlash against YA blockbusters. Articles that condemn adults for reading children's books and examine the decline of teen culture have become popular in many mainstream newspapers and magazines. Cultural critics point to the upswing in YA blockbusters as the infantilizing of American culture.[10] The blockbuster is not going away, no matter how often cultural critics describe these extreme demonstrations of popularity and marketing prowess as a destructive force in our society, decimating our taste levels and cultural capital like the British bombs of old. However, those of us invested in children's literature should pay careful attention to the books being selected prior to publication for the blockbuster treatment and advocate for a more diverse cast of texts to receive these levels of support from children's literature institutions. Individuals concerned with the breadth and diversity of children's literature may not be able to undo the existing hyper-canon: however, they can work to create the word-of-mouth praise for a wider variety of texts so that the popularly elected blockbuster canon can begin to reflect a wider range of children's literature.[11]

Notes

1. According to Jacqueline Rose:

   > The association of money and childhood is not a comfortable one. Money is something impure. It circulates and passes from hand to hand (children are warned that coins are *dirty*). Money relies on traffic. The value of a piece of money depends on what it can be exchanged for (goods) and what it can be compared with (more, or less, money) [...]. It is contaminated by association and exchange. Not so childhood.

   (87)

2. *The New York Times Book Review* publishes bestseller lists every week; the *Publishers Weekly* list is released monthly.
3. Each bestseller list weeds out specific types of books, such as genre books, romance novels, religious texts, almanacs, cookbooks, dictionaries, encyclopedias, and game books. Specific organizations further regulate the content of their bestseller lists by creating niche lists for categories of books that don't fit their formation of a bestseller. For example, *The New York Times* introduced an "Advice, How-To and Miscellaneous" category in 1984 in order to remove self-help books from the main lists. For more see Mott (9), Hackett (11) and Bear (204).
4. This assertion about the list being editorial content protected by intellectual property law was upheld by the Supreme Court in 1984 (Bear 198).
5. See my essay "Testing the Tastemakers: Children's Literature, Bestseller Lists, and the 'Harry Potter Effect.'" *Children's Literature* 40.1, 78–107.
6. January 2001 *New York Times* Bestseller categories included: Hardcover Fiction, Nonfiction, Advice and Business; Paperback Trade Fiction, Popular Fiction, Advice and Nonfiction; Children's Literature.

7. 2010 *New York Times* Bestseller categories included: Hardcover Fiction, Nonfiction, Advice, and Business; Paperback Trade Fiction, Popular Fiction, Advice and Nonfiction; Children's Picture, Chapter, Series and Paperback; and Graphic Books.

8. December 2015 *New York Times* Bestseller categories: WEEKLY LISTS: PRINT & E-BOOKS (Fiction, Nonfiction), HARDCOVER (Fiction, Nonfiction), PAPERBACK (Trade Fiction, Mass-Market Fiction, Nonfiction), E-BOOKS (Fiction, Nonfiction), ADVICE & MISC. (Combined), CHILDREN'S (Picture Books, Middle Grade Hardcover, Middle Grade Paperback, Middle Grade E-Book, Young Adult Hardcover, Young Adult Paperback, Young Adult E-Book, Series), GRAPHIC BOOKS (Hardcover, Paperback, Manga).

   MONTHLY LISTS: Animals, Business, Celebrities, Crime, Culture, Education, Espionage, Expeditions, Family, Fashion, Food and Fitness, Games, Health, Humor, Indigenous, Politics, Race, Relationships, Religion, Science, Sports, Travel.

9. Trust me. As someone who has been writing about bestseller lists for almost a decade, the near constant changes to these lists is a research nightmare.

10. For more on this see Graham "Against YA" and Scott "The Death of Adulthood in American Culture."

11. The grass-roots organization We Need Diverse Books has been encouraging publishers to highlight more diverse titles in this way since early 2014.

12   The Archive Award, or the Case of de Grummond's Gold

Emily Murphy

In May 1969, the University of Southern Mississippi began a tradition of awarding the USM Medallion to authors of children's literature for "distinguished service in the field" ("History"). Cast in silver and featuring the bust of the winning author, the Medallion was intended to promote the de Grummond Collection of Children's Literature. The winning author not only received his or her medallion, but he or she also was invited to present a speech at the annual Children's Book Festival, where authors, librarians, researchers, and even children gathered to discuss the state of children's literature. Those who made donations but could not attend the Festival also received a cheaper bronze version of the medallion as a gift along with other promotional items, including the quarterly newsletter *Juvenile Miscellany*. Past winners include E.H. Shepard, Taro Yashima, Lois Lowry, and David Weisner, a list that demonstrates that both authors and illustrators alike are considered for the award. The award, too, is not limited to American authors, although historically winners have either been American or British. Although modest in its origins, the USM Medallion has grown in prestige since 1969. Now, in addition to donors, children's literature enthusiasts may purchase medallion replicas online from the "De Grummond Shoppe" and the collection has since added an additional four awards intended to recognize emerging authors as well as other contributors to the field of children's literature.[1]

The addition of new awards as a way of reflecting the diversity and range of contributors to the field of children's literature reflects de Grummond's vision for her collection. In *Growth of an Idea* (1972), de Grummond writes, "I was interested in building a fine collection for use by teachers and librarians, and, through them, the children—all children." With the help of Dr. Warren Tracy, chairman of the Library Science Department and university librarian for the University of Southern Mississippi, de Grummond's dream of building a "fine collection" of children's literature came closer to being realized. Tracy launched the annual Children's Book Festival in May 1968 as a way of attracting attention to de Grummond's children's literature collection, which was founded just two years earlier. An event that featured guest speakers such as Dr. Frances Lander Spain, the past president of the American Library Association and the head of the children's department of the New York Public Library, the Children's Book Festival was an instant success ("History of the Fay B. Kaigler"). The Festival quickly attracted specialists in children's literature, many of whom came to see the speech for the recipients of the USM Medallion. The USM Medallion continues to be an integral part of the Festival today, and has helped secure the Collection's status as an internationally recognized children's literature archive.[2]

In this essay, I argue that the USM Medallion was founded as a way of supporting the de Grummond Collection's central mission and main function as a protector of the value (both emotional and economic) of children's literature. More than just a way for the de Grummond Collection to showcase their materials, the USM Medallion also contributed to the collection's mission to preserve important works of children's literature. The award, as I will show, was one that many authors valued dearly and that fulfilled the goal of the USM award committee and the collection that it represented: to bring attention to materials or authors who might otherwise be overlooked or that, in the opinion of experts in the field, deserve praise and recognition for their intellectual labor. The USM Medallion, especially in the early years of the de Grummond Collection's formation, helped promote authors who made significant contributions to the field, and also rewarded those for more daring or creative work or those who were aspiring authors.

In addition to fulfilling a very specific and concrete need, the USM Medallion also demonstrates how the children's literature archive contributes to the process of canon formation. From the very beginning, the USM Medallion was meant to support the de Grummond Collection by promoting the materials it housed and encouraging more authors and illustrators to add their original materials to the collection. Judging works based on traditional notions of literary merit, the USM award committee fulfilled its role but only through indirect means. The USM Medallion often followed the lead of other award committees for children's book awards, including the Newbery and the Caldecott, and selected authors and illustrators who had previously won these nationally recognized prizes. However, as Robert Bittner and Michelle Superle note in their contribution to this volume, the decisions of the Newbery-Caldecott committee are often based on a single criterion—"excellence"—that is evaluated using formalist modes of literary criticism. This approach to the selection process disregards other types of value, such as the social value of books with representations of children from different racial and ethnic backgrounds, and increases the odds of these other valuable works being overlooked during the selection process.[3] Despite these drawbacks, the guidelines used by the American Library Association in the selection process for children's book awards continue to serve as a benchmark for making and breaking the literary canon in children's literature. Yet, as we shall see, the politics surrounding the selection process for the USM Medallion raised other concerns (namely how the prize might generate further donations) that were just as important as standards of "excellence," demonstrating how the politics of collecting shape the politics of prizing.

The Politics of Prizing in the Children's Literature Archive

Dr. Lena de Grummond nurtured her fledgling collection with her monumental letter-writing campaign that consisted of writing up to five hundred letters a week—in longhand—to authors and illustrators of children's literature, asking each if they might have something to donate to the collection. Established in 1966 in order to help her library science students understand the book-making process, the de Grummond Collection fulfilled a need for more collections dedicated to children's literature.[4] In one of her most famous lines, de Grummond invited authors and illustrators to send her their "trash basket" if they did not have anything to donate (*Growth*). While intended as a joke, many authors indeed felt that there was little need to save manuscripts, dummies, proofs, or other original materials once a book reached the press. There was simply no support structure to suggest otherwise. The development of several special collections of children's literature, including the Kerlan and the de Grummond Collection, however, began to convince authors and illustrators that this was no longer the case. Through her letters, de Grummond not only convinced donors that their work was valuable, but she also developed friendships that vastly increased the amount of donations the collection received and the quality of these donations. In the words of one reporter, de Grummond had the "Midas Touch" (Lambou 7). De Grummond received numerous letters from eager donors, who not only offered her their "gold," but who also made suggestions for future donations. Other, more seasoned veterans took the time to carefully label and sort their material (even going so far as to include information cards to direct future researchers), and often told de Grummond that they would do their best to find a little something to give.

I repeat this early history of the de Grummond Collection in large part because it informs the selection process of the USM Medallion, an award that in many ways supplemented de Grummond's successful letter-writing campaign. While letters were intended to foster friendships that would benefit the growth of the collection via donations, the USM Medallion was intended to showcase the highlights of the collection and to acknowledge those who had donated most generously. In a system dependent on the generosity of donors (i.e. financial compensation was largely given through tax breaks, a system that was abolished after the passage of the Internal Revenue Service Tax Reform Act of 1969), it was imperative that the collection staff find other means of attracting and maintaining a large pool of donors. For this reason, Dr. Warren Tracy, chairman of the Library Science Department, decided to establish the Children's Book Festival and the Medallion, which would become one of the highlights of the annual meeting. Unlike many other aspects of the collection, the Medallion was not something that de Grummond, the founder and curator of the collection, had complete control over. Instead, the award committee consisted of library staff who often had a different vision for the award, one that caused friction at times when de Grummond attempted to exert her power as collection founder and curator.

In keeping with her strategy to provide a personal touch to the donation process, de Grummond would do her best to make the USM Medallion her own. Folding the award into her other archive activities, de Grummond promoted the award and encouraged the Medallion committee to use it to reward rising authors and illustrators whose contributions had benefited the collection.

A dispute between de Grummond and the Medallion committee in 1981 reveals much about the politics behind the USM Medallion and the personal agenda of de Grummond. Intended to reward the most significant contributor to the field of children's literature while also showcasing the collection's strengths, the Medallion was an award developed in order to attract future donors and to reward existing ones. In an effort to fulfill these goals, de Grummond established a firm set of criteria for the Medallion, informing the 1981 award committee that a winner should be selected based on the following: 1) They have never received a Newbery or Caldecott award for their contributions to the field; 2) They show promise and will likely do well in the future; and 3) They have contributed a significant amount of materials to the collection. Outraged that that year's award went to Maurice Sendak, who had declined her invitation to contribute materials in a letter from 1968, de Grummond wanted to ensure that only collection contributors would receive the award in the future. In the same letter to the 1981 award committee, de Grummond stiffly claims, "In the future I would like to see the Committee not rubber-stamp the choices of the Newbery-Caldecott Committee, whose basis of selection is necessarily different from ours" (de Grummond, Letter, February 5, 1981).

Despite de Grummond's protestations, the USM Medallion committee continued to select authors whose work had already received recognition from the Newbery-Caldecott Committee. Lois Lenski, Taro Yashima, Madeleine L'Engle, and Lois Lowry were some of the celebrated authors who traveled to Hattiesburg to receive their medallion. Many of these authors were in fact dedicated to the growth of the collection and took seriously their position as award winners. For example, Lois Lenski, the first author to receive the Medallion award, made several suggestions regarding reprints of her award speech and possible duplicates of the medallion itself. Dazzled by the honor of receiving the USM Medallion despite her many accomplishments, Lenski also requested to have a special chain created so that she might wear the award around her neck and keep it close at all times (July 2, 1969). Lenski's ideas to turn the Medallion into a "unique association item" were put into action, and the collection began a policy of casting cheaper bronze copies of the medallion to give away to donors annually. The example of Lenski indicates how seriously even the "star" donors of the collection were when it came to the duties associated with being a Medallion winner. Since most of them were also collection contributors, they had an investment in the collection's success and they dedicated their personal time to aid the collection in its mission to grow and attract additional donors.

By awarding the Medallion to the collection's "star" donors, the Medallion committee used the prize as a way of attracting additional donors. This strategy may have fallen short of de Grummond's standards for evaluation, but it was a successful tactic for keeping high profile donors happy while also attracting new donors in the process. And, while de Grummond may have disagreed with the award committee's decisions at times, she wholeheartedly embraced the idea of rewarding her donors and building a stronger community that had the collection at its center. Indeed, de Grummond once traveled all the way to England to present E.H. Shepard with his medallion. A recipient of the 1970 award, Shepard was surprised that de Grummond had taken such pains to present him with this award.[5] De Grummond won many an artist over with her gracious attitude and charming personality, receiving praise such as the following by Elsa Posell: "Recently I have been approached by two different organizations asking for some of my original manuscripts—One a Ukranian Society. I have been so happy in all my dealings with you and should prefer to continue this relationship" (May 19, 1968). De Grummond's many contacts helped increase her relative power in the field of children's literature, and her impact during her time as curator might be compared to that of renowned New York librarian, Anne Carroll Moore. De Grummond attracted the attention of notable publishers such as Kaye Webb (Puffin Books), and she also helped struggling authors and artists by using her contacts to help them gain publishing contracts. One thankful contributor writes to de Grummond, claiming that "All that goes on now in the way of professional recognition is directly due to you" (Poole). Another letter from Gertrude Warner writes asking for new book suggestions for her *Boxcar Children* series (August 8, 1968). Letters such as these indicate the author's respect for de Grummond's opinion, and especially the way in which de Grummond's role in the field extended beyond the collection of original materials.

The Medallion was a crucial piece in de Grummond's larger mission to build a special collection of children's literature, and she was likely pleased when donors began writing to her rather than the USM Medallion committee requesting consideration for the upcoming award. Since the winner of the award had their original materials and published books displayed at the annual Children's Book Festival, authors hoping to increase book sales were eager to attract the attention of the award committee. One hopeful author addresses de Grummond, suggesting that he might be an ideal nominee for the Medallion:

> I would be highly honored should the Festival Committee ever consider my book of BRISTLE FACE. Many thousands of Mississippi children are familiar with it, as you probably know. I would really be thrilled to have your festival and award added to the book's honors.
>
> (Zachary Ball, March 24, 1969)

By combining her letter-writing campaign with the promotional activities for the Medallion, de Grummond attracted the attention of budding authors and artists in the field. The example of Zachary Ball, whose adventure stories for boys were good enough to land him several movie and television contracts, but whose style and plot was not imaginative enough to capture the attention of the American Library Association's Newbery award committee, was exemplary of what the Medallion sought to achieve for the de Grummond Collection. That is, it both gave the collection credibility by highlighting star donors while simultaneously increasing the interest of successful authors who had yet to receive the status of these stars due to the perceived literary merit of their work. In this respect, the Medallion committee did support the Newbery-Caldecott's decisions, yet they still indirectly challenged these yearly lists of award winners by enabling the preservation of the work of fellow donors like Ball.

Prizing in the Archive, or the Archive as Prize

Like any literary prize, the USM Medallion grew out of a debate about what was valuable and what was not. The award committee debated who the "most distinguished" of children's book authors/illustrators happened to be that particular year, and how they might go about supporting the contributions of dedicated artists who did not necessarily make this "best" list. This debate, as I have shown, was in large part dictated by the specific needs of a budding special collection, whose goal was first and foremost to attract donors. While the Medallion committee may have indeed "rubber-stamped the choices of the Newbery-Caldecott committee," as de Grummond herself suggested, they also continued to invite donors with work of varying literary merit to donate their material. In doing so, they initiated a two-tier system of prizing that worked to meet their individual needs and goals. This system was structured so that donors already accepted as talented authors by the literary community, especially through visible recognition such as national book prizes, would help build the reputation of the collection and attract additional donors. After successfully building up its reputation, a collection could then make an impact similar to that of other nationally recognized prizes by collecting other authors who did not receive the same recognition as prize-winning donors. While not all collections subscribed to this method—the Kerlan Collection, for example, originally focused exclusively on Newbery and Caldecott award-winning authors—the de Grummond Collection was built in large part through this strategy. Dedicated to collecting *all* authors, no matter the subject matter or genre, the collection ultimately challenged notions of value and worth through its collecting habits, a luxury that could not be extended to its award committee if the promotional activities were to be a success.

The unique status of the children's literature archive can in part attribute for the two-tier prizing system that the de Grummond Collection ultimately adopted. In her essay on children's literature archives, Karen Sánchez-Eppler argues that "archives hold what has been thought worth collecting" (220), yet she cautions readers that many of the items in these collections were only preserved as a happy accident, or because "someone did not bother to throw them away" (220). In cases where items were intentionally saved, she claims, it was often because of the "heartbreak of an early death" (220). As the early history of the de Grummond Collection indicates, the items first collected were often the result of luck, where de Grummond's letters reached an author before they had the chance to destroy their original materials. However, the progression of the collection over time indicates that collecting became more intentional as years passed, and that many an author was aware of the value associated with being collected by a children's literature archive. Kenneth Kidd adds,

> the idea of the archive ... operates not unlike the ideas of the classic and the canon, which, for all their problematic aspects, have helped shore up children's literature as a creative and critical field. More so than the classic or the canon, however, the archive valorizes research, adds academic value to children's materials.
>
> (2)

As Sánchez-Eppler and Kidd both suggest, it is the perceived "specialness" of an archive, especially those dedicated to childhood objects, that in part lends them value. Childhood, already a time considered by many to be precious, makes the children's literature archive an attractive destination. Many of these archives receive inquiries about a beloved childhood book from non-researchers hoping to rediscover a special item from their childhood. One of the de Grummond Collection's most frequently asked questions, for example, is "How can I find a book that I loved as a child?" suggesting that many regard the collection as an archive of childhood itself. Even in the collection's early days, those outside of the field believed that de Grummond's archive had a "special magic" that could reconnect them to childhood (Nagle),[6] and this became part of the archive's allure. The nostalgia and desire that is associated with children's literature collections is a central aspect of the way these special collections are understood by both professional and non-professional visitors. As Sánchez-Eppler notes, "In many ways, for each of us, childhood is the archive, a treasure box of the formative and the forgotten" (213). Like the nostalgia surrounding childhood, the children's literature archive generates a longing that is made all the more acute by its connection to childhood.

The connection between the archive and childhood is what in large part lends special collections of children's literature their value. Much like the "pricelessness" of the twentieth-century child, special collections of children's literature also house items deemed so valuable that a price tag is unthinkable.[7] Furthermore, these collections have an emotional value that is separate from the economic value of the objects housed in the collection. This value is increased exponentially through the collecting process, which Susan Stewart explains in *On Longing: Narratives of the Miniature, the Gigantic, the Souvenir, and the Collection* (1993):

> The collection cannot be defined simply in terms of the worth of its elements. Just as the system of exchange depends upon the relative position of the commodity in the chain of signifiers, so the collection as a whole implies value—aesthetic or otherwise—independent of the simple sum of its individual members.
>
> (166)

In his own reflections on collecting, Walter Benjamin adds that in a collection a collector "does not emphasize their [the collection item's] functional, utilitarian value—that is, their usefulness—but studies and loves them as the scene, the stage, of their fate" (60). In both of these reflections it is the collection as a whole rather than an individual item that produces the ultimate value of the archive.

This process of valuing the whole rather than the individual is reflected in anti-pricing campaigns of the de Grummond Collection. Former curator John Kelly, for example, remarks, "once in the collection, the original works, illustrations and volumes would never be sold" (qtd. in Lambou 7). Another de Grummond staff member adds, "The enclosed evaluation in no way reflects the true worth of this material to us, for it is invaluable" ("Letter to Phyllis," May 9, 1978). While the circumstances that generated these comments are quite different—Kelly was quoted in a newspaper article while the unidentified staff member was responding to a new collection donor—they both attest to the belief that the de Grummond Collection's value arises from the net sum of its content. That is, as Kelly notes, the value referred to in the 1978 letter is built as a result of the refusal to resell items once they make their way into the collection. For all practical purposes, these items are in fact priceless once they enter the collection. What both of these staff members understood is what Viviana Zelizer describes as the relationship between price and value. In Zelizer's words, the crude act of pricing "destroys value" (21). However, a "reciprocal 'sacralization' process" also occurs in which "value shapes price, investing it with religious, social, or sentimental meaning" (21). It is the knowing manipulation of both value and price that led to the phenomenal success of the de Grummond Collection, where collection staff emphasized the sentimental value of objects over their economic worth.[8]

Those in charge of building and maintaining the de Grummond Collection understood that a "priceless" item was far more valuable to them than one with a specific price tag, and this knowledge served them well as they continued to build the collection. By the time children's literature authors became accustomed to the fact that there were in fact collections willing and able to house their original materials, prizes were no longer necessary to entice these authors to donate. Rather, the collection itself became the prize. In the words of children's author Bruce Coville, "you never know if anyone is going to think your career is significant enough to WANT to archive your stuff!" As Coville attests, the archive is the ultimate prize, proof that one's career is "significant enough" to merit inclusion in this most valuable of collections. Operating from this new position of power, children's literature collections, such as the de Grummond, collect in a way that shapes our perception of the value of individual authors and their body of work. If an author is being collected, we presume that he or she is being collected for a reason, and it is our job to determine what makes his or her work so valuable. This is not to say that the older system of value production is not still in place, yet in the case of established collections it is no longer necessary to promote the collection in order to build one's value since that value has already been established through years of collecting.

As the very title of this edited collection suggests, prizing in children's literature is a political process, and this holds true for the USM Medallion. This award developed in an attempt to build the reputation of an individual collection and to attract potential donors. The case of the USM Medallion demonstrates how the archive award does more than identify books worthy of prizing; it also suggests that the institution giving the prize is also valuable. This distinct need to gain value while giving value distinguishes the archive award from other children's book prizes. Unlike other nationally recognized children's book prizes, the archive award is not given primarily to set a standard for literary merit—skewed as it might be by the literary preferences of award committees. Rather, the award is given in large part from a desire to build collections. It is only in building up the reputation of an individual collection that one can then act in a manner similar to the ALA committee.

Notes

1. New additions to the prizes awarded at the Fay B. Kaigler Children's Book Festival include the Coleen Salley Storytelling Award, the Ezra Jack Keats (EJK) Award, the Kaigler-Lamont Award, and the Magnolia Award. As Ramona Caponegro explains in her essay in this volume, the EJK Award was actually an existing award created by the Ezra Jack Keats Foundation. It was only in 2012 that the Foundation decided to partner with the de Grummond Collection (4), a decision that I believe may in part be due to the shared vision of the Foundation and the Collection. The EJK Foundation wanted to create an award that would support emerging authors and illustrators and be "as inclusive as possible on all fronts" (2–3), goals that Lena de Grummond certainly valued and promoted during her years as collection curator.
2. Since the initiation of the Medallion in May 1969, there have been a total of 45 award recipients. Many of these authors received nationally recognized awards (e.g. the Newbery or Caldecott Medal) before receiving the medallion.

3. Bittner and Superle provide other examples of the problems of current selection criteria based on their experience working on the award committees for a number of prizes in the field (e.g. the Michael L. Printz Award). See also, in this volume, Marilisa Jiménez García's discussion of the Pura Belpré Medal for more on the lack of representation of ethnic children's literature and how awards often fail to challenge racial segregation.

4. De Grummond started her collection well after the establishment of the University of Minnesota's Kerlan Collection. However, her collecting habits were distinct from Kerlan's since she was not just interested in collecting material from award winners. Unlike the Kerlan Collection, which is known for its vast collection of archival material for Newbery and Caldecott winners, de Grummond wanted to build a collection that reflected the contributions of all authors and illustrators in the field. By including non-award winners, de Grummond was able to satisfy a need for a more inclusive children's literature collection.

5. In "Lena de Grummond: Woman with a Dream," Yvonne Arnold writes, "Shepard was too ill to travel to Hattiesburg for the presentation, so de Grummond delivered the medallion to him personally, in England. 'I just wanted everyone to be happy,' she said" (5).

6. In a 1982 newspaper article "This children's literature collection isn't for kids" from *The Clarion-Ledger*, Margaret Nagle writes,.

> The de Grummond Collection also holds a special magic for anyone who was an avid reader as a child or still harbors a bit of childhood in his soul. It is here that the layman can not only visualize the creative process of writing and illustrating children's literature and thrill at the sight and touch of original works, but he can also relive a part of that innocence and charm that is growing up.

7. See Viviana Zelizer's *Pricing the Priceless Child* (1985) for an extensive discussion of the shift from economically useful to economically useless children in the twentieth century.

8. Despite the de Grummond staff's unwillingness to "price" collection items, there were practical concerns related to the issue of price that had to be addressed behind the scenes. I address some of these concerns in my article, "Unpacking the Archive: Value, Pricing, and the Letter-Writing Campaign of Dr. Lena Y. de Grummond," which appears in the Winter 2014 edition of the *Children's Literature Association Quarterly*.

13 *Apologia*

Michael Joseph and Joseph T. Thomas, Jr.

The Lion and the Unicorn Award for Excellence in North American Poetry has at least demonstrated that it can survive for a decade, has shown that contemporary children's poetry deserves and can sustain critical attention now and for the foreseeable future. First appearing in the pages of *The Lion and the Unicorn (LU)* in 2005, the award was created by Lissa Paul, the journal's editor, who modeled it on the British *Signal* Poetry Award, given by the journal *Signal Approaches to Children's Books*, edited by Nancy Chambers from 1979 to 2001. *The Lion and the Unicorn* Award owes a debt of influence to the exemplary Newbery and Caldecott awards. Unlike those awards, however, the *LU* prize has in recent years offered the winner five hundred dollars (a check from Johns Hopkins University Press, which publishes *The Lion and the Unicorn*), and bestows no golden or silver seal to affix to subsequent editions (should there be any). *The Lion and the Unicorn* award does not recognize the best or "most distinguished" book. As the 2005 judges of the award explain,

> Unlike *Signal*, which considered only books of poetry published

one might remark that there is perhaps a tautological element to our judging for *The Lion and the Unicorn* Poetry Award, one that leads us (as judges and essayists) to award our own readings—a tautology perhaps uneasily present in the critical enterprise itself, inasmuch as a work of art depends on one's aesthetic contemplations. Joseph Margolis believed that the right sort of attention was indispensable in order for the work to exist, and, according to Gianni Vattimo, in *Art's Claim to Truth*, the success or failure of an interpretation depends on "an unpredictable element of congeniality," that its destiny is not in the hands of the artist.[1]

By and large, we make some effort not to over-read, although our *modus operandi* tends toward

---

1 Joseph Margolis, 'The Mode of Existence of a Work of Art', *Review of Metaphysics* (1958 12:1): 26–34; Vatimo, Sabala intro. [unpaged, location 281]. However, congeniality in this sense implicates the text we're engaging as a work of art, as Peter Kivy, makes explicit: "texts which *are* works of art would be amenable to performance [interpretation] whereas texts which are not works of art would not be so amenable." Peter Kivy, *The Performance of Reading: An Essay in the Philosophy of Reading* (Oxford: Blackwell, 2006): 90.

in Great Britain, *The Lion and the Unicorn* Award focuses on North American poetry. But like [...] the *Signal* poetry award, this new award similarly resists the idea of "bestness" and focuses instead on excellence in children's poetry.

(Flynn et al. 428)

That is, the judges recognize the wide range of texts that fall within the category "children's poetry," suggesting that simply choosing "the 'best' book of poetry for children" would be impossible (428). Also like the *Signal*, the *LU* award coincides with a discursive essay written by the judges and with a dual focus: "[to] discuss the merits of the winning book of poetry alongside a handful of honor books, [and to] speculate on issues unique to the project of writing and publishing poetry for children" (Heyman et al., "The City" 296–7).

The essays to date have invested far more intellectual capital in critical evaluation than theoretical speculation. However, the diverse opinions and wide scope of awarded books make plain that the individual judges have represented various, disparate, and occasionally conflicting theoretical positions, critical methodologies, and tastes. Virtually all kinds of work—visual poetry, sound poetry, light verse, narrative poetry, novels in verse, what have you—have been given consideration, and differing (though related) artistic and aesthetic criteria evenly applied. Like the judges who served on the *Signal* award panels, the orientation

Vattimo's "congeniality," a tendency that reached new heights in the 2012 award essay, in which we "took it upon ourselves to treat our submissions in rough accord with the insights of William Blake's *The Marriage of Heaven and Hell*," justifying the approach as simply "an experiment in criticism" (288). And yet we are not always "congenial," our attention sometimes taking the form of enthusiastically negative criticism of poems we find less than congenial to the otherwise receptive reader. We're hard on books we don't like.[2]

In "The Meaning of Children's Poetry: A Cognitive Approach," Karen Coats criticizes our award essays for their negative criticism, which she claims make her "feel like a dolt for liking some of the poetry they reject as facile" (128), although she doesn't offer specific comments or specific choices (which is too bad, really, as we'd like to know what she likes and why). Her criticism may or may not reflect a more general dissatisfaction with the negativity of *LU* essays, but her argument strikes us as extreme inasmuch as it seems to advocate for a new definition of children's poetry as a form of IDS (Infant-Directed Speech) rather than a subcategory of poetry.[3]

2 Among the goals of our award: to spur poets to produce more interesting children's poetry, to encourage their presses to think hard about what poetry they publish and why, and to start conversation about children's poetry among readers—be they scholars, critics, poets, or some combination of the above. To put it in slogan form: if our negativity provokes, it provokes with purpose.

3 In the second half of her essay, Coats equates poetry with "a lilting, rhythmical

of the *LU* judges has been empirical. They have responded to the annual accumulation of children's poetry books by honoring books that moved them—books that possessed, in their considered view, the hard-to-define quality of "excellence" (Flynn et al. 428)—and by deprecating books in which excellence was woefully lacking. They have not noticeably attempted to read as children, or on behalf of actual or imaginary children, although they have included children's responses (see Thomas et al. 385) in their essays, and often indulged in childish jokes.[1]

The raison d'être of the award has been to celebrate the work of North American poets writing for children, and the *LU* judges have necessarily striven in their essays to counter a majoritarian disregard for children's poetry. Although part of a journal for the scholarly studies of children's literature, the essays have tended to address an ideal audience that includes poets and critics of poetry, as is implied in the first essay: "Even the most radically inclusive poets and critics of poetry tend to ignore children's poetry and leave it outside the world of 'real' poetry, that is, poetry for adults" (Flynn et al. 427–8). That ambiguous conceit—"the world of 'real' poetry"—confronts unconventionally "inclusive poets and critics," who have permitted arbitrary assumptions about "despised

Coats regards our negativity in relation to what she calls our "often elitist positioning of the criticism that seeks to tell us what is good, bad, or indifferent in terms of children's poetry" (128). This carefully phrased remark seems to suggest that we are transmitting moral attitudes, not confining ourselves to an analysis of the poems, alone. If that is what she means, well, there is something to that, since criticism reflects, sooner or later, however indirectly, on values that transcend questions of technique. Plato defines beauty in terms of luminosity and measure, writing that beauty is perceived as measure only when it is "lived as a moral attitude, measured in all the aspects of life, rather than in the perceptions of art only." This ancient aesthetic that joined life and art was what The New Criticism sought to bury by its rigorous evacuation of historical context and what has come back with a vengeance in subsequent methodologies. Yet, Coats's criticism seems actually not to be, or not to be entirely, focused on our old aesthetics ways, but rather our New Critical-esque formalism, our overly punctilious analysis of

---

1   Denouncing a book of anti-smoking limericks in 2005, the judges intoned that the book is "enough to make you reach for a cigarette" (Flynn et al. 431).

speech that replicates the shushing sounds of the womb and swinging rhythms of the moving body" (136). Although she doesn't name it as such, this is a form of speech called, variously, baby-talk, motherese or "infant-directed speech" (IDS). Researchers characterize IDS as having "a higher overall pitch, a wider range of pitch, longer 'hyperarticulated' vowels and pauses, shorter phrases and greater repetitions than are found in speech directed to older children and adults" (Singing Neanderthals 69). Interestingly, these attributes are also present in PDS (Pet Directed Speech) (74–5).

poems"[2] to limit their enjoyment and understanding of poetry. Yet it also allows for the possibility that poems might be real, or that there is such a thing as the (unqualified) real to which adult poetry does not have privileged or exclusive access, a thing (this "unqualified real") that children's poetry might have access to as well. The argument made by the *LU* judges on behalf of prizing children's poetry would seem to draw on the *prima facie* validity of the ontological question: what is real, or how is the real revealed? The real in this case is not what is actual or typologically accurate, or, as in Plato, real above or beyond the material, sensual, world, but in the sense of what is deeply meaningful, humanly necessary.[3] The genre of children's poetry is legitimate precisely because the humanly necessary (the really real) can be encountered in the act of reading and thinking about a children's poem. Gianni Vattimo's *Art's Claim to Truth* supports the notion that art is not mere play, but rather the sort of thing that can present readers or viewers with truth, characterizing this presentation as

meter, which she praises with notable ambivalence as a "game for gifted intellectual athletes, that can be beautiful and thrilling to watch but bruising to enter" (128). (One person's meter may be another person's poison?) But is the language of cognitive science clearer or closer to the vernacular than that of prosody? Surely to condemn formalism as esoteric and elitist and then adopt a cognitive approach to answer the ontological question of "what poetry is and what it means" (128) is to risk hoisting oneself on one's own rather dogmatic petard, though Coats's other insights seem both fresh and provocative.

Our essays participate in several, sometimes overlapping, critical traditions that involve the careful and largely congenial engagement with texts marked as poetry by their writers, their publishers, and the stores that sell them. And we certainly don't feel the need to evaluate the texts submitted to us more gently just because they're intended "for children." Indeed, a critic might argue—and we, in fact, do—that criticism ought to be criticism regardless of the object on which it is practiced. Besides, what would a kinder and gentler criticism be? What would it look like? Would it be "criticism" in the special sense that letting one's nieces and nephews win at cards is "poker"?

Toward understanding how the *LU* prize operates it may be useful to understand how negative criticism serves the overall project of valuing good children's poems *qua* the embodiments of poetic excellence—a term that we would suggest is homologous with the notion of ontological weight. An awareness of the strategic importance of negative

---

2 The reference is to William Carlos Williams' "Asphodel": "You will not find it there but in / despised poems." Our point is that the prejudice against poetry represented by Williams in the conceit lingers in the wholesale rejection of poems for children.

3 Understanding, after Roland Barthes and Jacques Derrida, that significance is not inherent in any particular object, and that different folks need and find meaning in different things—the ever-changing roster of *LU* essayists allows for a plurality of views regarding what might be meaningful and necessary.

the "ontological weight of art."[4] That is not to assert—contra post-structuralism—that ontological weight inheres in the object itself, but rather to suggest that a reader who is prepared (by personal predilection, education, and other factors) to experience the ontological weight of art in a poem, or more precisely within the contemplation of a poem, can do so.[5]

One directly encounters the ontological preoccupation in the award's stated purpose and title: it is the "award for excellence." It need hardly be said that there are readers on whom children's poetry will have little or no effect. For them, hymning the excellence of children's poetry probably seems quite nerdy if not utterly madcap. (One thinks here of the old anti-modern art cliché in which the disgruntled museumgoer, upon looking at a work by Jackson Pollock or Willem DeKooning, exclaims—belittlingly—"my kid could have done that.") But, there are others able to prize poetry—or "poetry for adults"—who may experience

criticism dates to the inception of the award, even as a more restrained variety can be found throughout the *Signal* essays. In our first essay (Flynn et al.), we write, "while we resist easy notions of 'best,' we still find pretty useful the notion of 'bad'" (428).[4] We conclude the essay by praising "a deeply ambiguous and ambitious poem," because "[i]t reminds us that children's poems can be [successful] works of art. And that is no small accomplishment" (440). Bad poems, then, are those that have the dangerous potential to cause one to forget that poems can be works of art, that one can experience excellence in a children's poem. This fall into forgetfulness is a catastrophe to be avoided—at any cost. "Books remember for us," poet Rachel Hadas reminds us in her poem, "Mnemonic."[5] And yet books are flimsy, insubstantial as the seasons. As Allen Grossman memorably writes: "A man is sitting in a room made quiet by him. / Outside, the August wind is turning the leaves of its book."[6] Books, then, themselves

---

4 Gianni Vattimo, *Art's Claim to Truth* (New York: Columbia University Press): 44.
5 Williams writes,

> My heart rouses / thinking to bring you news / of something / that concerns you / and concerns many men. Look at / what passes for the new. / You will not find it there but in / despised poems. / It is difficult / to get the news from poems / yet men die miserably every day / for lack / of what is found there.

One might say that the "what" Williams says "is found" in poetry may or may not actually *be* there, although it is certainly *found* there.

4 Nota bene: Michael Joseph and Joseph Thomas (the writers of the essay you're now reading) are both former *LU* judges and essayists, and therefore reject the deceptive objectivity of a "they." However, we have usurped the right to speak on behalf of all past essayists (probably ill advisedly), a decision that forces us occasionally to resort to locutions such as "we seem to be implying," when we (Joseph and Thomas) are speculating on "our" (judges not Joseph and Thomas) underlying motives.
5 Rachel Hadas, "Mnemonic," *The Ache of Appetite* (Providence: Copper Beach Press, 2010) 33.
6 Allen Grossman, "The Room," *The Ether Dome and Other Poems: New and Selected Poems 1979–1991* (New York: New Directions, 1991) 63.

an exhilarating pleasure in a children's poem: the pleasure of experiencing excellence. And, of course, there are young people who do not yet prize poetry but who also might experience excellence in a children's poem. For them, as Santiago Zabala suggests, that event might begin a process of thinking and feeling, leading to self-understanding, a process with pedagogical implications to which we will return.[6] Thus, the *LU* award essay provides a forum for the educated discussion and evaluation of children's poetry and encourages readers to discover poetic excellence.

In the second *LU* essay (2006), the judges write: "Children's poetry may be a special subset of poetry, but it is, nevertheless, poetry" (Thomas et al. 384). This full-throated assurance echoes throughout the accumulated body of work, without any loss of conviction, so that one finds—four years later—that JonArno Lawson's *A Voweller's Bestiary* "is not just this year's best book of children's poetry; it is one of the year's best books of poetry, period" (Heyman et al., "Lively" 379). Here the

are in need of shoring up. Invoking tradition (or competing—and even complementary—traditions) is an act of remembering outside of or alongside books, a process in which past and present are constantly mediated, as much an apotropaic maneuver as a critical one. It's an invocation to the muse of memory on behalf of the collective project of remembering, of rendering experience recognizable.

This argument appears elsewhere in that 2005 essay:

> The amount of bad children's verse [...] has us worried that publishing operates according to Gresham's law (the bad drives out the good), and we are quite certain that it operates according to Sturgeon's law (ninety percent of everything is crap).
>
> (Flynn et al. 431)

If 90 percent of everything lacks excellence, then the critic must try to understand how 90 percent of everything fails and make his or her understandings transparent so readers might judge for themselves. Not only do good poems worthy of memorializing with prizes serve the ends of memory, but the critique of the bad ones does so as well.

We try to mark our negative criticisms in rich and memorable ways. Again, in the 2005 essay, we note, lamentingly, "as book upon book arrived and we began our discussions, we initially despaired" (Flynn et al. 428). With a similar dramatic rise in the second essay (2006), we posit that most books under examination disappoint: "Sifting through the piles of this year's books, the

---

6 In the introduction to *Art's Claim to Truth*, Santiago Zabala writes

> In this experience [of truth via contemplation of art] we not only understand the object we are confronting but also become better acquainted with ourselves because understanding always brings self-understanding, and therefore a certain circularity which Heidegger referred to as the "hermeneutical circle."
>
> (Vattimo, [unpaged location 303])

judges insist that Lawson's poetry deserves precisely the same kind of heightened attention commanded by *The Shadow of Sirius*, by W. S. Merwin (Pulitzer), *Versed*, by Rae Armantrout (National Book Critics Circle Award), or *Transcendental Studies: A Trilogy*, by Keith Waldrop (National Book Award for Poetry), to name just three of the year's books of poems to score prizes. Whatever issues are unique to the project of writing poetry for children, they do not impinge on its efficacy as art: excellence is excellence, whether we are talking Mozart or The Slits, Jack Kirby or Rembrandt, Shel Silverstein or Marilyn Nelson.

In 2009, the judges prodded publishers and book designers to draw on European rather than tried and true English design traditions. They complain, "there's not much out there exploring the trails blazed by proponents of literary Cubism, Dada, Surrealism, Fluxus, or Lettrism, movements well-suited to the world of children's literature" (Heyman et al., "Lively" 377). Anticipating skepticism, they point readers to two texts they believe will illustrate just how "well suited to the world of children's literature" these notoriously difficult literary schools might be: Gertrude Stein's "unforgivably neglected children's book" *To Do: A Book of Alphabets and Birthdays* and Kurt Schwitters's *Lucky Hans* (377). These two books are marked by a self-conscious sense of textual experimentation, their excellence rooted in a ludic playfulness that resists conventional notions

bad and indifferent threatened to overwhelm us. We were, it could be said, on the point of despair" (Thomas et al. 384). Consider: had we been examining these books as instruments for cultural or ideological analysis, we would have found no cause for "despair," no cause to feel "threatened," but as we're engaged with excellence and with the standing accusation that children's poetry is bereft of the same, the theatrically overwrought term, "despair," comes into play as a sign-vehicle of self-parody and self-recollection. We behave as if the dreadful revelation that the books of children's poetry we have in hand threatens this project as well as our self-possession in order to assure ourselves, ironically, and implicitly the reader (ye of little faith?) of the soundness of our thesis. Anagnorisis leads to peripeteia. Naiveté to profundity. Not *all* children's poetry is poetry, but then, neither is all or even most of what is published as poetry in the literary journals—even in *Poetry*—poetry.

Prizing children's poetry is inextricably bound up with disprizing children's poetry, and perhaps the enthusiasm for one must square with the enthusiasm for the other. When Polonius comments, "And oft 'tis seen the wicked prize itself / Buys out the law," he is evidently thinking along the same lines. In order to recognize excellence, "wickedness" must be denounced (and renounced) for the sake of balance.

But, problematically, we've constructed for our denunciations a privileged position that empowers us to say what is excellent and of maturity and seriousness that inform the worlds of "high art." Of course, critics tended to use this playfulness as a bludgeon. Willard Bohn reminds us that the Dadaists in particular have been discounted, historically, for their capricious irrationality, their work unflatteringly associated with "infantile behavior" (xv). And yet this idea of play is central to many discussions of children's literature. While there are usages of "play" that are sophisticated (e.g. to perform, to bet, or to trick or con; the sexual dalliance or swordplay), the general or most commonly occurring one, having to do with pleasure and delight, draws its form and influence from childhood.

However, especially in criticism of poetry for adults, "play" appears as a praise word. One finds, for example, Vasilis Papageorgiou asserting to John Ashbery that his work is "so playful."[7] Likewise, *The Oxford Encyclopedia of American Literature* uses this positively-inflected *play* repeatedly: to describe Andrew Marvell ("in its playfulness has a strength that Herrick's has not—a seriousness that does not make it less playful"), Philip Roth ("darkly sardonic but always incorrigibly playful. He has said that Sheer Playfulness and Deadly Seriousness are my closest friends"), Oliver Wendell Holmes (who "was more often wry and playful"), Delmore Schwartz

what wicked. Were we to assert our adequacy, it would not be excellence we were commending but our own authority and the ontology of the structure that confers such authority on us. In fact, it may be that charges of elitism are incited by the apprehension that critics—in general—are doing precisely that. Therefore, in order to truly prize children's poetry, rather than to prize oneself, and to avoid acts if not accusations of elitism, one must renounce one's authority—disprize oneself—and to some extent, quarrel with the structure of award-giving. The prestige of the award cannot overshadow the excellence of the poetry, this side farce. Therefore, prizing involves a negotiation between the excellent, the wicked, the self, and the structure by which the award, perhaps every award, is given. One must praise excellence, set it in dialectical relation to the wicked, and, while drawing upon one's own experience and the lexicon and grammar of prizing, deny that one is acting on behalf of the self or behalf of the committee, or even the community. One acts as a lone and disinterested agent of excellence. If we prize our interpretations, our wit, our verbal athleticism, it is, as Plato would wish, as a measure of the excellence we are praising in the poetry. As *LU* judges (The "Lion and the Unicorn" is itself a parody and self-parodying image), we attempt to encompass just such an ecology through irony, parody, absurdity, overstatement, and other distancing devices within and along with our venomous barbs.

In essay three (2007), for example, after announcing that we have

7   John Ashbery interviewed by Vasilis Papageorgiou, New York, April 5, 1989, *Chromata* http://chromatachromata.com/interview-with-john-ashbery/ accessed date August 20, 2016

("in the playful yet serious poem 'The Kingdom of Poetry'"), David Mamet ("his playful intellect delights in obfuscation"), and again John Ashbery ("[...] the playful diminishment of this traditional form, a plenty that is more postmodern than modern, unanchored as it is from the very traditions it mocks"), among many others.[8] Play as praise takes many meanings, joyful rather than solemn, experimental or independent rather than rigidly conventional or sentimental, breezy rather than morbid. All of them are positive and often combined in some binary-abusing relationship to seriousness.

However similar in appearance to these playful/serious locutions, the phrase describing American children's verse in the *Oxford* appears with rather a whiff of condescension. ("American verse for children was more moral than playful, though, of course, the two were often blended").[9] Here playful has an obligatory sense—the iron hand "of course" in the velvet glove—reminiscent of Miss Havisham explaining, "I sometimes have sick fancies, [...] and I have a sick fancy that I want to see some play. There, there!" with an impatient movement of the fingers of her right hand; "play, play, play!"[10]

The important distinction can be described with reference to the work of Nicolai Hartmann (the

received more books of good poetry than in previous years, we add that we are

> hesitant to conclude that we are now entering some Golden Age of children's poetry, even as we are cognizant of the always-witty Randall Jarrell's remark in his essay "The Taste of the Age" that "the people who live in a Golden Age usually go around complaining how yellow everything looks."
> (qtd. in Sorby et al., "Messages" 264)

We try to engender a sense of suspicion about our own pronouncements, even as we warn that the false or meretricious is everywhere; we assert our credentials, even as we self-deprecate. For instance, in commending reissues of children's poetry we write that while we were unable to honor them, these texts "*reassured* us that poetry expressly written for children *matters*" [emphases ours] (265). The implication that we needed to be "reassured" that poetry for children "matters" (the hyperbolic echo) recalls our earlier "despair" (Flynn et al. 384). We continue in this vein a little later:

> We desperately wish we would see something other than recycled nursery rhymes, sentimental poems about nature, and haiku published for the very young. Even when we love the sharp, lively language play—the real poetry, not just rhymed prose—of something like *Once around the Sun*, by Bobbi Katz, we're almost hurt

---

8 *The Oxford Encyclopedia of American Literature*, ed. Jay Parini (New York: Oxford University Press, 2004) pp. 245, 497, 23, 534, 16, 64.

9 *Oxford*, 275.

10 Charles Dickens, *Great Expectations* (New York: Gregory, 1861) 81.

teacher of Hans-George Gadamer), who differentiated the usages of "play" according to belief. The child supposedly becomes lost in imaginative play, unable to distinguish the imaginative from actuality, but for the adult, play "remains fiction."[11] The contradiction is exemplary: a playful adult poem inspires critics with positive and profound thoughts of childhood, its joy, surprises, innocence, discoveries, daring, its ease with contradiction, but a children's poem marked as playful is assumed to indulge in an unavoidable escapism and betray a dangerously seductive lack of depth. A poet writing this latter sort of playful verse for adults (generally in traditional stanzas) would be abused for writing light. Such a writer distances himself or herself from the dark or heavy aspects of life or refuses to acknowledge critical demands, lazily asserts Blakean or Wordsworthian innocence in the face of harsh truths or intractable complexities. If not avoidance, there is a sense of faux enlightenment and transcendence about this incorrigible attitude: death / shmeth. Such playfulness suggests an unsympathetic denial of the ferocious energies poetry is supposed to celebrate or at least kick back at. A playful children's poem is not really a poem, the critic admits, but *at least* it is developmentally appropriate. A playful adult poem that is not light verse, or a sentimental journey, is really a poem: playfulness as a kind of *sprezzatura* or grace under pressure

by the fact that the subject matter is terribly mundane.

(Sorby 267)

Reflecting on our desperation, we concede that it somehow places us within (while simultaneously querying) the camp of mainstream critics who hold no brief for poetry for children. Yet our theatrical pain also seems to divide us from the (yellow) authority to judge. (Wanting to be a judge reveals self-interest, the most egregiously bad judgment.) Flamboyant turns of language betray us. We are not rational and cool but subjective, hot, injudicious. Furthermore, by ironizing our despair, we suggest that our problem is the reader's problem. We are recycling or re-*playing* a universal despair, inasmuch as the antagonist of good children's poetry is the recognized difficulty of doing *anything* well. Writing poetry, the real stuff, is difficult, much harder than it looks, kids, regardless of who one supposes the audience to be. Judgment begins with this childlike awareness.

Revisiting our past essays for this chapter, we found many examples of self-ironization. In essay seven (2011), for example, we write, "[w]e nearly came to loggerheads over *Sail Away with Me: Old and New Poems*, by Jane Collins-Philippe" (Heyman et al., "The City" 302). The contrast between coming to blows and the volume's sweet title (a contrast heightened by being encapsulated in such a whimsical old and vaguely nautical word) widens the lens so that readers are permitted, as it were, to glimpse the judges' sense of unworthiness at being entrusted with the sober duty of determining what

11 Nicolai Hartmann, Ästhetik (Berlin: De Gruyter, 1953) 53.

is thus an earmark of excellence. Of course, let us remind ourselves that the distinction we have carefully been drawing may be perspectival, and exists not as a product of the artist's activity, but rather within a reader's aesthetic or contemplative experience.

The critical use of "play" throughout the nine *LU* essays makes consistent use of "play" in the "good" (adult) sense, associating the poetry with Marvell, Schwartz, Ashbery, and so on, and exemplifies the intent of the *LU* judges to abolish the spurious divide between poetry and children's poetry. In their first essay (Flynn et al.), half-heartedly praising Allan Wolf's *New Found Land: Lewis and Clark's Voyage of Discovery*, the judges write, "Its narrative scope is impressive, as is its use of multiple registers of language and multiple types of text," but they stress that it "lack[s] energy and linguistic play. That is, as poetry, the texture of language (or even the absence of that texture—perhaps willful prosiness) just isn't engaging" (435). The judges carefully delineate the sense of play intended—linguistic—and in doing so conflate "play" (childhood) with the communicative verve, the charm, of poetry, a mode of freedom from the dead hand of the conventioneer. In the second essay (2006), the judges observe that "Marsalis's musical tour de force [*Jazz A·B·Z*] and the other fine and playful honor books we discuss here are certainly excellent poetry" (Thomas et al. 383). Here "playfulness" is not merely compatible with poetry, but indispensable to it—"certainly"—and naturally occurring alongside "excellence."

is real, and perhaps as well their uneasiness in the presence of the real, whose shadow is palpable in the light phrase. Being at "loggerheads" characterizes for readers our disregard for the popular misconception that it is we who determine what is or is not excellent. We are merely intending to honor excellence, but our dramatic self-deprecation (sometimes sincere) is emblematic of a hard-fought resistance to the conventional, 'real'-world stance of condescending to children's poetry. If in dispraising ourselves—and in dispraising certain select books of children's poetry—we appear to be complicit in the general logger-headed prejudice, at the same time, our complicity appears disingenuous. Rereading the essays for this chapter, we found ourselves thinking that they tend toward the subversive, not mock-subversive, their intent seeming to be the inoculation of readers of poetry against such virulent contempt as they dissimulate, an intent rooted in a desire to enable readers to wholeheartedly experience excellence. In our eighth essay (2012), as we turn from praising poetry to dispraising faux poetry, we invoke the authority of none other than William Blake in support of our seemingly inconsistent attitude: "However, we begin not with the best but rather by taking up a few submissions worthy of—if not our scorn—then at least a little medicinal teasing ('Listen to the fools reproach. It is a kingly title!' [pl. 9])" (Heyman et al., "Roses" 289). If all children's poetry is profane, then those who find the sacred in children's poetry must be fools; by inference, that which fools deem profane must be the sacred. But, offered as irony, as trickster

The third award essay (2007) organically connects play to the avant-garde: "Hoberman classics are playfully onomatopoetic in the manner of Gertrude Stein [...]" (Sorby et al., "Messages" 265) and to "*New Yorker* sophistication" (266), and it is balanced against the childish, pusillanimous play found in bad "poetry." The essayists write: "Too much of what we received tends toward this (low) level of language play" (268). Their ambiguity suggests that a "(low) level of language play," that is, a paucity of linguistic freedom and experimentation (note how "low" is materially constrained, appearing between parentheses, as if in custody) equates to the lack of seriousness or excellence found in admirable work. The judges themselves self-consciously foreground the difference, punning on the sexual usage of "play": "Lawson is in a class by himself: he plays, but he does not pander. His book is a lot of smart fun because it keeps changing gears" (276). Lawson's "play" is not condescending (low play), nor merely fun. It is smart play, smart fun.

In the 2008 essay, as one might expect from a maturing award, there are fewer (three) and more sophisticated instances of "play." For example, in praising *The Moon Is La Luna: Silly Rhymes in English and Spanish*, by Jay M. Harris, the judges associate "play" with "cleverness" ("smart fun," again) and declare "the language play evident here is at the heart of poetry. These are poems about language first and foremost." While solidly associating play with intelligence and control, the judges still

foolishness (because, remember, it is the fool offering the advice), then the result reads in the reverse, to wit: that which fools deem profane (since you cannot trust someone who says s/he is untrustworthy) *may be profane*, or that which fools deem sacred *may be sacred*. This is, if you will, a kind of vaudevillian play, the spirit of which is evident elsewhere in the essay. In this same essay, critiquing a picture book poem by Kathi Lee Gifford (yes, that Kathi Lee), we write:

> A fair parody of Robert Service, *The Legend of Messy M'Cheany* reminded one of the judges of another in this esteemed genus, sometimes called the "Ballad of Mangy Nell and Pisspot Pete," that warhorse of a filthy folk poem similarly preoccupied by gender relations and cultural constructions of chastity— although one certainly less coy in its celebration of the Blakean proverb, "the lust of the goat is the bounty of God." (pl. 8 qtd. in Heyman et al., "Roses" 289)

Cramming Robert Service, Blake, and the "Ballad of Mangy Nell and Pisspot Pete" in one sentence appraising the poetry of a talk show host is high vaudeville, a carnivalesque subversion of the structure of prizing as well as of the ostensible legitimacy of the jury. One might see it as a kind of self-sacrifice in service to a project that would—at least beyond the pages of a few scholarly journals of relatively minor importance in literary and cultural studies—be thought quixotic, in the sense that few poets or critics are admit the lowest sense of "play" implicitly by referencing "bathroom humor," however they might deprecate it (Sorby et al., "from brain" 352). But this low "play" sits on a continuum that ultimately rises to language play, and merits the judges' highest praise. Language play is not only a sine qua non to excellence in poetry, but might be seen to gesture at definition: Poetry is "language play," or a unique instance of it.

Here we see an impression of that definition (again with reference to *The Moon is La Luna*): "language-learning becomes synonymous with language-play" (355). One of the conversations in this particular essay (the award's fourth) is about the relationship of pedagogy and children's literature. Poems that are mere tinsel and wrapping paper for lectures or lessons are unsatisfactory, even though pedagogy is not incompatible with poetry. Learning occurs through meaningful experience. Good, successful poems model and teach effective language skills by enabling readers through the experience of excellence to enter the hermeneutic circle. The "language play" indispensable to poetry is also indispensable to learning.

Bearing in mind that "play" is closely aligned with childhood, and so references to "play" encode emanations of childhood, we might read the commentary as making the extraordinary claim that not only are good children's poems real poetry (that is, they contain or provoke in the receptive reader an experience of excellence, of ontological weight), but that all poetry is or derives from children's

likely to accept the idea that childhood endows poetry with poetic excellence. More likely, and more common, is the view that entering into dialogue with a children's poem as though it were a work of art is nothing short of capricious and naively idealistic: childish. But then, that of course is part of why it might be excellent.

The materiality or material packaging of children's poetry remains a source of discussion, if not anxiety, in part presumably because children's books are often marked as unserious by commodifying cliché and kitsch decorations. And yet, the materiality of children's books not only affords avenues of expression for talented illustrators and book designers but figures into the experience of the poetry and conditions interpretation of the text in ways that cannot simply be brushed aside. The material stratum of a book of poems is the basis for the reader's imaginative engagement with the poetry, and together, imaginative engagement and physical substrate mesh to form his or her aesthetic experience, an experience that further conditions interpretation, a sense of the poetry's excellence. Perhaps it is in regard to this union, and a recognition that the poetry is not autonomous, that the *LU* judges have praised excellent *books* of children's poetry:

> But we are proud that the books we've selected to recognize as this year's most accomplished volumes of children's poetry share a concern with language as *matter*: the sounds, the grammatical textures, and the look of language. Unlike the bad and indifferent books, all the short-listed collections recognize the

poetry. In the five essays subsequent to 2008 (as of this writing, the 2014 award essay has not been published), this radical claim is not developed, but one hears its heartbeats elsewhere.

For example, in the fifth essay, the judges write "*The Year I Was Grounded* is different, because it is composed of poems that play with language as they reflect—playfully, but deeply—on the life cycle" (Heyman et al., "Lively" 387). The adjectival phrase set off in dashes (like dueling knives) sharpens our earlier claim that "play" is not superficial—we used the term *escapism*. A more conservative claim than the one levied the previous year, this contrast is still well-within the discourse and anchored to language: Adult poetry and children's poetry alike are constituted by a certain linguistic facility. Language is a watery element within which the undifferentiated sphere of poetry lolls like a sunken treasure ship, its moieties fused together, or re-fused, by play.

The fusion of "play" and language continues into 2010. "[Marion Dane] Bauer's play with language and the twilight paintings elevate the work above the average nature poetry" (Heyman et al., "It's [Not]" 355), say the judges (though not far enough to earn her an award—indeed, no award was bestowed that bleak year, although Bauer's poetry was commended). Bauer's playfulness is linked to nonsense (a variety of "play" very seldom mentioned in discussions of adult poetry). The judges

serious nature of play. And though we have reservations about the interplay between text and pictures in at least one of our honor books, there is no doubt that our winner displays playfulness not only in its superior poetic language, but also in its design.

(Thomas et al. 384–5)

Contrariwise, we have as well taken to task books, that is to say, book objects, that we judge to be of uneven quality. In 2006, we preferred Wynton Marsalis's *Jazz A·B·Z*, illustrated by Paul Rogers, for the award over Marilyn Nelson's *A Wreath for Emmett Till*, even though we admired Nelson's poetry more, describing her book as an

unfortunate marriage of image and text, of the book's design and the content so designed. Of course, this marriage is an arranged marriage—a marriage of convenience not rooted in love, but in economics, in the desire for a safe, saleable product. It's a shame.

(Thomas et al. 392)

And a shame it was, but so perhaps is our clumsy, ideologically bounded intent to identify and prize poetic excellence. Still, we make the attempt at critical evaluation, out of an altruistic impulse to share our excitement about the aesthetic potential of children's poetry; we judge, that is, with hopeful hearts: the hope, in this instance, that we can encourage congenial readers to think about what express a liking for nonsense, but the endorsement might strike one as weak, nominal even, principally because the engagement with "play" is strained. However, there is a final reference to "play" in the essay's concluding endnote that takes us back to the subversive idea that play (childhood) is integral to poetry. In this evocation of playfulness, judge Joseph Thomas recalls sharing Christian "Bök's performance of [Kurt] Schwitters's *Ursonate* with his students," who apparently agreed that "its complex rhythms, syncopated repetitions of linguistic fragments, and the apparent joy both the writer and performer seem to take in the piece's nonsensical proto-language would be ideal for adventurous children[.]" Thomas continues, noting that, "indeed, at times [the performance] sounds much like the joyful babbling or, as Lyn Hejinian puts it, the 'glossolaliac chants and rhyme' typical of childhood play" (362–3). The density of mutually valorizing meanings in "play" comes once again into focus in 2013—perhaps more explicitly and self-consciously than in any essay to date, in a brief discussion of JonArno Lawson's poem "I Played with Toys":

I played with toys, and later,
I learned to play inside them.
Inside them was the only way
to keep them,
because I couldn't find a way
to hide them.
While inside them, I learned to
play without them

they like and why, to agree or disagree with the partisan views we make explicit in discursive prose, to think about poetry for children, at least for a moment, not as cultural symptoms, but, instead, as works of art that have the potential to produce that singular experience we've come to call, for lack of a better word, the aesthetic.

As we write these words, *The Lion and the Unicorn* Award for Excellence in North American Poetry is in its eleventh year. The tenth essay has been written and will be published in the fall, well before this book will have appeared, and the *LU* judges are soon to receive submissions for the eleventh annual award. Lissa Paul, who transported the award from the *Signal* and served as de facto poetry editor, organizing the process of acquiring the books, selecting judges, and, when she was an *LU* editor, publishing the essay, has handed the baton to Joseph Thomas, whom *The Lion and the Unicorn* officially designates, on its masthead, as its Poetry Editor, and she has joined the jury, for the first time. Her voice will have been added to recent essays beginning in 2015.

The *LU* judges have included: Joseph Thomas (2005–2012), Richard Flynn (2005–2008), Kelly Hager (2005), JonArno Lawson (2006), Angela Sorby (2007–2010), Michael Heyman (2009–2012), Michael Joseph (2011–2013), Donelle Ruwe (2013–), Craig Svonkin (2013–), and Lissa Paul (2014–).[7] To date, the Award has been bestowed on six

7 The *LU* judges serve no set terms. JonArno Lawson, the only professional children's poet on the list, agreed to step

and within them (so without them)
I no longer thought about them.

(47)

In the reference to "toys," the judges see a shift from literal toys to language. They write,

he plays toylessly ["without them"] with the toys of language, a toy he can never be without [i.e. outside of] insofar as our consciousness is always boxed in or constituted by language. It's a perfectly enigmatic mental amusement ride of a poem.

(Joseph et al. 340–1)

Their playful yet highly sophisticated reading presupposes that "play" must relate to language, a presupposition fostered by the ongoing, underlying conversations about play. Otherwise, one might have interpreted the enigmatic "toys" to mean a number of things— emotions, for example, or some ineffable internalized pluralized otherness, the "them" that is not "me." The interpretation of the poetry here may have been conditioned by the force of the project, and hence

poets: Arnold Adoff, Susan Blackaby, JonArno Lawson (3 times), Wynton Marsalis, Marilyn Nelson, and Linda Sue Park. Fourteen poets have received an honorable mention: Helen Frost and Walter Dean Meyers received it three times and the following poets once: Nan Forler, Jay M. Harris, Rob Jackson, Paul B. Janeczko, X.J. Kennedy, JonArno Lawson, Marilyn Nelson, William New, Naomi Shahib Nye, Shel Silverstein (posthumously), Carole Boston Weatherford, and Allan Wolf.

During the short tenure of the award, scholarly activity around children's poetry has shown a bit of an uptick. There have been panels on children's poetry at the annual Modern Language Association conference as well as the annual conference of the Children's Literature Association and the Pacific Ancient and Modern Language Association, and a children's literature panel at the American Literature Association Symposium on American Poetry (as well as two chapters in the *Cambridge History of American Poetry* [2014]). If not a "tradition of professional commentary,"[8] the award has at least acquired a critic. While it appears uncertain at best that it will wield cultural influence among the wider community of literary scholars or serve as an "effective mechanism for publicity, sales [or] scandal,"[9]

off the committee after one year because of potential conflicts of interest.

8 Kenneth Kidd, "Prizing Children's Literature: The Case of Newbery Gold," *Children's Literature* 35 (2007): 168.

9 Kidd, 166.

14 Prizing in the Children's Literature Association

Kenneth B. Kidd

In *Homo Academicus*, his study of French academic society, sociologist Pierre Bourdieu insists that the academic or professional scholar has an obligation to self-scrutinize. Such scrutiny is necessary, he says, because academic research "has been socially licensed as entitled to operate as objectification which lays claim to objectivity and universality" (xii). Academics don't just happen to feel removed from the things we investigate, asserts Bourdieu; we are positioned that way by our training and credentialing. Burton Bledstein makes a similar observation in *The Culture of Professionalism: The Middle Class and the Development of Higher Education in America*. Literary scholars professionalized in the late nineteenth century, Bledstein reminds us, around the same time as other academics as well as professional types like doctors and lawyers. Ever since, we've been busy asserting our autonomy and naturalizing our practices. We tend to think of ourselves as especially sensitive to cultural ideology and practice, since we research these things. But when it comes to prizing, we are not only observers. We are also practitioners and even champions.

That's why Joseph and I see this volume as part of the prizing scene, not an objective commentary on such. In our respective chapters, we consider what scholars have to gain and lose in the game of prizing. In this chapter, I examine the prizing activities of my major professional organization, the Children's Literature Association (ChLA). Founded in 1973, and international if primarily North American in membership, the ChLA is an association of scholars, librarians, teachers, and other professionals interested in children's literature and its scholarship. ChLAers prize children's literature, and we also prize prizing. I've won academic prizes from the Association, all the more meaningful because they were conferred by colleagues. I've also been on the giving end, serving on the Book Award Committee as well as the Grants Committee, which selects the Hannah Beiter and Faculty Research Awards, prizes for scholarly work in progress. But our biggest and most significant prize is a literary one, the Phoenix Award, an early and major project of the Association. Established in 1985 and given annually to "a book originally published in the English language" 20 years prior, the Award is intended to recognize books of high literary merit [...] Phoenix books [like the fabled bird] rise from the ashes of neglect and obscurity and once again touch the imagination and enrich the lives of those who read them.

("Phoenix Award")[1]

What, I ask in this chapter, does ChLA academic and literary prizing do for us within and beyond the Association? Why would an organization of literary scholars want to award a literary prize, and in particular one concerned with works from the past? How does the Phoenix Award actually function within and outside the Association, and has our sense of its purpose and/or urgency changed over the years?

Prize Proliferation, Canon-Making, and the Phoenix Award

Prizing, notes James English in *The Economy of Prestige*, facilitates what he calls "capital intraconversion," or the conversion of one kind of capital into another—money into symbolic capital, say. Early-twentieth-century prizes such as the Nobels and the Pulitzers, he explains, were exercises in such intraconversion and reputation laundering, transforming the great wealth of industrial capitalism into philanthropic culture (10–11). The prizing of scholarship is more modest and perhaps goes in the other direction, helping to secure an academic reputation and contribute toward tenure, promotion, and professional mobility. The prizing of scholarship takes place within a culture of middle-class professionalism. Like most, if not all academic organizations, ChLA participates energetically in prize proliferation. If we are sometimes ambivalent about prizing, we've been quick to jump on the bandwagon, adding new awards as our organizational and professional "needs" develop. Recent examples are the Edited Book Award, inaugurated in 2011, and the Mentoring Award, launched in 2014.

ChLA prizing is in many ways typical of academic prizing at large. The Modern Language Association (MLA) likely set the stage, establishing its first academic prize in 1964, the William Riley Parker Award. Five years later saw the debut of the first book award, the James Russell Lowell Prize. There are now 25 book or article prizes sponsored by the MLA, for the study of various national literatures, for instance; for scholarly editions; for translations; for work on the teaching of languages other than English; for independent scholarship. There's also the MLA Award for Lifetime Scholarly Achievement, established in 1996. One award gestures beyond the academy proper—the Phyllis Franklin Award for Public Advocacy of the Humanities, founded in 2003 and awarded to NPR's Terry Gross and the late Senator Edward M. Kennedy, among others.

Formed in 1973, ChLA is a younger, smaller, and more specialized organization, claiming a measly ten awards by comparison.[2] First on the scene was the article award, debuting in 1977. The book award came next, first made in 1981. Next up was the Phoenix Award, the Association's first and only literary prize, in 1985. Then in 1992, the Anne Devereaux Jordan Award, a kind of lifetime achievement award for children's literature. In 1998 the Carol Gay Award was repurposed as an award for best undergraduate essay (it was formerly an award for high school students). In 2010, the Phoenix Picture Book Award came onto the scene. The Graduate Student Essay followed in 2011, and divided into MA- and PhD-level Awards. I have already mentioned the Edited Book Award and the Mentoring Award, the latter requiring nomination letters from people outside the nominee's home institution. Overall, the pattern of ChLA prizing is one of increasing professional expansion and specification. We have awards targeting kinds of participants: undergraduate student, MA student, PhD student, faculty member, senior eminence, etc. And we have awards for genres of work: article, scholarly book, edited book, mentorship. About the only thing we don't award (like the MLA) is teaching; that is folded into mentorship.[3] We can see in ChLA prizing both an increasing diversification of children's literature studies and an ongoing centralization of such. The book and article prizes, for instance, sometimes approach but rarely indulge in non-literary analysis.

ChLA is distinctive in its combination of literary with academic prizing. The MLA sponsors no literary awards, nor do most smaller scholarly organizations. Why this concern with literary prizing on the part of ChLA? In short, in the early years of the organization, ChLA members felt the need to emphasize that our field was real and substantial. The Phoenix Award was part of a broader effort at canon-making by the Association, an effort central to its bid for professional legitimacy. Jon C. Stott's 1978 presidential address to the Association explicitly called for the establishment of a canon of children's literature, which led to a panel discussion in 1980 and to various exercises in—and arguments about—canon-making. A Canon Committee was formed, which produced a list of masterworks but also considerable debate about the viability and even desirability of canon-making. This project was taking shape around the time of the first canon wars in the academy, so it's not surprising that ChLA members had reservations about not only specifics but the whole affair. One of the Canon Committee members, Peter F. Neumeyer, registered his disillusionment in a short report for the *ChLA Quarterly* in 1983, writing that "the very word 'canon' has become offensive. It implies a sacredness and authority and inevitability that none of my friends on the Committee would seriously claim for themselves or their choices" (35). Neumeyer objected to the "preposterously Anglo-Saxon" nature of the list, decrying "our collective linguistic ignorance" and "our parochial myopia" (35). Some improvements were made to the list, and eventually the project morphed into a three-part collection of critical essays, *Touchstones: Reflections on the Best in Children's Literature*, edited by Perry Nodelman. Volume 1 of *Touchstones* focuses on exemplary texts of fiction; Volume 2, on folk literature, legend, myth, and poetry; and Volume 3, on picture books (and includes essays describing the selection process).

Nodding to Matthew Arnold's use of the term in *The Study of Poetry* (1880), Nodelman and his colleagues chose *touchstone* over *classic* as their keyword, opting for something more humble and nimble while retaining the sheen of excellence.[4] What's interesting to me about the *Touchstones* project is its pairing of literary works with critical essays about them. The implication is that the essays are themselves touchstones, valuable in their powers of illumination. The project, in other words, not only offered the quasi-consecration of literary texts, but also established the cultural and even aesthetic value of scholarship. What is scholarship if not the professional prizing of literature?

The ChLA's strategy of professionalization through canon-making and prizing should sound familiar, as it was first the strategy of librarians earlier in the century in both the U.S. and Great Britain. Children's literature had essentially been outsourced to librarians because librarians work with children and their materials, and because literary scholars didn't want much to do with either.[5] Only later did specialists of children's literature emerge within literary studies. The establishment of the Phoenix Award, as a literary award in particular, represents in part an assertion of domain and expertise on the part of children's literature scholars, in response to both the historical authority of the librarians and the ongoing resistance to children's literature as a respectable or legitimate field by literary critics. The Award complements the other canon-making activities of the organization.

As the ChLA Phoenix Award webpage explains, the award is chosen "by an elected committee of ChLA members that considers nominations made by members and others interested in promoting high critical standards in literature for children."[6] But the most interesting thing about the Phoenix Award is that it's made retroactively, to books published 20 years prior that did not receive the recognition they deserved (overlooked by major awards, insufficiently reviewed, and so forth). The Phoenix Award mounts a rescue operation across time. Books die, but sometimes revive. The Phoenix Award offers recuperation and reparation both. It stands in for the test of time, a very specific test of 20 years. Alethea Helbig, one of the award's founders, confirms that she and her colleagues settled on the twenty-year mark "to emphasize the idea that really good books last." Twenty years represents a respectable midpoint between too soon and too late, calibrated to the lifespan of both the books and their authors. Any sooner, and the award might not be so meaningful; any longer, and the book and its author might both be dead, and some of the Award's intent, of course, is to affirm the author. In fact, the ChLA invites winning authors to the annual banquets, celebrating them and their work. Authors are typically very touched by the recognition, even when they've been more successful with other titles, and the whole affair can be pretty moving. In any case, the Phoenix Award must represent the passage of time but also insist on currency. Its work is not only reparative; it also constructs an alternative history in which the winning title *has always been* significant. The prize, that is, fills in as much as makes up for the lost time, replacing years of neglect with years of enduring merit, now duly noted and affirmed. No other book award works quite so. Moreover, the recuperative function of the Phoenix extends into literary criticism, further confirming the interweaving of literary and academic prizing within the Association. The annual ChLA meeting features a panel of academic papers about the winners and nominees, and over the years those papers have been made available to the community of scholars. The hope is that literary criticism on the Phoenix titles will help galvanize scholarly interest.

I've never served on the selection committee, and so to better understand the original Award I queried long-time ChLA members involved with its founding and administration.[7] Helbig explained that the idea came up one day when she, Agnes Perkins, Helen Hill and Mary Ake were chatting over lunch about the mission of the ChLA and the need for a literary award. "We wanted to emphasize the literary aspects," she writes, "because it seemed to us that so many people felt that children and young people should learn from the books they read—that is, [we wanted] to deemphasize the didacticism." She credits Ake with the name, quickly agreed upon. She further clarifies: "We thought it best to avoid picture books, because we didn't feel qualified to judge, and besides, the fiction award was quite enough to start with." Helbig served as the first committee chair and continued on the committee for some time. The award has been made annually by an elected committee of four ChLA members elected for staggered terms, headed by a chair appointed by the ChLA Executive Board. Phoenix Honor books were instituted four years later but are not always awarded.

The administration of the Phoenix is time- and labor-intensive. The first task is assembling a comprehensive book list of potential contenders, a daunting exercise in reconstruction. The process involves the suppression of award winners as well as the revival or identification of lesser-known texts. Barbara Garner reports that the committee "as a whole worked on generating the lists; hence it was valuable to have a librarian as a member of the committee." Getting the books isn't so simple or easy either, with many out of print and unavailable even through inter-library loan. A good deal of book-swapping goes on among committee members. The evaluation process involves reading and reading over a period of several years. For many years, committee members read titles for multiple award years simultaneously, but as former Phoenix Committee Chair Lisa Rowe Fraustino reports, the process was recently streamlined to make the workload more manageable. Now committees work on one year at a time. The process is still laborious. For each year's batch, multiple rounds of discussion and elimination are typical. The evaluation process involves both email exchanges and face-to-face meetings of the committee, usually at the annual conference. Drawing on her experience with the Phoenix Award and also the Tomás Rivera Mexican-American Children's Book Award, Marilynn Olson remarks that "around-the-table discussion" at meetings was "particularly important when discussing racial fairness and depiction."

Reports vary as to the number of books read by each committee member, but a ballpark seems to be 50 books, even when first-pass reading lists are divided up among members. Garner notes that while members of the selection committee are typically heroic in their efforts, not everyone understands the time commitment required, or the responsibilities entailed. "The committee's work has always been intensive," she notes. Committee chairs have made occasional adaptations to the process with workload in mind. For instance, when she chaired the committee, Priscilla Ord established a methodology of reading four years ahead, pairing readers for each group of books, which changed as the lists were shortened. The committee chair plays a particularly important role in the process. Everyone responding to my questionnaire agrees that the work of the committee is substantial, important, and generally congenial. Reports Michael Levy:

> We were each assigned a long list of books to read, though I don't remember how the titles were originally chosen. The lists were certainly long enough to include everything or nearly everything of note including some very obscure, hard to find volumes. We read and we read. We came up with favorites. Everyone read the favorites. We ended up with a short list, discussed it at length and voted. It was an amiable discussion, as I remember.

Content analysis isn't my goal in this essay, but a few quick observations. Winners of the Phoenix Award are sometimes experimental in form and/or topic. They are aimed at older readers and are indeed pretty literary, with innovative and often challenging storylines and narrative elements. Most of the books were published in the United States or Great Britain, although they were not necessarily popular (or even known) in both.[8] Phoenix titles feature boy and girl protagonists about equally, with a slight edge for the girls; they do not generally engage issues of racial or ethnic diversity, although many protagonists are underdogs. Eleven of the 30 titles are historical fiction, with several others a mix of historical fiction with magical realism. Eleven are realistic novels, and only five are fantasy or science-fiction. There's no poetry or non-fiction (not even biography), despite the lack of genre specification in the award criteria. There's only one story collection, E.L. Konigsburg's *Throwing Shadows*.

This is roughly the same genre distribution observable in the Newbery Medal winners, where historical fiction is even more dominant. I wonder if the Phoenix Award might be more receptive to historical fiction in part because it's a historical award, dedicated to honoring and preserving the past. Historical fiction may also seem more literary for various reasons, its imaginative energies held in check by its historicist commitments. One of my questions to those serving on the committee was thus whether or not they saw or experienced a bias in favor of historical fiction. Most said no. Olson stressed that the Phoenix Award process "teaches one that there aren't very many good books in any one year and that the other prizes at the time are pretty much picking up the books that we would have considered, too." Donna White likewise emphasizes that Phoenix consideration depends upon the leavings of other awards. "We were getting the books the Newbery committee and others overlooked," she writes, "which means THEIR biases affected our available contenders." Several committee members did report having to defend fantasy as sufficiently literary.

Most of my informants tolerated the fuzziness of "literary excellence" as a criterion. Olson, White, and Levy all report that literary excellence was never defined per se but rather worked out through the discussions. White points out that perspectives on quality vary, and also that not all committee members are literary critics. During her service, she reports, there was debate about the value of diversity in relation to "more traditional literary values." Adrienne Kertzer, who served on the committee from 1993–97 and then chaired it from 2000–2003, notes an ongoing faith in "enduring literary quality as something we could all recognize," which could lead to difficulties when sufficiently "literary" books were too obviously racist, homophobic, or otherwise offensive. Kertzer reports that "I felt pressure sometimes to say that X book is unworthy because it lacks enduring literary quality." She recalls that there wasn't much discussion of what actually constitutes such quality, or how readers might recognize it. Some of the same tension marks the evaluation of ALA award contenders which, even if they are not identity-based, cannot sanction overt racism or homophobia.

Kertzer observes further that the tension between an ostensibly universal ideal of excellence and the ever-pressing realities of cultural change is observable in the forewords to the second and third installments of Phoenix Award literary criticism, covering 1990–94 and 1995–99. In their respective forewords, Nancy Huse and Kathy Piehl address the issue of literary quality and its endurance in a fast-changing cultural environment. "The Phoenix Award signifies the ongoing life of books in a changing culture," asserts Huse in the first line of her foreword to the earlier volume (vii). Huse positions Phoenix titles amid but also against "rapid technological and ideological change" (vii), sometimes implying, as Kertzer puts it, that literary value "is assumed to be beyond cultural change." At the same time, Huse recognizes that they are not static objects but rather part of a dynamic global culture, underscoring our general expectation that "classic" works simultaneously preserve the past and remain current. Piehl claims more confidently that the twenty-year test can ensure "enduring literary quality," because titles "that depend heavily on language, fads, and obsessions of a particular era quickly reveal their age, like parents using slang from their teenaged years to try to communicate with their own adolescents" (ix).

Whatever we make of such comments, the debates in and around the Phoenix selection process clearly echo those of better-known book awards: issues of genre, topicality, "literary excellence," social relevance, and so forth. Olson rightly underscores that the question of a book's excellence or lack thereof isn't an isolated question, but rather part of a broader conversation about that book and the other work of its author. Timing and context matter, she points out, and sometimes, as has been said of the major ALA awards, "the right people got the prize but for the wrong book." "I would guess," she continues, "that some of our winners, at least, failed to win the Newbery or other prizes because they came out in a year in which another major writer had the edge." Phoenix committees, in other words, participate in a broader conversation about excellence, in which case it doesn't matter much if Phoenix winners are Newbery losers. Seen from this perspective, the fuzziness of excellence benefits prizing and the professionalism it endorses.

The Least Known Award in Children's Literature?

Blogger Elizabeth Bird has called our Phoenix Award "Quite Possibly the Least Known Award in Children's Literature" (that's the subtitle of her entry for September 30, 2010). "When it is bestowed the press is positively silent," she writes. "Blogs do not discuss it. Twitter remains mute. Even reliable listservs like child_lit rarely note its passing. I say, revivify it! It serves a magnificent purpose, after all." Bird goes on to praise ChLA itself: "Here we have a group that should be better known to the greater online children's literary community." The ALA awards scene, by contrast, generates much public intrigue, especially in the case of the Newbery and Caldecott Medals. The blogosphere lights up. There are press releases and book parties and interviews on national talk shows. The most public aspect of the Phoenix Award, in contrast, are the speeches given by winning authors at the ChLA annual conference banquet.

What explains the (in)difference? Most obviously, ChLA is a small and specialized operation, whereas the ALA reports some 57,000 members and serves a more diversified group of professionals and their clients (3). In part the difference is a matter of scale. But it's also a matter of professional culture and the aim of the prizing activity. I suggest there's some tension between the function of the Award within the ChLA and its ostensible investment in generating broader publicity. There's no question that ChLA members want the Phoenix books to be recognized and affirmed outside the organization. The Award does encourage broader discussion of underappreciated books, especially by other professional stakeholders in children's literature, especially librarians. The Award has met with some success in that respect. It's probably not the least known award in children's literature (although, how would we know?). It's unclear how much the Award has helped keep titles in print; there are too many variables to consider. It may have helped in that direction. It was 2015 that marked the thirtieth anniversary of the first award, made in 1985. The winner in 1985 was Rosemary Sutcliff's *The Mark of the Horse Lord* (1965), and it is no longer in print, despite the popularity of Sutcliff's historical fiction. The next two winners, however, are currently in print: Robert Burch's *Queenie Peavy* (1966) and Leon Garfield's

Smith: The Story of a Pickpocket (1967). Nineteen of the 30 Phoenix Award winners are in print, and those include many early winners. Not as high a percentage as for the Newbery or Caldecott Medals, but not bad. The longevity of these titles may owe something to their Phoenix designation, in combination with other factors—a book's prior reputation among scholars and librarians, the popularity of an author's other works, and so forth.[9] For many years, if a winning title was no longer in print, committee chair Priscilla Ord tried to get it republished, and others followed this practice, with mixed results.

Even so, it would be easy enough to take to Twitter and other social media platforms to promote the Phoenix. Certainly Phoenix titles deserve to be better known. I can't help but wonder, though, if promoting the Phoenix more energetically might risk ChLA's ownership of the award, or if there's unspoken anxiety to that effect among its members. In an earlier draft of this essay, I speculated that if the Phoenix speeches were televised, or if the winning authors were whisked off to morning talk shows, we might lose that warm, fuzzy feeling we get at the conference banquet. Kertzer was quick to reassure me that there'd be no loss of such feeling on her part. She'd be quite happy to see the Phoenix get more attention, by whatever means necessary. She's not alone; there's a general sense among the membership that the Phoenix deserves a bigger spotlight. At the same time, I can't shake the perception that we haven't really wanted the Phoenix to go public. The Award's very fashioning seems poised against "publicity"—not only its administration by a relatively small group of scholars, but also its historical tenor. The Award was designed in large measure to bolster children's literature studies as an academic field; it helped to expand our canon. The Phoenix Award is arguably *still* a canon-making activity, continued after other canon-making ventures of the organization have been abandoned. A significant part of the challenge is that these are not new titles. Virtually every other literary award recognizes new work, in keeping with the general economy of commodity capitalism. The Phoenix is a countermeasure to the fast tempo and planned obsolescence of the contemporary book business. In any case, the recuperative or maintenance mission of the Phoenix, bound up with the professional culture of ChLA, is an obstacle to wider dissemination. Another and related obstacle is our relative lack of engagement as scholars with the public. Librarians and teachers interact more regularly with children and parents than do we. Our claim to children's literature has required a certain distance or remove from the work of education, librarianship, and publishing. I'll be curious, then, to see what current and future members of ChLA really want with or through the Award. In re-envisioning its status or role, will we also re-visit its original purpose or mission?

Moreover, while the Phoenix was once central to ChLA's identity, it has since become more peripheral as the organization has expanded and diversified. I mean no disrespect with that observation. I hope I've made clear my admiration of the Award and all those who participate in its administration.

But we are no longer so concerned with canonicity, and I'm not sure that the Award keeps its titles in scholarly circulation. The annual Phoenix conference panels aspire toward this end, of course. In 2003, ChLA stopped publishing the Phoenix Papers in book form—sales had been less than brisk (itself telling)—and launched an electronic site, The Phoenix Award Papers, which archives each year's Phoenix conference panel as well as acceptance speeches. ChLA members generously give their time and labor not only to Phoenix selection but also Phoenix literary criticism. But I'm not sure how widely these Papers are read. The organization has diversified to the point that our range is vast and our sense of field quite varied. The generation of scholars who launched ChLA long presided over the Phoenix Award, and while some younger scholars have taken up the cause, most have not. I don't think younger scholars are reading the Phoenix Papers as regularly as they are reading the field's refereed journals. I'm guilty as charged, having never served on the Phoenix Committee, having not read most of the winning titles, and having read only some of the Phoenix Papers.

An interesting development within the ChLA was the introduction of the Phoenix Picture Book Award in 2010. This award represents both the maintenance of the Phoenix tradition and a modernization of such. The Picture Book Award also observes the twenty-year test of time, functioning also to recuperate lesser-known works.[10] It repeats a familiar pattern of expansion toward works for young readers—Caldecott after Newbery, Kate Greenaway Medal after Carnegie—but also reflects recent enthusiasm for imagetexts forms more generally (comics, graphic novels, etc.). Those involved explain that the creation of the Phoenix Picture Book Award was both timely and opportunistic. Fraustino points out that

> the idea of having a second committee probably wasn't even thinkable in the years when the ChLA could barely make ends meet. While the award doesn't offer prize money, we do always pay expenses for speakers, and the winners would presumably have to be invited. There was also the issue of finding people to serve on committees—it hasn't always been easy. I'm guessing that the timing wasn't right for it to become a viable idea until after the organization grew to a certain size and the financial picture became reliably healthy after Project MUSE took our publications digital.

Also, a new format for showcasing the Phoenix Awards within the ChLA— an evening reception—will be piloted at the 2015 conference, alongside the usual Phoenix academic panel. The Phoenix Award winner will speak at this event rather than at the Awards Banquet (as traditionally). Fraustino and current Phoenix Picture Book Award committee chair Andrea Schwenke Wyile hope the reception will help raise the profile of the Awards within the organization, and perhaps generate discussion about their status and function.

Academic Rewards of Merit

The Phoenix Award is a literary prize serving our professional academic interests. But what about our prizes for scholarship? I'll close out with a few observations on such, although a deeper treatment will have to wait. Academic prizes are pretty obviously oriented inward or toward the profession itself, part of a broader apparatus of credentialing and academic capital. There's surprisingly little analysis of the topic, however. The only two essays I encountered in my research are S.F. Johnson's 1952 PMLA article "Honors and Prizes in the MLA Field," essentially a survey,[11] and William W. Savage's biting if not bitter assessment "Eyes on the Prize: The Transom" (2009). Savage worked in scholarly editing before becoming an academic historian, and he pulls no punches, calling out academic prizing as inflationary and egocentric. To hear Savage tell it, it's an absurd and pretentious affair, bringing out the worst in all parties:

> Sadly, there is nothing like the success of others (or the prospect of it) to bring grumbling to the halls of ivy. One finds among some PhDs a low tolerance for news of the prize nominations and awards bestowed upon persons other than themselves. A brief word of congratulation is the most of which such people are capable, if they're capable even of that. Were jealousy and envy coin of the realm, universities would have no fiscal concerns. One is occupied with one's own chances for success, not with the chances of others. This is an attitude developed in graduate school, and it flourishes at the next level, in competitions for employment, for tenure, and for promotion. It is a near-feral thing, living in the shadow of collegiality but never far from the light.
>
> (113)

I've not found any materialist or sociological analysis of academic prizing. English makes no mention of such, although he does discuss academic societies of the past. Bourdieu doesn't discuss prizing directly, but like English he provides useful insights, exploring how academic power is "founded principally on control of the instruments of reproduction of the professional body" (78). (And like Savage, he is pretty down on Homo Academicus.) He mentions examinations in particular, but we could think of prizing as another such instrument. Like other components of the academic game as Bourdieu explains it, prizing requires patience and the willingness to wait for recognition, essential to the academic "establishment of *durable* relations of authority and dependency" (89). For better and for worse, we wait for our work to be affirmed, just as we wait through a long apprenticeship as scholars. If prizing can speed things up, standing in for the test of time, it also insists that good things come to those who wait.

The paucity of scholarship is all the more surprising given that literary prizing has partial origins in academic prizing, specifically in the nineteenth-century tradition of recognizing good performance in school with "rewards of merit." Those rewards included certificates, medals, and also gift books, and the tradition of the book-as-prize led in turn to prizes *for* books. In other words, academic prizing, understood broadly, isn't a recent offshoot of the contemporary prizing craze but a return to prizing's longer history. Moreover, prizing belongs to middle-class professionalism as much as to popular culture.

ChLA prizes for scholarship take the classical form of rewards of merit: certificates (with the accompanying checks a welcome innovation). The selection process for our academic prizes, not as onerous as the process for the Phoenix but still demanding, is handled by committee, with six elected committee members serving a three-year term, alongside a committee chair appointed by the organization's Executive Board. The awards are given for work published one or two years previously. As with most literary awards, there are categories for runners-up or honor books. In the case of the Article Award, established in 1977, the category "Honor Article" was introduced in 1986, and "Honorable Mention" in 1989. The latter hasn't been awarded since 1994, however, and we haven't seen two Honor Article awards made since 2002. Not surprisingly, most of the winning articles have been published in children's literature journals, with *Children's Literature* sweeping 1996–2007 with one exception, and with three of the four most recent awards going to articles published in *The Children's Literature Association Quarterly*. Occasionally winning or honor articles have appeared in non-children's literature venues: *Genre, Poetics Today, Arizona Quarterly, Yale Review, Victorian Studies, 19th-Century Fiction*. In terms of people, there are some repeat winners, but it's a diverse lot, with many active ChLA members. I see a nice distribution of topic and methodology, too, although with some interesting pairings; two winning articles focus on Philip Pullman's *Clockwork*, two on Frances Hodgson Burnett's *The Secret Garden*, and two on Maurice Sendak. I'm sure a more careful content analysis would turn up interesting patterns in the scholarship. For instance, many of the winning articles became chapters in books, although I don't know how that compares to published articles not singled out for recognition.

The Book Award, launched in 1981, but not really given annually until 1987 (when there were two winners),[12] likewise reflects the achievements as well as emphases of ChLA professionalism. Most winners of the award are ChLA members, but that's not a requirement. Only one scholar has won the award twice. Winning titles vary considerably in concern, scope, and method. Here, too, "Honor Book" and "Honorable Mention" categories were introduced but have not been used consistently, as the organization struggles to strike a balance between selective and singular prize-giving and the need to recognize scholarly excellence in a more comprehensive and/or representative way. In 2006, the Book Award began to feature a list of recommended titles beyond the winner and/or honor book, with six books on the list that year. But even this practice has been in flux. In 2007, only one title was recommended, in 2008, five titles were recommended, followed by none in 2009, one in 2010 and 2011, and none in 2012. The expansion of book and article award categories underscores our sense that while some scholarship does seem exemplary, much scholarship is excellent, making difficult the identification of the best. There's no twenty-year test of time. Like serious books and films, most research projects unfold across the space of many years, so there's a test of time built into the production side, but as yet there's no award for research published 20 years prior that didn't receive the recognition it should have. Surely much of our research would qualify!

All the tweeting in the world wouldn't have much impact on the scale or visibility of these prizes, but that's ok, since they are not meant for the world, exactly. Rather they are modest if successful mechanisms for prestige assertion and reputation leveraging, at once bound up with and separate from professional and institutional contexts. ChLA is a scholarly organization, and we identity with and through it, perhaps as much as with or through our own universities or programs. Literary and academic prizes are an integral part of the Association's networked identity, along with the conferences, the journals, the academic gossip and bar escapades. Prizes work not only for the individual but also for the collective. Even so, like literary prizing, academic prizing makes us a little uncomfortable. We know that for better and for worse, prizing risks devaluing the many by celebrating the few. We are ambivalent about principles of selectivity and distinction even when they benefit us. It's striking that the word "best" is nowhere in our titles or descriptions—instead we have "distinct," and "significant" and especially "outstanding." From its beginnings, ChLA has struggled with the rhetorics of exceptionality, treating them as a necessary evil. If we haven't really confronted our investments in prizing, neither do we love prizing unconditionally or uncritically.

So far, however, we haven't refused it. What would happen if, as a professional organization, we gave up our prizes? Would we gain or lose standing in the academic world? Would we think differently about our work—about what quality means, what kind of work is valuable, and so forth? Would there be any serious consequences for our careers? Could we find other ways to encourage, certify, promote ourselves? Queer theory has lately made much of "failure" and its potential for rethinking success as normative. Is it possible to affirm and rethink failure or prize-losing, or at least not to prize? If we can't refuse prizing, we might at least temper our enthusiasm for it. We might study whether prizing does indeed function to encourage scholarly excellence and/or innovation, or if it tends to enforce normativity, or both, or something else entirely. At the least, we must recognize that our insights into *other* prizing ventures are more persuasive when we also confront our own.

Notes

1. While the ChLA's Phoenix came first, there are a number of other Phoenix Awards, all invoking "the fabled bird who rose from its ashes with renewed life and beauty," to quote from the ChLA webpage. Phoenix Awards are presented annually by the Metro Atlanta Chamber Bioscience-Health IT Leadership Council to individuals and companies making an outstanding contribution to the health IT industry in Georgia (founded in 2011). The Restoration Industry Association administers Phoenix Awards, for innovation in the restoration and reconstruction of damaged buildings. The Council of Editors of Learned Journals also makes an annual Phoenix Award, for Significant Editorial Achievement; this one goes back to 1987 and seems to be the second-oldest Phoenix, after ours. There's even another Phoenix Book Award, inaugurated in 2007 by the Network of Educational Librarians in London, and promoting "reading for pleasure among Year 6 and Key Stage 3 pupils in the London Borough of Lambeth."
2. For a history of the first ten years of ChLA, see Carol Gay, "ChLA: 1973–1983." Gay was ChLA Historian until her death in 1987. See also Anne H. Lundin's comparative history of librarian and scholarly professionalization around children's literature.
3. From the ChLA website:

   > The Children's Literature Association is pleased to announce the ChLA Mentoring Award. The award recognizes excellence in mentoring taking place within the ChLA and extending beyond the boundaries of the mentor's own university. Awardees will have contributed in significant ways to enhancing others' scholarship and/or professional careers within the field of children's literature over a substantial period of time. Such mentorship may take place in a variety of contexts, including but not limited to organizational committee work, journal or other professional editing work, ChLA discussions of teaching and/or career-building, and informal contacts.

4. The project was undertaken, as John Cech explains in his presidential address to the Association, "not to dictate or mandate certain books while ignoring or rejecting others, but rather, to serve as a starting point" (177). Patricia Demers concurs: "Never ends in themselves, these aids usually serve modest instructional aims: surveying the field for a neophyte and easing the chronological trudge by erecting signposts. Their purpose is initiatory" (142–3). Even so, the enterprise was not without critics, some of whom complained that the Association was sending mixed messages about literary value.
5. Rebekah Fitzsimmons traces this "outsourcing" and its consequences in her dissertation, "The Chronicles of Professionalization." See also Lundin for context.
6. Actual trophies are awarded for the Phoenix, brass statues individually cast and inscribed with the name of each year's winner, reminiscent of the Oscar trophies.
7. Here's the questionnaire I sent:

   1 Most children's book awards are selected and administered by librarians, not literary critics. Was the establishment of the award in part an effort to claim that authority for scholars or for the ChLA itself? I'm thinking about not only what the prize does for its authors, but what it does for us, as members of the Association.

   2 The Award emerged out of the Touchstones Project, and that the "touchstone" conceit is a kind of alternative to "canon," retaining the idea of

excellence or distinction but refusing the more elitist tendencies of canonicity. Has the Phoenix Award been understood as a kind of canon- or touchstone-building exercise? I ask especially because the selection of titles has long been linked with scholarly interpretations of those titles (the conference panel, the online archive, etc.).

3 How does the process of selection actually work, in terms of procedure and logistics? I know anyone in the organization can make nominations. Once nominations are all in, how does the committee go about the business of selection? What kinds of negotiations go on in the discussions?

4 There's a lot of accusation around "adult" literary awards that their selection process is either "political" or "subjective" or sometimes both. There's a touch of that concern around the Newbery, Carnegie, etc., although my sense is that most people are less suspicious about children's book awards (maybe for unfortunate reasons). Has there been any such concern around the Phoenix Award over its history? If so, what were the issues?

5 How is excellence or distinction actually decided in evaluating the nominees? The criteria for evaluation for most book awards are notoriously vague or flexible, and I'm curious if there's any preliminary discussion of what excellence means, or if the assumption is that committee members will know excellence when they see it and/or will make arguments on behalf of the excellence of contenders.

6 Why 20 years? My guess is that 20 years is a respectable midpoint between too soon and too late, calibrated to the lifespan of both the books and their authors. Any sooner, and the award might not be so meaningful; any longer, and the book and its author might both be dead, and some of the Award's intent, of course, is to affirm the author. Am I close?

7 A quick glance at the 30ish winners suggests that historical fiction is the dominant genre, also true of some major awards (the Newbery for sure). Is this because historical fiction is better (more literary), or is perceived that way—and perhaps is also more neglected at first pass (or has been)? It occurred to me also that the award is historical, committed to preserving and honoring the past, so maybe that plays a role? Any ideas about this tend are welcome. In discussions by the selection committee, is genre a guiding factor?

8 Some of the winning authors are famous/established through other books or overall body of work (as with Gary Soto this year); some authors are less known. Does an author's identity play any role in the decision process, and in particular, is there any sense that lesser-known authors "need" the recognition more (or that their books do)?

9 What else should I know—should we all know—about the Phoenix awards?

8. Olson observed that her experience with the award made her aware "that a book could be a perpetual bestseller in another English-speaking country and be entirely unknown in the United States," which led her to seek out more international contenders.

9. Deborah Stevenson persuasively asserts that scholars have little chance of rescuing lost or fading children's classics, because we preside over the "canon of significance" rather than the better-circulating "canon of sentiment" (1997).

10. The selection process is handled by a separate ChLA committee, also composed of five members with four elected to staggered terms.

11. Johnson takes a general approach to prize culture, discussing things such as membership in honors societies, postgraduate fellowships or grants, academies and learned societies, endowed professorships, festschrifts, elected academic office, invited talks, and manuscript prizes. Quoting "one observer," Johnson notes that the competitions for fellowships or scholarships are "more likely to foster opportunism than independent thought" (57). The closest thing to analysis is Johnson's conclusion that prizes "are finally less valuable as honors conferred on their recipients than as the means of defining, maintaining, or even raising the standards of scholarly and critical writing, and they might best be awarded with this fact in mind" (58). There is of course a Wikipedia entry for Academic awards, with useful links to specific awards, including named lectures and professorships.

12. One award was given for the years 1981–84, and one for 1985–86.

Contributors

Katlyn M. Avritt graduated in 2014 from Kansas State University with a BS in Psychology and a BS in Secondary English Education. She is currently a high school English teacher at Oxford High School in Oxford, KS.

Robert Bittner is a doctoral candidate at Simon Fraser University, working with transgender narratives in children's and young adult literature. He has served on a number of book award committees including the Sheila Egoff Children's Literature Award, the Stonewall Award, the John Newbery Medal, the TD Canadian Children's Literature Prize, and the Michael L. Printz Award.

Clare Bradford is Alfred Deakin Professor at Deakin University in Melbourne, Australia. Her books include *Reading Race: Aboriginality in Australian Children's Literature* (2001), *Unsettling Narratives: Postcolonial Readings of Children's Literature* (2007), *New World Orders in Contemporary Children's Literature: Utopian Transformations* (2009) (with Mallan, Stephens and McCallum); and *The Middle Ages in Children's Literature* (2015). She is coeditor of *Contemporary Children's Literature and Film: Engaging with Theory* (2011), and *Girls, Texts, Cultures* (2015).

Ramona Caponegro is Associate Professor of English and the Coordinator of the Children's Literature Program at Eastern Michigan University. She has published essays about juvenile delinquents and girl detectives in children's literature and about the Jane Addams Children's Book Award, and she was a member of the 2015 Pura Belpré Award Committee.

Kynsey M. Creel is a native of New Mexico who graduated in 2014 from Kansas State University with a BA in English Literature and a specialization in Women's Studies and Spanish. She is now enrolled in the MA program in the English Department at K-State.

June Cummins is Associate Professor in the Department of English and Comparative Literature at San Diego State University. Having published articles on topics ranging from Beatrix Potter to Harry Potter, around subjects such as feminism, colonialism, consumerism, and ethnicity, she is currently working on the first biography of Sydney Taylor, author of the

All-of-a-Kind Family books. Taylor gives her name to the identity-based award for Jewish children's literature.

Rebekah Fitzsimmons earned her PhD in English from the University of Florida, and is now appointed with the Writing and Communication Program at the Georgia Institute of Technology. She has published articles in *Children's Literature* and the *Journal of the Fantastic in the Arts* and has a chapter in *The Early Reader in Children's Literature and Culture*, edited by Jennifer M. Miskec and Annette Wannamaker. Her dissertation focused on how the professionalization of children's literature experts has shaped definitions of children's literature and vice versa.

Marilisa Jiménez García, Assistant Professor of English at Lehigh University, graduated from the University of Florida with a PhD in English, specializing in American literature/studies and children's literature. She is currently revising her dissertation, *"Every Child is Born a Poet": The Puerto Rican Narrative within American Children's Culture*, which won the Puerto Rican Studies Association Dissertation Award 2012 and the University of Florida's Dolores Auzenne Dissertation Award. Her scholarship appears in *Changing English: Studies in Culture and Education* and *CENTRO Journal*. She has also published reviews in *International Research in Children's Literature* and *Latino Studies*.

Erica Hateley is Associate Professor of English at Sør-Trøndelag University College in Trondheim, Norway. Her research into award-winning Australian children's literature was funded by an Australian Research Council Discovery Early Career Researcher Award (project DE120101948). Erica continues to explore issues of gender, nation, and capital in her research into literature for young people.

Michael Joseph is a poet, scholar, and rare books librarian at Rutgers University Library. His recent publications include a co-authored work of collaborative fiction with Sarah Stengle, *Juvenile Fantasies and Innocent Dreams* (2013), and *La Nouvelle Chatte Blanch* (Lucia Press, 2013), a re-imagination of a seventeenth-century fairy tale, with illustrations by Henry Charles and serigraphs by MaryAnn L. Miller.

Kenneth B. Kidd is Professor of English at the University of Florida. He is the author of *Making American Boys: Boyology and the Feral Tale* (2004) and *Freud in Oz: At the Intersections of Psychoanalysis and Children's Literature* (2011), both with University of Minnesota Press. He is also coeditor of *Wild Things: Children's Culture and Ecocriticism* (Wayne State University Press, 2004) and *Over the Rainbow: Queer Children's and Young Adult Literature* (U of Michigan P, 2011).

Peter C. Kunze holds a PhD in English from Florida State University and is currently completing a second PhD in media studies at the University of Texas-Austin. His research examines children's media and digital culture.

His children's literature criticism has appeared in *Children's Literature Association Quarterly*, *The Lion and the Unicorn*, and *Signal*.

Charlie C. Lynn earned his BA in English Education at Kansas State University in 2014 and is now an AP language teacher at Junction City High School.

Barbara McNeil, PhD, is Associate Professor in the Language and Literacy Subject Area at the University of Regina, Saskatchewan, Canada. She teaches courses in reading as well as children's and young adult literature.

Emily Murphy earned her PhD from the University of Florida and is now Writing Lecturer at NYU Shanghai. She has published essays on children's literature in *The Lion and the Unicorn*, *Children's Literature Association Quarterly*, and *Jeunesse: Young People, Texts, and Cultures*. She is currently working on revising her book manuscript, *Growing Up With America: Myth, Childhood, and National Identity from 1945–2011*.

Michelle Superle is Assistant Professor at the University of the Fraser Valley and has served as a jury member twice for both the George Ryga Award for Social Awareness in Literature and the TD Canadian Children's Literature Award. Her feminist and post-colonial theory-focused research on Indian children's literature has been published in *Papers*, IRSCL, and in the monograph *Contemporary, English-language Indian Children's Literature* (Routledge, 2011).

Joe Sutliff Sanders is Associate Professor of English Department at Kansas State University. He is finishing a monograph on children's non-fiction and editing a collection of essays on the Belgian cartoonist Hergé.

Joseph T. Thomas, Jr. is Professor of English and Comparative Literature at San Diego State University, where he also serves as Director of the National Center for the Study of Children's Literature. Thomas is the author of a handful of essays and two books, *Poetry's Playground: The Culture of Contemporary American Children's Poetry* (Wayne State University Press, 2007) and *Strong Measures* (Make Now P, 2007). His book on Shel Silverstein's life and work—*Shel Silverstein, The Devil's Favorite Pet* is forthcoming. His interest in literary awards emerged during his term as the first Poetry Award Editor of *The Lion and the Unicorn: A Critical Journal of Children's Literature*.

Abbie Ventura is UC Foundation Assistant Professor and Associate Chair of English at the University of Tennessee at Chattanooga. She has published essays on issues of social justice, economic citizenship, and national identities in children's and YA literature; her current research focuses on international children's texts, and the economic conditions that grant and limit non-Western children's books' visibility on the Western market.

Bibliography

"The 1997 Erza Jack Keats New Writer Award." Ezra Jack Keats Foundation and the Early Childhood Resource and Information Center. Apr. 17, 1997. Ezra Jack Keats Foundation, Brooklyn, New York. Print.

"2014 Awards Guidelines." *Lambda Literary: Celebrating Excellence in LGBT Literature since 1989.* Lambda Literary Foundation, 2014. Web. Sep. 9, 2014.

"5/01 Draft Procedures/Guidelines, Ezra Jack Keats New Writer Award/Ezra Jack Keats New Illustrator Award." Ezra Jack Keats Foundation and New York Public Library. May 19, 2001. Ezra Jack Keats Foundation, Brooklyn, New York. Print.

Ablavsky, Gregory. "The Savage Constitution." *Duke Law Journal*, 63.5 (Feb. 2014): 999–1089. Print.

"About BC Book Prizes: Categories and Criteria, Sheila A. Egoff Children's Literature Prize." *BC Book Prizes*, n.d. Web, Mar. 10, 2014.

"About IBBY." International Board on Books for Young People, 2014. Web, May 3, 2014.

"About Three Percent." *Three Percent: A Resource for International Literature*, 2014. Web, Jun. 1, 2014.

"About Us: Astrid Lindgren Memorial Award." Astrid Lindgren Memorial Award, 2014. Web, May 4, 2014.

Abrams, M.H. *A Glossary of Literary Terms.* Boston: Wadsworth, 2008. Print.

"Academic Awards." *Wikipedia.* Wikimedia Foundation, Inc., n.d. Web, Jun. 6, 2014.

"A History of the Ezra Jack Keats Foundation." *Ezra Jack Keats.* Ezra Jack Keats Foundation. 2014. Web, Oct. 11, 2014.

Allen, Ruth. *Children's Book Prizes: An Evaluation and History of Major Awards for Children's Books in the English-Speaking World.* Aldershot and Brookfield: Ashgate, 1998. Print.

Alloway, Nola. "Swimming Against the Tide: Boys, Literacies, and Schooling: An Australian Story." *Canadian Journal of Education* 30.2 (2007): 582–605. Print.

Alvarez, Julia. *Before We Were Free.* New York: Alfred A. Knopf, 2002. Print.

"Amazon Best Sellers." Amazon.com. 2014. Web, Jun. 27, 2014.

Apter, Emily. "Untranslatables: A World System." *New Literary History* 39.3 (2008): 581–98. Print.

Arnold, Yvonne. "Lena Young de Grummond: Woman with a Dream." *Juvenile Miscellany* 28.2 (2008): 4–6. Print.

Aronson, Marc. "Slippery Slopes and Proliferating Prizes." *The Horn Book Magazine* May/June 2001. *The Horn Book.* Web, Apr. 12, 2014.

Ashman, Linda. *Rain!* Ill. Christian Robinson. Boston: Houghton Mifflin, 2013. Print.

Attree, Lizzy. "The Caine Prize and Contemporary African Writing." *Research in African Literatures* 44.2 (Summer 2013): 35–47. Print.

Auerbach, Rita. Letter to Paul Zelinksy. Aug. 5, 2003. Ezra Jack Keats Foundation, Brooklyn, New York. Print.

"Awards Guidelines." *Lambdaliterary.org*. Web, Aug. 24, 2016.

Aylward, Carol A. *Canadian Critical Race Theory: Racism and the Law*. Halifax: Fernwood Publishing, 1999. Print.

Bailey, Em. *Shift*. Richmond: Hardie Grant Egmont, 2011. Print.

Baker, Dierdre, and Ken Setterington. *A Guide to Canadian Children's Books in English*. Toronto: McClelland and Stewart, 2003. Print.

Baker-Whitelaw, Gavia. "How the 'Sad Puppies' Internet Campaign Gamed the Hugo Awards." *Daily Dot*. Apr. 5, 2015. Web, Apr. 20, 2015.

Bakhtin, M.M. *The Dialogic Imagination*, editor Michael Holquist. Trans. Caryl Emerson and Michael Holquist. Austin, TX: University of Texas Press, 1981. Print.

Ball, Zachary. Letter to Lena de Grummond. Mar. 24, 1969. TS. Lena de Grummond and Lynn Delaune Papers, box 8, folder 7. de Grummond Children's Literature Collection. University of Southern Mississippi, Hattiesburg.

Banet-Weiser, Sarah. *Kids Rule! Nickelodeon and Consumer Citizenship*. Durham, NC: Duke University Press, 2007. Print.

Barker, Keith. "Prize-fighting." In *Children's Book Publishing in Britain Since 1945*, editors Kimberley Reynolds and Nicholas Tucker. Aldershot, England: Scolar Press, 1998. 42–59. Print.

Barnes, Henry. "Quentin Tarantino Plans *Django Unchained* TV series." *The Guardian*, May 23, 2014. Web, Jun. 10, 2014.

Bar-Tal, Daniel. "Delegitimation: The Extreme Case of Stereotyping and Prejudice." In *Stereotyping and Prejudice*, editors Daniel Bar-Tal, Carl F. Graumann, Arie W. Kruglanski, and Wolfgang Strobe. New York: Springer-Verlag, 1989. 169–82.

Bartoletti, Susan Campbell. *Hitler Youth: Growing Up in Hitler's Shadow*. New York: Scholastic Inc., 2005. Print.

"Batchelder Award." American Library Association, 2014. Web, May 1, 2014.

Battiste, Marie. Introduction. *Reclaiming Indigenous Voice and Vision*, editor Marie Battiste. Vancouver: UBC Press, 2009. xvi–xxx. Print.

Bausum, Ann. *Freedom Riders: John Lewis and Jim Zwerg on the Front Lines of the Civil Rights Movement*. Washington DC: National Geographic, 2006. Print.

Bear, John. *The #1 New York Times Bestseller: Intriguing facts about the 484 books that have been #1 New York Times bestsellers since the first list in 1942*. Berkeley, CA: Ten Speed Press, 1992. Print.

Beck, Scott A. "Children of Mexican Farmworkers in Picture Storybooks: Reality, Romanticism, and Representation." *Children's Literature Association Quarterly* 34.2 (Summer 2009): 99–137. Print.

Belpré, Pura. "Multi-ethnic Literature." The Pura Belpré Papers, n.d. Archives of the Puerto Rican Diaspora, Center for Puerto Rican Studies, Hunter College, City University of New York.

Benjamin, Walter. "Unpacking My Library: A Talk about Book Collecting." *Illuminations: Essays and Reflections*, editor Hannah Arendt. New York: Schocken Books, 1968. 59–68. Print.

Berger, Maurice. "One Small Step." *The Snowy Day and the Art of Ezra Jack Keats*, editor Claudia J. Nahson. New York and New Haven: The Jewish Museum and Yale University Press, 2011. 28–39. Print.

"Best Sellers: Children's Chapter Books." *New York Times*. New York Times. Sep. 28, 2008. Web, Jun. 30, 2014.

"Best Sellers: Children's Chapter Books." *New York Times*. New York Times. Sep. 20, 2009. Web, Jun. 30, 2014.

"Best Sellers." *New York Times*. New York Times. Jan. 21, 2001. Web, Nov. 10, 2014.

"Best Sellers." *New York Times*. New York Times. Jan. 3, 2010. Web, Nov. 10, 2014.

"Best Sellers." *New York Times*. New York Times. Nov. 2, 2014. Web, Nov. 10, 2014.

Bird, Elizabeth. "Quite Possibly the Least Known Award in Children's Literature." *School Library Journal* Blog. Sep. 30, 2010. Web, Aug. 4, 2014.

Bishop, Rudine Sims. "Reflections on the Development of African American Children's Literature." *Journal of Children's Literature* 38.2 (2012): 5–13. Print.

Bledstein, Burton J. *The Culture of Professionalism: The Middle Class and the Development of Higher Education in America*. New York: W.W. Norton & Co., 1976. Print.

Bloem, Patricia. "International Literature for U.S. Children and Young Adults: In Search of Difference." In *Building Bridges to Literacy*, editors Patricia E. Linder, Mary Beth Sampson, JoAnn R. Dugan and Barrie Brancato. Texas A&M, 2006. 207–20. Print.

Bloom, Harold. "Can 35 Million Book Buyers Be Wrong? Yes." *Wall Street Journal*, Jul. 11, 2000: *Factivia*. Web, Feb. 24, 2010.

Bode, Katherine. *Reading by Numbers: Recalibrating the Literary Field*. London: Anthem Press, 2012. Print.

Bordwell, David, Janet Staiger, and Kristin Thompson. *The Classical Hollywood Cinema: Film Style & Mode of Production to 1960*. London: Routledge, 1985/2004. Print.

Bosman, Julie. "With One Word, Children's Book Sets Off Uproar." *The New York Times*. Feb. 19, 2008. Web, Feb. 8, 2015.

Bourdieu, Pierre. *Homo Academicus*. Trans. Peter Collier. Oxford: Polity Press, 1988. Print.

———. "The Production of Belief: Contribution to an Economy of Symbolic Goods." 1986. In *The Field of Cultural Production: Essays on Art and Literature*, editor Randal Johnson. New York: Columbia University Press, 1993. Print.

———. *Distinction: A Social Critique of the Judgment of Taste*.London: Routledge, 2010. Print.

Bowskill, Sarah. "Politics and Literary Prizes: A Case Study of Spanish America and the Premio Cervantes." *Hispanic Review* (Spring 2012): 289–311. Print.

Bradford, Clare. *Unsettling Narratives: Postcolonial Readings of Children's Literature*. Waterloo, ON: Wilfrid Laurier University Press, 2007. Print.

Brady, Mary Pat. "Children's Literature." In *The Routledge Companion to Latino/a Literature*, editors Suzanne Bost and Francis R. Aparecio. New York: Routledge, 2013. 375–82. Print.

Breed, Clara E. "The Newbery Medal: A Plea for Understanding." *Wilson Library Bulletin* 16:9 (May 1942). 724. Print.

Bridges, Ruby. *Through My Eyes*. New York: Scholastic Press, 1999. Print.

Brier, Evan. *A Novel Marketplace: Mass Culture, the Book Trade and Postwar American Fiction*. Philadelphia: University of Pennsylvania Press, 2010. Print.

Brimner, Larry D. *Birmingham Sunday*. Honesdale: Calkins Creek, 2010. Print.

Brodkin, Karen. *How Jews Became White Folks and What That Says About Race in America*. New Brunswick: Rutgers University Press, 1998. Print.

Brooks, Peter. *The Melodramatic Imagination: Balzac, Henry James, Melodrama, and the Mode of Excess*. New Haven: Yale University Press, 1996. Print.

Brown, Noel. *The Hollywood Family Film: A History, from Shirley Temple to Harry Potter*. New York: I.B. Tauris, 2012. Print.

Brubaker, Rogers and Frederick Cooper. "Beyond Identity." *Theory and Society* 29.1 (Feb. 2000): 1–47. Print.

Burd-Sharps, Sarah. "About Human Development." Measure of America, 2014. Web, May 22, 2014.

"Burt Award for First Nations, Métis and Inuit Literature." *Code*. Web, Jan. 9, 2016.

Cadden, Mike. Untitled. Message to Kenneth Kidd. Jan. 30, 2015. Facebook mail.

Campbell, K.G. *Lester's Dreadful Sweaters*. Toronto: Kids Can, 2012. Print.

Canada Council for the Arts. "The Governor General's Literary Awards: About the GGS—History—In search of a 'Canadian' Voice." Ottawa: Canada Council for the Arts. Web, Jun. 6, 2014.

———. Equity Framework: Summary 2014. Canada Council for the Arts. Web, Jun. 10, 2014.

Caponegro, Ramona. "Prizing Social Justice: The Jane Addams Children's Book Award." In *Ethics and Children's Literature*, editor Claudia Mills. Burlington, VT: Ashgate Publishing, 2014. 207–221. Print.

Capra, Frank. *The Name Above the Title: An Autobiography*. 1971. New York: Da Capo, 1997. Print.

Capshaw Smith, Katharine 2004. *Children's Literature of the Harlem Renaissance*. Series: Blacks in the diaspora. Bloomington: Indiana University Press. Print.

———. 2014. "Ethnic Studies and Children's Literature Studies, A Conversation Between Fields," Keynote Address, 2014 Children's Literature Association Annual Conference, Columbia, South Carolina.

Cart, Michael. "A New Literature for a New Millennium? The First Decade of the Printz Awards." *Young Adult Library Services* 8.3 (2010): 28–31. Print.

Casanova, Pascale. *The World Republic of Letters*. Trans. M. B. DeBevoise. Cambridge: MA: Harvard University Press, 2007. Print.

Cave, Alfred A. "Canaanites in a Promised Land: The American Indian and the Providential Theory of Empire." *American Indian Quarterly*, 12.4 (Autumn 1988): 278–98. Print.

Cech, John. "Touchstones and the Phoenix: New Directions, New Dimensions." *Children's Literature Association Quarterly* 10.4 (Fall 1986): 177. Print.

Chapman, Lindsey. "Critics Debate Value of Newbery Medal for Children's Literature." *Finding Dulcinea*, Dec. 18, 2008. Web, Feb. 27, 2014.

"The Children's Book Council of Australia Judges' Report 2007." *Reading Time* 51.3 (2007): 5–12. Print.

Children's Books Awards & Prizes. New York: Children's Book Council, 1999. Print.

Childs, Donald J. "New Criticism." In *Encyclopedia of Contemporary Literary Theory: Approaches, Scholars, Terms*, editor Irena R. Makaryk. Toronto: University of Toronto P, 2000. 120–24. Print.

Christopher, Lucy. *Stolen: A Letter to my Captor*. Frome: Chicken House, 2009. Print.

Clark, Beverly Lyon. *Kiddie Lit: The Cultural Construction of Children's Literature in America*. Baltimore: Johns Hopkins University Press, 2003. Print.

Clark, Roger, Rachel Lennon, Leanna Morris. "Of Caldecotts and Kings: Gendered Images in Recent American Children's Books by Black and Non-Black Illustrators." *Gender and Society* 7.2 (Jun. 1993): 227–45. Print.

Clarke, Judith. *One Whole and Perfect Day*. Crows Nest: Allen & Unwin, 2006. Print.

Cohen, Lizabeth. *A Consumers' Republic: The Politics of Mass Consumption in Postwar America*. New York: Alfred A. Knopf, 2003. Print.

Collier, Bryan. *Uptown*. New York: Henry Holt, 2000. Print.

Collins, Patricia Hill. Foreword. *Emerging Intersections: Race, Class, and Gender in Theory, Policy, and Practice*. Bonnie Thornton Dill and Ruth Enid Zambrana. New Brunswick: Rutgers University Press, 2009. Print.

Condon, Bill. *Confessions of a Liar, Thief and Failed Sex God*. North Sydney: Woolshed Press, 2009. Print.

Connell, R.W. *Masculinities*. 2nd ed. Crows Nest: Allen & Unwin, 2005. Print.

Conrad: The Factory-Made Boy. Amazon, 2014. Web, Jul. 19, 2014.

Conrad: The Factory-Made Boy. Barnes & Noble, 2014. Web, Jul. 19, 2014.

Conrad: The Factory-Made Boy. Goodreads, 2014. Web, Jul. 19, 2014.

"Convention on the Rights of the Child." United Nations Human Rights: Office of the High Commissioner for Human Rights. Web, May 28, 2014.

Coville, Bruce. Message to Emily Murphy. Nov. 7, 2008. E-mail.

Crenshaw, Kimberle, Gotanda, Neil, Peller, Gary, and Thomas, Kendall. "Introduction." *Critical Race Theory: The Key Writings that Formed the Movement*. New York: The New Press. 1996. xiii–xxxii. Print.

Crisp, Thomas. "It's Not the Book, It's Not the Author, It's the Award: The Lambda Literary Award and the Case for Strategic Essentialism." *Children's Literature in Education* 42 (2011): 91–104. Print.

Crispin: The Cross of Lead. Amazon, 2014. Web, Jul. 19, 2014.

Crispin: The Cross of Lead. Barnes & Noble, 2014. Web, Jul. 19, 2014.

Crispin: The Cross of Lead. Goodreads, 2014. Web, Jul. 19, 2014.

"Criteria for Entry into This Competition." *George Ryga Award for Social Awareness in Literature*, n.d. Web, Mar. 10, 2014.

Crowley, Cath. *Graffiti Moon*. 2010. Sydney: Pan Macmillan, 2011. Print.

Cummins, Julie. Letter to Deborah Pope. Apr. 24, 2000. Ezra Jack Keats Foundation, Brooklyn, New York. Print.

Damrosch, David. *How to Read World Literature*. Chichester: Wiley-Blackwell, 2008. Print.

Darder, Antonia, Baltodano, Marta P. and Torres, Rodolfo D. "Critical Pedagogy: An Introduction." In *The Critical Pedagogy Reader*, 2nd ed., editors Darder et al. New York: Routledge. 1–20. 2009. Print.

Dargis, Manohla. "Defending Goliath: Hollywood and the Art of the Blockbuster." *New York Times* (1923- Current file): 2. May 6, 2007. ProQuest. Web, Jun. 27, 2014.

Davila, Arlene. *Latinos, Inc.: The Marketing and Making of a People*. Berkeley: University of California Press, 2001. Print.

Davis, Kenneth C. *Two-Bit Culture: Two-Bit Culture*. Boston: Houghton Mifflin, 1984. Print.

DeAnda, Roberto. "Ernesto Galarza and Mexican Children's Literature in the United States." *Camino Real* 4.7 (2012): 11–28. Print.

Dear Mr. Henshaw. Amazon, 2014. Web, Jul. 19, 2014.

Dear Mr. Henshaw. Barnes & Noble, 2014. Web, Jul. 19, 2014.

Dear Mr. Henshaw. Goodreads, 2014. Web, Jul. 19, 2014.

Décoste, Rachel. "Blackface is a Black Eye to Canadian Values." *The Huffington Post Canada: The Blog*, Oct. 22, 2013. Web, Jun. 5, 2014.

De Grummond, Lena. *Growth of an Idea: The de Grummond Collection*. Hattiesburg: University of Southern Mississippi, 1972. Print.

———. Letter to Dr. Onva Boshears. Feb. 5, 1981. TS. Lena de Grummond and Lynn Delaune Papers. No Box or Folder Listed. de Grummond Children's Literature Collection. University of Southern Mississippi, Hattiesburg.

Delgado, Richard and Stefancic, Jean. "Introduction." In *Critical Race Theory: The Cutting Edge* 2nd ed., editors Richard Delgado and Jean Stefancic. Philadelphia: Temple University Press. 2000. Print.

Demers, Patricia. "Classic or Touchstone: Much of a Muchness?" *Children's Literature Association Quarterly* 10.3 (Summer 1985): 142–3. Print.

"The Development of Circus Acts." Victoria and Albert Museum. Web, May 27, 2014.

Diaz, Shelley. "Librarians Sound off: Not a Lack of Latino Lit for Kids, but Awareness." *School Library Journal*, Jan. 22, 2013. Web, Jan. 8, 2016.

Dickens, Charles. *Great Expectations*. New York: Gregory, 1861. Print.

Dill, Bonnie Thornton and Ruth Enid Zambrana. *Emerging Intersections: Race, Class, and Gender in Theory, Policy, and Practice*. New Brunswick: Rutgers University Press, 2009. Print.

Dillon, Leo. Letter to Louann Toth, Bee Cullinan, and Julie Cummins. Apr. 10, 2000. Ezra Jack Keats Foundation, Brooklyn, New York. Print.

Dimock, Wai Chee. *Through Other Continents: American Literature Across Deep Time*. Princeton, NJ: Princeton University Press, 2008. Print.

Doherty, Thomas. *Hollywood's Censor: Joseph I. Breen and the Production Code Administration*. New York: Columbia University Press, 2007. Print.

Driscoll, Beth. "The Politics of Prizes." *Meanjin* 68.1 (2009): 71–8. Print.

Dubosarsky, Ursula. *The Red Shoe*. Crows Nest: Allen & Unwin, 2006. Print.

Dubrow, Heather. Foreword. In *New Formalisms and Literary Theory*, editors Verena Theile and Linda Tredennick. New York: Palgrave, 2013. vii–xviii. Print.

Duyvis, Corinne. "Diverse Characters: Corinne Duyvis on the Decline of 'Issues' Books." *The Guardian*. Guardian News and Media Limited, Oct. 17, 2014. Web, Oct. 20, 2014.

Eagleton, Terry. "The Subject of Literature." *Cultural Critique* 2 (Winter, 1985–1986): 95–104. Print.

Eagleton, Terry and Fuller, Peter. 1983. "The Question of Value: A Discussion." *New Left Review* I.42 (Nov. to Dec.). Web, Jun. 6, 2014.

Eddy, Jacalyn. 2006. *Bookwomen: Creating an Empire in Children's Book Publishing, 1919–1939*. Madison, WI: University of Wisconsin Press. Print.

Egoff, Sheila, and Judith Saltman. *The New Republic of Childhood: A Critical Guide to Canadian Children's Literature in English*. Toronto: Oxford University Press, 1990. Print.

Elberse, Anita. *Blockbusters: Hit-Making, Risk-Taking, and the Big Business of Entertainment*. New York: Henry Holt and Company, 2013. Print.

Eliot, T.S. "Tradition and the Individual Talent." 1919. *The Sacred Wood*. 1920 New York, Dover, 1997. Print.

Elliott, Zetta. *Bird*. Ill. Shadra Strickland. New York: Lee & Low, 2008. Print.

Emerson, Ralph Waldo. "Experience," *Self-Reliance and Other Essays*. New York: Dover, 1993. Print.

English, James F. "Winning the Culture Game: Prizes, Awards and the Rules of Art." *New Literary History* 33.1 (2002): 109–35. Print.

———. *The Economy of Prestige: Prizes, Awards, and the Circulation of Cultural Value*. Cambridge: Harvard University Press, 2005. Print.

"Ezra Jack Keats New Writer and Illustrator Awards for Children's Books." *Ezra Jack Keats.* Ezra Jack Keats Foundation, 2014. Web, Dec. 12, 2014.

"The Ezra Jack Keats New Writer and New Illustrator Book Awards Come to the de Grummond Collection of Children's Literature." Ezra Jack Keats Foundation Press Release. Dec. 2011. Ezra Jack Keats Foundation, Brooklyn, New York. Print.

"Ezra Jack Keats New Writer Award and the Ezra Jack Keats New Illustrator Award." The de Grummond Children's Literature Collection and The Ezra Jack Keats Foundation. 2014. Ezra Jack Keats Foundation, Brooklyn, New York. Print.

"FAQ—About the Ezra Jack Keats New Writer & Illustrator Awards." *Ezra Jack Keats.* Ezra Jack Keats Foundation. 2014. Web, Oct. 11, 2014.

Feldman, Irving. *Collected Poems 1954–2004.* New York: Schocken Books, 2004. Print.

Fenn, Patricia, and Alfred P. Malpa. *Rewards of Merit: Tokens of a Child's Progress and a Teacher's Esteem as an Enduring Aspect of American Religious and Secular Education.* The Ephemera Society of America, 1994. Printed and bound in Hong Kong. Distributed by Howell Press, Inc. Print.

Fitzsimmons, Rebekah. "Testing the Tastemakers: Children's Literature, Bestseller Lists, and the 'Harry Potter Effect.'" *Children's Literature* 40.1 (2012): 78–107. Print.

———. *The Chronicles of Professionalization.* PhD diss., University of Florida, 2015. Print.

Fleischman, John. *Black and White Airmen: Their True History.* Boston: Houghton Mifflin Company, 2007. Print.

Flora & Ulysses: The Illuminated Adventures. Amazon, 2014. Web, Jul. 19, 2014.

Flora & Ulysses: The Illuminated Adventures. Barnes & Noble, 2014. Web, Jul. 19, 2014.

Flora & Ulysses: The Illuminated Adventures. Goodreads, 2014. Web, Jul. 19, 2014.

Flournoy, Valerie. *The Patchwork Quilt.* Ill. Jerry Pinkney. New York: Dial, 1985. Print.

Flynn, Richard et al. "It Could Be Verse: The 2005 Lion and the Unicorn Award for Excellence in North American Poetry." *The Lion and the Unicorn* 29 (2005): 427–41. Print.

Foetry's goodbye message at http://poetry-arts-confidential.blogspot.com/2011/04/foetrycom-inside-poetry-site-i-only.html accessed Aug. 24, 2016.

Fraustino, Lisa Rowe. "Re: Phoenix Picture Book Award." Message to Kenneth Kidd. Jan. 30, 2015. E-mail.

Freedman, Russell. *The Voice that Challenged a Nation: Marian Anderson and the Struggle for Equal Rights.* New York: Clarion Books, 2004. Print.

———. *Freedom Walkers: The Story of the Montgomery Bus Boycott.* New York: Holiday House, 2006. Print.

Freire, Paulo. *Pedagogy of the Oppressed.* Trans. Myra Bergman Ramos. New York: Seabury, 1970. Print.

"Frequently Asked Questions about Old Books" *de Grummond Collection of Children's Literature.* de Grummond Collection, n.d. Web, Nov. 11, 2008.

Gardner, Scot. *The Dead I Know.* Crows Nest: Allen & Unwin, 2011. Print.

Garner, Barbara. "Re: Phoenix Award research." Message to Kenneth Kidd. Jul. 15, 2014. E-mail.

Garza, Melita Marie. "Blacks, Hispanics Are Rare Heroes with Newbery Kids Books Medal." *Bloomberg*, Dec. 30, 2008. Online.

———. "Newbery Kids Books Medal." *Bloomberg*. Dec. 30, 2008. Web, Feb. 27, 2014.

Gay, Carol. "Newbery Kids Books Medal." *Bloomberg*, Dec. 30, 2008. Web, Feb. 27, 2014.

———. "ChLA: 1973–1983." Children's Literature Association website, n.d. Web, May 7, 2015.

Gelder, Ken. "Proximate Reading: Australian Literature in Transnational Reading Frameworks." *JASAL* (2010): 1–12. Print.

Giles, Paul. *Virtual Americas: Transnational Fictions and the Transatlantic Imaginary*. Durham: Duke University Press, 2002.

Gillborn, David. "Education policy as an act of white supremacy: whiteness, critical race theory and education reform." *Journal of Education Policy* 20.4 (Jul. 2005): 485–505. Print.

———. "Critical Race Theory and Education: Racism and anti-racism in educational theory and Praxis." *Discourse: studies in the cultural politics of education* 27.1 (Mar. 2006): 11–32. Print.

Gillespie, John T., and Corinne J. Naden. *The Newbery Companion: Booktalk and Related Materials for Newbery Medal and Honor Books*. Englewood, CO: Libraries Unlimited, 1996. Print.

Goldberg, David Theo. *The Threat of Race: Reflections on Racial Neoliberalism*. Malden, MA: Blackwell Publishing. 2009. Print.

"The Governor General's Literary Awards." Canadian Encyclopedia. Web, Jun. 29, 2014.

Graham, Ruth. "Against YA." *Slate*. The Slate Group. Jun. 5, 2014. Web, Nov. 15, 2014.

Griffin, Sean P. *Tinker Belles and Evil Queens: The Walt Disney Company from the Inside Out*. New York: New York University Press, 2000. Print.

Grossman, Allen. *The Ether Dome and Other Poems: New and Selected Poems 1979–1991*. New York: New Directions, 1991. Print.

"Guidelines." *Inside a Dog*. State Library of Victoria, n.d. Web, Jan. 9, 2016.

Guillory, John. *Cultural Capital: The Problem of Literary Canon Formation*. Chicago: University of Chicago Press, 1993. Print.

Hackett, Alice Payne. *70 Years of Best Sellers: 1895–1965*. New York: R.R. Bowker Co, 1967. Print.

Hadas, Rachel. *The Ache of Appetite*. Providence: Copper Beach Press, 2010. Print.

Hall, Stuart. "The Spectacle of the 'Other.'" In Hall, *Representation: Cultural Representations and Signifying Practices*. London: Sage/Open University, 1997. 225–79. Print.

Hames-García, Michael. *Identity Complex: Making the Case for Multiplicity*. Minneapolis: University of Minnesota Press, 2011. Print.

"Hannah Nuba, Pioneer in Field of Early Childhood Services in Libraries, Dies." The New York Public Library Press Release. Dec. 5, 2000. Ezra Jack Keats Foundation, Brooklyn, New York. Print.

"Hans Christian Andersen Awards." International Board on Books for Young People, 2014. Web, May 7, 2014.

Harasty, Amy S. "The Interpersonal Nature of Social Stereotypes: Differential Discussion Patterns about In-Groups and Out-Groups." *Personality and Social Psychology Bulletin* 23.3 (Mar. 1997): 270–82. Print.

Harding, Robert. "Historical Representations of Aboriginal People in the Canadian News Media." *Discourse & Society* 17.2 (2006): 205–35. Print.

Harrington, Janice N. *Going North*. Ill. Jerome Lagarrigue. New York: Farrar, Straus and Giroux, 2004. Print.

Hateley, Erica "'In the hands of the receivers': The Politics of Literacy in *The Savage* by David Almond and Dave McKean." *Children's Literature in Education* 43.2 (2012): 170–80. Print.

———. "Paranoid Prizing: Mapping Australia's Eve Pownall Award for Information Books, 2001–2010." *Bookbird: A Journal of International Children's Literature* 51.1 (Jan. 2013): 41–50. Print.

Havens, Timothy, and Amanda D. Lotz. *Understanding Media Industries.* New York: Oxford University Press, 2011. Print.

Hegamin, Tonya Cherie. *Most Loved in All the World.* Ill. Cozbi A. Cabrera. Boston: Houghton Mifflin, 2009. Print.

Helbig, Alethea. "Re: Phoenix Award research." Message to Kenneth Kidd. Jul. 15, 2014. E-mail.

Helbig, Alethea and Agnes Perkins, editors. *The Phoenix Award of the Children's Literature Association, 1985–1989.* Metuchen, NJ: The Scarecrow Press, 1993. Print.

———. *The Phoenix Award of The Children's Literature Association, 1990–1994.* Lanham, MD: The Scarecrow Press, 1996. Print.

———. *The Phoenix Award of The Children's Literature Association, 1995–1999.* Lanham, MD: The Scarecrow Press, 2001. Print.

Hendershot, Heather. *Nickelodeon Nation: The History, Politics, and Economics of America's Only TV Channel for Kids.* New York: New York University Press, 2004. Print.

Henderson, Laretta. "The Black Arts Movement and African American Young Adult Literature: An Evaluation of Narrative Style." *Children's Literature in Education* 36.4 (Dec. 2005): 299–323. Print.

The Hero and the Crown. Amazon, 2014. Web, Jul. 19, 2014.

The Hero and the Crown. Barnes & Noble, 2014. Web, Jul. 19, 2014.

The Hero and the Crown. Goodreads, 2014. Web, Jul. 19, 2014.

Hewstone, Miles. "Changing Stereotypes with Disconfirming Information." In *Stereotyping and Prejudice*, editors Daniel Bar-Tal, Carl F. Graumann, Arie W. Kruglanski, and Wolfgang Stroebe. New York: Springer-Verlag, 1989. 207–23. Print.

Heyman, Michael, Angela Sorby, et al. "Lively Rigor: The 2009 *Lion and the Unicorn* Award for Excellence in North American Poetry," *The Lion and the Unicorn* 33 (2009): 376–96. Print.

———. "It's (Not) All Small Stuff: The [2010] *Lion and the Unicorn* Award for Excellence in North American Poetry." *The Lion and the Unicorn* 34.3 (Sep. 2010): 354–63.

Heyman, Michael, Michael Joseph, et al. "'The City, the Country, and the Road Between': The 2011 *Lion and the Unicorn* Award for Excellence in North American Poetry." *The Lion and the Unicorn* 35 (2011): 296–313. Print.

———. "'Roses are planted where thorns grow': The 2012 *Lion and the Unicorn* Award for Excellence in North American." *Lion and the Unicorn* 36 (2012): 288–307. Print.

Heyman, Michael, Angela Sorby et al. "It's (Not) All Small Stuff: The [2010] *Lion and the Unicorn* Award for Excellence in North American Poetry." *The Lion and the Unicorn*, 34.3 (Sep. 2010): 354–63. Print.

"History of the Fay B. Kaigler Children's Book Festival." *Fay B. Kaigler Children's Book Festival.* University of Southern Mississippi, n.d. Web, Oct. 10, 2014.

Holson, Laura M. "The Gold Starts With the Nomination." *New York Times* Feb. 13, 2002: E1, E12. Print.

———. "As Animation Goes Digital, Disney Fights for Its Crown." *New York Times* Feb. 10, 2003: C1, C6. Print.

Holt, Jennifer, and Alisa Perren, editors. *Media Industries: History, Theory, and Method*. Malden, MA: Wiley-Blackwell, 2009. Print.

hooks, bell. "No Love in the Wild." *NewBlackMan (in Exile)* Blogspot, Sep. 5, 2012. Web, Jun. 27, 2014.

Hoose, Phillip. *Claudette Colvin: Twice Toward Justice*. New York: Farrar Straus Giroux, 2009. Print.

Horning, Kathleen. *From Cover to Cover: Evaluating and Reviewing Children's Books*. 2nd ed. New York: HarperCollins, 2010. Print.

———. "The Search for Distinguished." *Horn Book*. Jun. 2012. Web, Mar. 27, 2014.

Houdyshell, Mara L., and Janice J. Kirkland. "Heroines in Newbery Medal Award Winners: Seventy-Five Years of Change." *Journal of Youth Services in Libraries* 11.3 (Spring 1998): 252–62. Print.

"How the Newbery Medal Came to Be." *Association for Library Service to Children*. American Library Association, n.d. Web, Mar. 10, 2014.

Huck, Charlotte, et al. *Children's Literature in the Elementary School*. New York: McGraw Hill, 2003. Print.

Huggan, Graham. "Prizing 'Otherness': A Short History of the Booker." *Studies in the Novel* 29.3 (Fall, 1997): 412–33. Print.

———. *Australian Literature: Postcolonialism, Racism, Transnationalism*. Oxford: Oxford University Press, 2007. Print.

"Human Development Index – 2012 Report." United Nations, 2013. Web, Mar. 1, 2014.

Hunt, Peter, editor. *International Companion Encyclopedia of Children's Literature*. New York: Routledge, 1996. Print.

Huse, Nancy. "Foreword." In *The Phoenix Award of The Children's Literature Association, 1990–1994*, editors Alethea Helbig and Agnes Perkins. Lanham, MD: The Scarecrow Press, 1996. vii–ix. Print.

Hwang, Sun-mi. *The Hen Who Dreamed She Could Fly*. New York: Penguin, 2013. Print.

"Intermediate Fiction." The Horn Book Guide to Children's and Young Adult Books.18.2 (Fall 2007). Web, Nov. 6, 2014.

The Island on Bird Street. Amazon, 2014. Web, Jul. 19, 2014.

The Island on Bird Street. Barnes & Noble, 2014. Web, Jul. 19, 2014.

The Island on Bird Street. Goodreads, 2014. Web, Jul. 19, 2014.

Itzkoff, Dave. "Study Finds Less Diversity in Newbery Books." *The New York Times*. Dec. 30, 2008. Web, Feb. 27, 2014.

"Jacqueline Woodson on Growing Up, Coming Out and Saying Hi to Strangers." *Fresh Air*. National Public Radio. Dec. 10, 2014. Radio.

Jameson, Fredric. *The Political Unconscious: Narrative as a Socially Symbolic Act*. Ithaca: Cornell University Press, 1981. Print.

Jenkins, Christine A. "Women of ALA Youth Services and Professional Jurisdiction: Of Nightingales, Newberies, Realism, and the Right Books, 1937–1945." *Library Trends* 44.4 (Spring 1996): 813–39. Print.

Jiménez García, Marilisa. 2014. *"Every Child is Born a Poet": The Puerto Rican Narrative within American Children's Culture*. Diss. University of Florida: UMI. Print.

———. "Pura Belpré Lights the Storyteller's Candle: Reframing the Legacy of a Legend and What It Means for Latino Studies and Children's Literature." *CENTRO Journal* 26.1 (Spring 2014): 1–28. Print.

John Newbery Award Committee Manual." *Association for Library Service to Children.* American Library Association, n.d. Web, Mar. 10, 2014.

Johnson, Angela. *Tell Me a Story, Mama.* Ill. David Soman. New York: Orchard Books, 1989. Print.

Johnson, D. B. *Henry Hikes to Fitchburg.* Boston: Houghton Mifflin, 2000. Print.

Johnson, S. F. "Honors and Prizes in the MLA Field." *PMLA* 67.1 (Feb. 1952): 37–58. Print.

Joseph, Michael et al. "Outside the Inside of the Box: The 2013 *Lion and the Unicorn* Award for Excellence in North American Poetry," *The Lion and the Unicorn* 37 (2013): 327–45. Print.

Justice, Keith L. *Bestseller Index: All Books, by Author, on the Lists of Publishers Weekly and the New York Times Through 1990.* Jefferson, NC: McFarland & Co, 1998. Print.

Kachka, Boris. *Hothouse: The Art of Survival and the Survival of Art at America's Most Celebrated Publishing House, Farrar, Straus and Giroux.* New York: Simon and Schuster, 2014. Print.

Keats, Ezra Jack. *The Snowy Day.* 50th Anniversary Edition. New York: Viking, 2011. Print.

Kertzer, Adrienne. "Re: Phoenix Award research." Message to Kenneth Kidd. Jul. 13, 2014. E-mail.

Khan, Rukhsana. *Silly Chicken.* Ill. Yunmee Kyong. New York: Viking, 2005. Print.

Kidd, Kenneth "Children's Culture, Children's Studies, and the Ethnographic Imaginary." *Children's Literature Association Quarterly* 27.3 (2002): 146–55. Print.

———. 2005. "A" is for Auschwitz: Psychoanalysis, Trauma Theory, and the "Children's Literature of Atrocity." *Children's Literature* 33.120–49. Print.

———. "Prizing Children's Literature: The Case of Newbery Gold." *Children's Literature* 35 (2007): 166–90. Print.

———. "'Not Censorship but Selection': Censorship and/as Prizing." *Children's Literature in Education* 40.3 (Sep. 2009): 197–216. Print.

———. "The Child, the Scholar, and the Children's Literature Archive." *The Lion and the Unicorn* 35.1 (2011): 1–23. *Project MUSE.* Apr. 22, 2011.

Kivy, Peter. *The Performance of Reading.* Oxford: Blackwell, 2006. Print.

Klingberg, Göte. *Children's Fiction in the Hands of the Translators.* GWK Gleerup, 1986. Print.

Klingman, Lee, editor. *Newbery and Caldecott Books 1956–1965: With Acceptance Papers, Biographies, and Related Material Chiefly from the Horn Book Magazine.* Boston: Horn Book, 1965. Print.

———. *Newbery and Caldecott Books 1966–1975: With Acceptance Papers, Biographies, and Related Material Chiefly from the Horn Book Magazine.* Boston: Horn Book, 1975. Print.

———. *Newbery and Caldecott Books, 1976–1985: With Acceptance Papers, Biographies, and Related Material Chiefly from the Horn Book Magazine.* Boston: Horn Book, 1986. Print.

Korda, Michael. *Making the List: A Cultural History of the American Bestseller, 1900–1999.* Barnes & Noble Publishing Inc. New York. 2001. Print.

Kroyer, Bill, and Barry Weiss. "Today's Toons Should Draw Praise." *Variety* Feb. 5, 2003: 15. Print.

Ladson-Billings, Gloria. "The evolving role of critical race theory in educational scholarship." *Race Ethnicity & Education* 8.1 (Mar. 2005): 115–19. Print.

Ladson-Billings, Gloria and Tate, William F. "Toward a critical race theory of education." *Teachers College Record* 97.1 (Fall 1995): 47–68. Print.

Lambou, Madeline G. "The Midas Touch of Lena de Grummond." *The Pen Woman.* Dec. 1969: 7. Lena de Grummond and Lynn Delaune Papers, box 1A, folder 3. De Grummond Children's Literature Collection. University of Southern Mississippi, Hattiesburg.

Lanagan, Margo. *Black Juice.* New York: HarperCollins, 2004. Print.

———. *Red Spikes.* New York: Alfred A. Knopf, 2006. Print.

———. *Tender Morsels.* New York: Alfred A. Knopf, 2008. Print.

Lanthier, Jennifer. *The Stamp Collector.* Ill. François Thisdale. Markham, Ontario: Fitzhenry & Whiteside, 2012. Print.

Larrick, Nancy. "The All-White World of Children's Books." *Saturday Review*, Sep. 11, 1965: 63–5. Print.

Lathey, Gillian, editor. *The Translation of Children's Literature: A Reader.* London: Cromwell, 2006. Print.

———. *The Role of Translators in Children's Literature: Invisible Storytellers.* New York: Routledge, 2010: 145–60. Print.

Leitch, Thomas M. "Know-Nothing Entertainment: What to Say to Your Friends on the Right, and Why It Won't Do Any Good." *Literature/Film Quarterly* 25.1 (1997): 7–17. Print.

Lenski, Lois. Letter to Dr. Warren Tracy. Jul. 2, 1969. TS. Lois Lenski Papers, box 1, folder 3. de Grummond Children's Literature Collection. University of Southern Mississippi, Hattiesburg.

Lesley, Naomi. "Internal Diversity and the Market for 'Diverse' Children's Books." Unpublished conference paper, Children's Literature Association Conference. Columbia, South Carolina, 2014. Print.

Letter to Phyllis Reynolds Naylor. May 9, 1978. TS. Unprocessed. De Grummond Children's Literature Collection. University of Southern Mississippi, Hattiesburg.

Levinson, Cynthia. *We've Got a Job: The 1963 Birmingham Children's March.* Atlanta: Peach Tree Publishers. 2012. Print.

Levy, Emanuel. *All About Oscar: The History and Politics of the Academy Awards.* New York: Continuum, 2003. Print.

Levy, Michael. "Re: Phoenix Award research." Message to Kenneth Kidd. Jul. 4, 2014. E-mail.

Lewis, Oscar. 1966. *La vida: A Puerto Rican family in the culture of poverty—San Juan and New York.* New York: Random House. Print.

Lindsay, Nina. "The 2015 Youth Media Awards: A Crossover Year for Diversity." *School Library Journal.* Mar. 2, 2015. Web, Apr. 13, 2015.

Loewen, James W. *Lies My Teacher Told Me: Everything Your American History Textbook Got Wrong.* New York: Touchstone, 1995. Print.

Lundin, Anne. *Constructing the Canon of Children's Literature: Beyond Library Walls and Ivory Towers.* New York: Routledge, 2004. Print.

Lyman, Rick. "Animators Say, 'That's All, Folks.'" *New York Times* Jul. 24, 2000. Web, Jun. 24, 2014.

Lyons, A. and Kashima, Y. "The Reproduction of Culture: Communication Processes Tend to maintain Cultural Stereotypes." *Social Cognition* 19.3: 372–94. Print.

Mackintosh, Paul St. John. "Jacqueline Woodson Answers the Daniel Handler Watermelon Gaffe." *TeleRead.* Dec. 3, 2014. Web, Feb. 2, 2015.

Marchetta, Melina. *Looking for Alibrandi.* New York: Afred A. Knopf, 1992. Print.

——. *Saving Francesca*. New York: Alfred A. Knopf, 2004. Print.

——. *Jellicoe Road*. New York: HarperCollins, 2006. Web, Nov. 6, 2014.

Marcus, Kendra. "Buying and Selling International Children's Book Rights: A Literary Agent's Perspective." *Publishing Research Quarterly* 19.2 (2003): 51–6. Print.

Marcus, Leonard S. *Minders of Make-Believe: Idealists, Entrepreneurs, and the Shaping of American Children's Literature*. Boston: Houghton Mifflin, 2008. Print.

Martínez-Roldán, Carmen. 2013. "The Representation of Latinos and the Use of Spanish: A Critical Content Analysis of Skippyjon Jones." *Journal of Children's Literature*, 39 (1): 5–14. Print.

Maughan, Shannon. "And the Winner Is …" *Publishers Weekly*. Dec. 2, 2011. Web, Mar. 10, 2014.

"Melina Marchetta." Penguin Books Australia. n.d. Print.

Metzenthen, David. *Jarvis 24*. Camberwell: Penguin, 2009. Print.

"Midnight Edict is Blockbuster to Manhattan." *Chicago Daily Tribune* (1923–1963): 2. Feb. 20 1945. ProQuest. Web, Jun. 27, 2014.

The Midwife's Apprentice. Barnes & Noble, 2014. Web, Jul. 19, 2014.

The Midwife's Apprentice. Amazon, 2014. Web, Jul. 19, 2014.

The Midwife's Apprentice. Goodreads, 2014. Web, Jul. 19, 2014.

Miller, Bonnie J. F. "What Color is Gold? Twenty-One Years of Same-Race Authors and Protagonists in the Newbery Medal." *Joys* (Fall 1998): 34–9. Print.

Miller, Carl F. "Precious Medals: The Newbery Medal, the YRCA, and the Gold Standard of Children's Book Awards." In *Little Red Readings: Historical Materialist Perspectives on Children's Literature*, editor Angela E. Huber. Jackson, MS: University Press of Mississippi, 2014. 57–74. Print.

Miller, Laura J. "Best-Seller List as Marketing Tool and Historical Fiction." *Book History* 3 (2000): 286–304. Print.

——. *Reluctant Capitalists: Bookselling and the Culture of Consumption*. University of Chicago P: Chicago, 2006. Print.

——. "The making of a blockbuster: Salon exclusive: The behind-the-scenes story of the readers and booksellers who launched the *Hunger Games* franchise." *Salon*. Salon Media Group. Mar. 18, 2012. Web, Jun. 30, 2013.

Miller, Leo R. "Reading-Grade Placement of the First Twenty-Three Books Awarded the John Newbery Prize." *The Elementary School Journal* 46.7 (Mar. 1946): 394–99. Print.

Millett, Fred B. "Literary Prize Winners." *The English Journal* 24.4 (Apr. 1935): 269–82. Print.

Mister Orange. Amazon, 2014. Web, Jul. 19, 2014.

Mister Orange. Barnes & Noble, 2014. Web, Jul. 19, 2014.

Mister Orange. Goodreads, 2014. Web, Jul. 19, 2014.

Mitchell, David, T. and Hearn, Melissa. "Colonial Savages and Heroic Tricksters: Native American in the American Tradition." *Journal of Popular Culture* 32.4 (1999): 101–17. Print.

Mithen, Steven. *The Singing Neanderthals: The Origins of Music, Language Mind and Body*. Cambridge: Harvard University Press, 2006. Print.

Moloney, James. *Silvermay*. Sydney: Angus and Robertson, 2011. Print.

Mott, Frank Luther. *Golden Multitudes: The Story of Best Sellers in the United States*. New York: The Macmillan Co, 1947. Print.

Murphy, Emily. "Unpacking the Archive: Value, Pricing, and the Letter-Writing Campaign of Dr. Lena de Grummond." *Children's Literature Association Quarterly* 39.4 (2014): 551–68. Print.

Myers, Christopher. "Young Dreamers." *The Horn Book Magazine* Nov/Dec 2013: 10–14. Print.

———. "The Apartheid of Children's Literature." *The New York Times. The New York Times.* Mar. 15, 2014. Web, Mar. 16, 2014.

Myers, D. G. "The New Historicism in Literary Studies." *Academic Questions* 2.1 (Winter 88/89): 27–36. Print.

Myers, Walter Dean. "One Step Forward, Two Steps Back: The Black Experience in Children's Literature." In *The Black American in Books for Children: Readings is Racism,* editors Donnarae MacCann and Gloria Woodard. London: Scarecrow Press, 1985. 222–6. Print.

———. "Children's Books; 'I Actually Thought We Would Revolutionize the Industry.'" *New York Times* Nov. 9, 1986. Print.

———. "Where Are the People of Color in Children's Books?" *The New York Times. The New York Times.* Mar. 15, 2014. Web, Mar. 16, 2014.

Nagle, Margaret. "This Children's Book Collection Isn't for Kids." *Jackson Daily News.* Aug. 22, 1982: 1H, 4H. Lena de Grummond and Lynn Delaune Papers, box 1A, folder 3. de Grummond Children's Literature Collection. University of Southern Mississippi, Hattiesburg.

Nahson, Claudia J. Preface. The Snowy Day *and the Art of Ezra Jack Keats,* editor Claudia J. Nahson. New York and New Haven: The Jewish Museum and Yale University Press, 2011. vi–xi. Print.

Neale, Steve. "Hollywood Blockbusters: Historical Dimensions." In *Movie Blockbusters,* editor Julian Stringer. London: Routledge, 2003. Print.

Nel, Philip, and Lissa Paul, editors. *Keywords for Children's Literature.* New York: New York University Press, 2011. Print.

Neumeyer, Peter F. "Spanish Kids Got No Books?" Children's Literature Association Quarterly 8.2 (Summer 1983): 35. Print.

"Newbery Medal Terms and Criteria." *Association for Library Service to Children.* American Library Association, n.d. Web, Mar. 10, 2014.

"Newbery Medal Winners and Honors." American Library Association, 2014. Web, May 1, 2014.

Newton, Robert. *When We Were Two.* Melbourne: Penguin, 2011. Print.

Ng, Lynda. "Inheriting the World: German Exiles, Napoleon's Campaign in Egypt,and Australia's Multicultural Identity." In *Scenes of Reading: Is Australian Literature a World Literature?* editors Robert Dixon and Brigid Rooney. North. Melbourne: Australian Scholarly Publishing, 2013. 156–67. Print.

Nieto, S. 1995. A History of the Education of Puerto Rican Students in U.S. Mainland Schools: "Losers," "Outsiders," or "Leaders." Handbook on Multicultural Education. 388–410. Print.

———. 2000. *Puerto Rican Students in U.S. Schools.* Mahwah, NJ: Lawrence Erlbaum Associates. Print.

Nöstlinger, Christine. *Conrad: The Factory-Made Boy.* London: Heinemann, 1975.

Olsen, Sylvia. *Working with Wool: A Coast Salish Legacy and the Cowichan Sweater.* Winlaw: Sono Nis, 2010. Print.

Olson, Marilynn. "Re: Phoenix Award research." Message to. Jul. 24, 2014. E-mail.

Orlev, Uri. *The Island on Bird Street.* Trans. Hillel Halkin. 1981. Boston: Houghton Mifflin, 1984. Print.

Osborne, Robert. *80 Years of the Oscars: The Official History of the Academy Awards.* New York: Abbeville Press, 2008. Print.

O'Sullivan, Emer. *Comparative Children's Literature*. New York: Routledge, 2005. Print.

Pallant, Chris. *Demystifying Disney: A History of Disney Feature Animation*. London: Continuum, 2001. Print.

Papageorgiou, Vasilis. "John Ashbery interviewed by Vasilis Papageorgiou," New York, Apr. 5, 1989, *Chromata*. Web, Jun. 3, 2014.

Patron, Susan. *The Higher Power of Lucky*. New York: Atheneum Books, 2006. Print.

Peck, Harry Thurston. "Books in Demand." *The Bookman*. Feb. 1895. Web, Jan. 3, 2010.

"Phoenix Award." *Children's Literature Association*, n.d. Web, Jun. 23, 2014.

Pickford, Susan. "The Booker Prize and the Prix Goncourt: A Case Study of Award-Winning Novels in Translation." *Book History* 14 (2011): 221–40. Print.

Piehl, Kathy. "Foreword." In *The Phoenix Award of The Children's Literature Association, 1995–1999*, editors Alethea Helbig and Agnes Perkins. Lanham, MD: The Scarecrow Press, 1996. ix–xii. Print.

Pinkney, Andrea Davis. "Awards That Stand on Solid Ground." *The Horn Book Magazine* September/October 2001. The Horn Book. Web, Apr. 12, 2014.

———. Address. May Hill Arbuthnot Lecture. Kerlin Collection of Children's Literature, Minneapolis, Minnesota. May 3, 2014. Print.

Poole, Gray Johnson. Letter to Lena de Grummond. Mar. 18, 1974. TS. Lena de Grummond and Lynn Delaune Papers, box 9, folder 2. de Grummond Collection of Children's Literature. University of Southern Mississippi, Hattiesburg.

Pope, Deborah. Personal interview. Jul. 8, 2014.

Posell, Elsa. Letter to Lena de Grummond. May 19, 1968. TS. Lena de Grummond and Lynn Delaune Papers, box 7, folder 7. de Grummond Children's Literature Collection. University of Southern Mississippi, Hattiesburg.

"Printz Award." YALSA. n.d. Web, Nov. 6, 2014.

Raibmon, Paige. "Theaters of Contact: Theatres of Contact: The Kwakwaka'wakw Meet Colonialism in British Columbia and at the Chicago World's Fair." *Canadian Historical Review* 81.2 (Jun. 2000): 157–92. Print.

Readings, Bill. "The Idea of Excellence." *The University in Ruins*. Cambridge, MA: Harvard University Press, 1996. 21–43. Print.

Reid, Raziel. *When Everything Feels Like the Movies*. Vancouver, BC: Arsenal Pulp Press, 2014. Print.

———. "Smells Like Teen Dispirit." *The Walrus*. Jan. 28, 2015. Web, Feb. 11, 2015.

Reynolds, Kimberley. *Radical Children's Literature: Future Visions and Aesthetic Transformations in Juvenile Fiction*. Houndmills: Palgrave Macmillan, 2007. Print.

———. "Ch. 10. Rewarding Reads? Giving, Receiving and Resisting Evangelical Reward and Prize Books." In *Popular Children's Literature in Britain*, editors Julia Briggs, Dennis Butts, and M.O. Grenby. Aldershot: Ashgate, 2008. 189–207. Print.

Rich, Motoko. "Muggle Soirees Herald 'Harry' Finale. *The New York Times*. New York Times. Jul. 20, 2007. Web, Jun. 30, 2014.

———. "For Young Latino Readers, an Image Is Missing." *The New York Times*. Dec. 4, 2012. Web, Jan. 8, 2016.

Robinson, Catherine J. "Buffalo Hunting and the Feral Frontier of Australia's Northern Territory." *Social & Cultural Geography* 6.6 (2006): 885–901. Print.

Rodman, Mary Ann. *My Best Friend*. Ill. E.B. Lewis. New York: Viking, 2005. Print.

Rogers, Stan and James, Matt. *Northwest Passage*. Toronto: Groundwood Books. 2013. Print.

Romøren, Rolf and John Stephens. "Representing Masculinities in Norwegian and Australian Young Adult Fiction: A Comparative Study." In *Ways of Being Male: Representing Masculinities in Children's Literature and Film*, editor John Stephens. New York: Routledge, 2002. 216–33. Print.

Rose, Jacqueline. *The Case of Peter Pan: or, The Impossibility of Children's Fiction*. Philadelphia: University of Pennsylvania P, 1984. Print.

Ross, Trevor. "Canon." In *Encyclopedia of Contemporary Literary Theory: Approaches, Scholars, Terms*, editor Irena R. Makaryk. Toronto: University of Toronto Press, 2000. 514–16. Print.

Rubin, Rita. "PG-rated Rango has Anti-smoking Advocates Fuming." *USA Today*, Mar. 8, 2011. Web, Jun. 10, 2014.

"Rule Seven: Special Rules for the Animated Feature Film Award." *Oscars.org*. The Academy of Motion Pictures Arts and Sciences, n.d. Web, Jun. 12, 2014.

Ruscher, Janet B. "Prejudice and Stereotyping in Everyday Communication." *Advances in Experimental Social Psychology* 30 (1998): 241–307. Print.

Ryan, Caitlin L., and Jill M. Hermann-Wilmarth. "Already on the Shelf: Queer Readings of Award-Winning Children's Literature." *Journal of Literacy Research* 45.2 (2013): 142–72. Print.

Ryan, Pam Muñoz. *When Marian Sang*. New York: Scholastic Press, 2002. Print.

Said, Edward. "Orientalism." *The Post-Colonial Studies Reader*, 2nd ed., editors Bill Ashcroft, Gareth Griffiths and Helen Tiffin. New York: Routledge. 24–27. 1978/2006. Print.

Sammond, Nicholas. *Babes in Tomorrowland: Walt Disney and the Making of the American Child, 1930–1960*. Durham, NC: Duke University Press, 2005. Print.

Sánchez-Eppler, Karen. "In the Archives of Childhood." In *The Children's Table: Childhood Studies and the Humanities*, editor Anna Mae Duane. Athens: University of Georgia Press, 2013. 213–37. Print.

Sánchez González, Lisa. 2001. *Boricua Literature*. New York University Press. Print.

———. 2013. *The Stories I Read to the Children*. Centro Press. Print.

Sasser, M. Tyler. "*The Snowy Day* in the Civil Rights Era: Peter's Political Innocence and Unpublished Letters from Langston Hughes, Ellen Tarry, Grace Nail Johnson, and Charlemae Hill Rollins." *Children's Literature Association Quarterly* 39.3 (2014): 359–84. Print.

Savage, William W. Jr. "Eyes on the Prize: The Transom." Journal of Scholarly Publishing 41.1 (Oct. 2009): 110–115. Print.

Schatz, Thomas. *The Genius of the System: Hollywood Filmmaking in the Studio Era*. New York: Pantheon, 1988. Print.

Schneider, David J. *The Psychology of Stereotyping*. New York: The Guilford Press, 2004. Print.

Scott, A. O. "A Maiden Voyage to Where the Live Action Isn't." *New York Times* Mar. 10, 2002: B4, B14. Print.

———. "The Death of Adulthood in American Culture." *New York Times Magazine*. New York Times. Sep. 11, 2014. Web, Nov. 14, 2014.

Seiter, Ellen. *Sold Separately: Children and Parents in Consumer Culture*. New Brunswick, NJ: Rutgers University Press, 1993. Print.

Sellers, John A. "A Dark Horse Breaks Out: The Buzz is on for Suzanne Collins's YA series debut." *Publishers Weekly*. Publishers Weekly. Jun. 9, 2008. Web, Jun. 30, 2014.

Sendak, Maurice. Letter to Lena de Grummond. Apr. 2, 1968. MS. Lena de Grummond and Lynn Delaune Papers, box 7, folder 4. de Grummond Children's Literature Collection. University of Southern Mississippi, Hattiesburg.

Serrato, Philip. 2014. "Working with What We've Got." *The Unjournal of Children's Literature.* Vol. 1. No.1. 1–11. Print.

Sharrad, Paul. "Which World, and Why Do We Worry About It?" In *Scenes of Reading: Is Australian Literature a World Literature?*, editors Robert Dixon and Brigid Rooney. North Melbourne: Australian Scholarly Publishing, 2013. 16–33. Print.

Silvey, Anita. Introduction. *Keats's Neighborhood: An Ezra Jack Keats Treasury.* New York: Viking, 2002. 7–11. Print.

———. "Has the Newbery Lost Its Way?" *School Library Journal* (Oct. 2008): 39–41. Print.

Sims, Rudine. *Shadow & Substance: Afro-American Experience in Contemporary Children's Fiction.* Urbana, Illinois: National Council of Teachers of English, 1982. Print.

Sito, Tom. *Moving Innovation: A History of Computer Animation.* Cambridge, MA: MIT Press, 2013. Print.

Sklar, Robert. *Movie-Made America: A Cultural History of American Movies.* Revised and updated. New York: Vintage, 1994. Print.

Skow, John, and Elaine Dutka. "What Makes Meryl Magic." *Time* 118.10 (1981): 56. Print.

Smith, Henrietta M. *The Coretta Scott King Awards, 1970–2009.* 4th ed./40th Anniversary. Chicago: American Library Association, 2009. Print.

Smith, Irene. *A History of the Newbery and Caldecott Medals.* New York: Viking Press, 1957. Print.

Solomon, Charles. "New Oscar Category Will Change Animation." *Los Angeles Times* Oct. 11, 2000. Web, Jun. 29, 2014.

Sorby, Angela et al. "Messages in a Bottle: The 2007 *Lion and the Unicorn* Award for Excellence in North American Poetry." *The Lion and the Unicorn* 31 (2007): 264–81. Print.

———. "'from brain all the way to heart': The 2008 *Lion and the Unicorn* Award for Excellence in North American Poetry." *The Lion and the Unicorn* 32 (2008): 344–56. Print.

Spurlock, Donna, and Karen Boss. "'Why Did That Book Win?': A Children's Books Boston Discussion." *Publishers Weekly.* Feb. 25, 2014. Web, Mar. 10, 2014.

Staples, Terry. *All Pals Together: The Story of Children's Cinema.* Edinburgh: Edinburgh University Press, 1997. Print.

Stevenson, Deborah. "Sentiment and Significance: The Impossibility of Recovery in the Children's Literature Canon, or, The Drowning of *The Water-Babies*." *The Lion and the Unicorn* 21.1 (Jan. 1997): 112–130. Print.

Stewart, Susan. *On Longing: Narratives of the Miniature, the Gigantic, the Souvenir, and the Collection.* Durham: Duke University Press, 1993. Print.

"Stonewall Book Awards." *American Library Association*, n.d. Web, Mar. 10, 2014.

"Stonewall Book Awards Committee." *American Library Association*, n.d. Web, Mar. 10, 2014.

Strassel, Kimberley A. "Movie-Goers Toon Out Sex and Violence." *Wall Street Journal* Oct. 10, 2000: A–26. Print.

Stratton, Jon and Ien Ang. "Multicultural Imagined Communities: Cultural Difference and National Identity in Australia and the USA." *Continuum: Journal of Media & Cultural Studies* 8.2 (1994): 124–158. Print.

Strauss, Valerie. "Plot Twist: The Newbery May Dampen Kids' Reading." *The Washington Post*, Dec. 16, 2008. Web, Feb. 27, 2014.

Sutton, Roger. "Editorial: Books Built from the Ground Up." *The Horn Book. The Horn Book.* Aug. 30, 2013. Web, Sep. 3, 2013.

——— "The Elephant Was in the Room." *Read Roger. The Horn Book Magazine.* May 15, 2014. Web, Mar. 5, 2015.

"TD Canadian Children's Literature Award." *The Canadian Children's Book Centre*, n.d. Web, Mar. 10, 2014.

Teller, Janne. *Nothing.* Trans. Martin Aiken. New York: Atheneum Books, 2010. Print.

Telotte, J. P. *The Mouse Machine: Disney and Technology.* Urbana: University of Illinois Press, 2008. Print.

———. *Animating Space: From Mickey to WALL-E.* Lexington: University Press of Kentucky, 2010. Print.

Theile, Verena. "Introduction." In *New Formalisms and Literary Theory*, editors Verena Theile and Linda Tredennick. New York: Palgrave, 2013. 3–26. Print.

Thomas, Jr. Joseph T. "Aesthetics." In *Keywords for Children's Literature*, editors Philip Nel and Lissa Paul. New York: New York University Press, 2011. 5–9. Print.

Thomas, Jr. Joseph T. et al. "'It Don't Mean a Thing (If It Ain't Got That Swing)': The 2006 *Lion and the Unicorn* Award for Excellence in North American Poetry." *The Lion and the Unicorn* 30 (2006): 383–97. Print.

Thomson, Ruth. *Terezin: Voices of the Holocaust.* Sommerville: Candlewick, 2011. Print.

Three Percent: A Resource for International Literature at the University of Rochester. Web, http://www.rochester.edu/College/translation/threepercent/ accessed Aug. 24, 2016.

Tomlinson, Carl. *Children's Books from Other Countries.* Lanham, MD: Rowman and Littlefield, 1998. Print.

———. "The International Children's Literature Movement." *World Literature Today* 77.1 (2003): 68–70. Print.

Treviño, Rose Z. *The Pura Belpré Awards: Celebrating Latino Authors and Illustrators.* Chicago: American Library Association, 2006. Print.

Van Coillie, Jan, and Walter P. Verschueren, editors. *Children's Literature in Translation: Challenges and Strategies.* New York: Routledge, 2014. Print.

Vattimo, Gianni. *Art's Claim to Truth.* Trans. Luca D'Istanto. New York: Columbia University Press, 2010. Print.

Venuti, Lawrence. *The Translator's Invisibility: A History of Translation.* New York: Routledge, 1995. Print.

Villeneuve, Anne. *The Red Scarf.* Toronto: Tundra Books. Print.

Warner, Gertrude. Letter to Lena de Grummond. Aug. 8, 1968. TS. Gertrude Warner Papers, box 1, folder 1. de Grummond Children's Literature Collection. University of Southern Mississippi, Hattiesburg.

Warren, Andrea. *Surviving Hitler: A Boy In The Nazi Death Camps.* New York: HarperCollins, 2001. Print.

Wasko, Janet. *Understanding Disney: The Manufacture of Fantasy.* Malden, MA: Polity, 2001. Print.

Webby, Elizabeth. "Literary Prizes, Production Values and Cover Images." In *Judging a Book by Its Cover*, editors Nicole Matthews and Nickiannae Moody. Aldershot: Ashgate, 2007. 63–70. Print.

Weigman, Robyn. *Object Lessons.* Durham: Duke University Press, 2012. Print.

Weikle-Mills, Courtney. *Imaginary Citizens: Child Readers and the Limits of American Independence, 1640–1868*. Baltimore: The Johns Hopkins University Press, 2013. Print.

Weinberger, Stephen. "Joe Breen's Oscar." *Film History* 17.4 (2005): 380–91. Print.

The Westing Game. Amazon, 2014. Web, Jul. 19, 2014.

The Westing Game. Barnes & Noble, 2014. Web, Jul. 19, 2014.

The Westing Game. Goodreads, 2014. Web, Jul. 19, 2014.

White, Donna. "Re: Phoenix Award research." Message to. Jul. 7, 2014. E-mail.

Whiteside, Thomas. *The Blockbuster Complex: Conglomerates, Show Business and Book Publishing*. Middletown; Wesleyan University Press, 1980. Print.

Wiles, Deborah. *Freedom Summer*. Ill. Jerome Lagarrigue. New York: Aladdin, 2001. Print.

Wiley, Mason, and Damien Bona. *Inside Oscar: The Unofficial History of the Academy Awards*, editor Gail MacColl. New York: Ballantine Books, 1996. Print.

Winstanley, Nicola. *Cinnamon Baby*. Ill. Janice Nadeau. Toronto: Kids Can, 2011. Print.

Wojcik-Andrews, Ian. *Children's Films: History, Ideology, Pedagogy, Theory*. New York: Routledge, 2000. Print.

Woodson, Jacqueline. "The Pain of the Watermelon Joke." *The New York Times*. Nov. 28, 2015. Web, Mar. 6, 2015.

Wyile, Andrea Schwenke. "Re: Phoenix Picture Book Award." Message to. Jan. 30, 2015. E-mail.

Yahr, Emily. "'Lemony Snicket' Author Apologies for 'Watermelon' Joke at National Book Awards." *The Washington Post*. Nov. 20, 2014. Web, Mar. 8, 2015.

Yazzie, Robert. "Indigenous Peoples and Postcolonial Colonialism." *Reclaiming Indigenous Voice and Vision*, editor Marie Battiste. Vancouver: UBC Press, 2009. 39–49. Print.

Yingling. "Small Rant on Newbery Awards." *Ms. Yingling Reads*. Nov. 12, 2008. Web, Mar. 2, 2014.

Yum, Hyewon. *Mom, It's My First Day of Kindergarten!* New York: Farrar, Straus and Giroux, 2012. Print.

Zelizer, Viviana A. Rotman. *Pricing the Priceless Child: The Changing Social Value of Children*. 1985. Princeton, NJ: Princeton University Press, 1994. Print.

———. *Happily Ever After: Fairy Tales, Children, and the Culture Industry*. New York: Routledge, 1997. Print.

Zipes, Jack. *The Oxford Encyclopedia of Children's Literature*. London: Oxford University Press, 1996. Print.

Zusak, Markus. *I Am the Messenger*. New York: Random House, 2002. Print.

———. *The Book Thief*. Sydney: Pan Macmillan, 2005. Print.

Index

Page numbers followed by an italic *t* point to a table.

Award; USM Medallion). *See also
specific prizes*
progressive prizing 13
publication and previous prizewinning,
relationship between 21–22
Publishers Weekly 43n7, 87, 156, 163
Puffin Books 171
Pulitzer Prizes 2, 194
Pullman, Philip, *Clockwork* (1996) 204
Pura Belpré Award and Latino/a
children's literature 12, 104–15;
author identity requirements 92,
94; Canada's need for analogous
award 141–42; commodification
of literature and 113; criteria 104;
definition of Latino/a 94, 113;
difficulties in construction of literary
tradition 106–10; in history of
children's book awards 3; in history
of diversity-based awards 122;
immigration/migration narratives,
focus on 105, 115; "issues" books
and 127; name-branding *latinidad*
and 105, 113–14, 116n3; Newbery
compared 106, 109–11; origins of
110; paucity versus availability of
Latino/a titles 104, 110; political
objectives of 95; problem, Latin/a
children seen as 105, 107, 115;
scholarly study and literary valuation
of 110–13; segregation of American
children's literature and 104–6, 109,
111–12; specialized diversity-based
awards, emergence of 84–85; writing
and activism in Latino/a community,
relationship between 108, 113,
114–15

queer literary theory 74, 205. *See also*
LGBTQ community
Quest for Camelot (film) 150
Quigley, Martin 147

racial diversity. *See* diversity and
identity-based prizing
Random House 24
Rango (film) 151
Raskin, Ellen, *The Westing Game*
(1978) 41t
readers' choice awards: book-of-the-
month clubs and 100; hegemonic
masculinity in top-down awards
versus 45–46, 55–57; Inky Awards
(Australia) 11, 45–46, 48–49, 50t

55–56; scandals associated with 7;
selection criteria 73
Readings, Bill, *The University in Ruins*
(1996) 78
Reese, Debbie 115n2
REFORMA 110, 141
Reid, Raziel, *When Everything Feels
Like the Movies* (2014) 7
Rembrandt van Rijn 78, 183
Revere, Anne 145
Reynolds, Kimberley 45
rhetoric of excellence. *See* formalism
and the rhetoric of excellence
Riha, Bohumil 43n10
Riordan, Rick 94
Rios Balderrama, Sandra 104, 110
Rivera, Diego 114
Robert F. Silbert Award 11, 58. *See also*
non-fiction, humanization of victims
and villains in
Robinson, Catherine J. 139
Robinson, Christian 126
Rockefeller Foundation 44n14
Rodman, Mary Ann, *My Best Friend*
(2005) 126
Rogers, Paul 190
Rogers, Stan, and Matt James,
Northwest Passage (2013)
137–40, 143
Rollins, Charlemae Hill 124
Roman Holiday (film) 29
Roosevelt, Eleanor 67–69
Rose, Jacqueline 165n1
Rosoff, Meg 20
Ross, Trevor 79
Roth, Philip 184
Rowling, J. K. 37; *Harry Potter* books
155, 160, 161, 164
Ruscher, Janet B. 59, 69
Rushdie, Salman 37
Ruwe, Donelle 191
Ryan, Pam Muñoz, *When Marian Sang*
(2002) 67–68

The Sad Puppies 6, 7, 16n7
Saeed, Aisha 87, 94
Sáenz, Benjamin Alire, *Aristotle and
Dante Discover the Secrets of the
Universe* (2012) 114
Salinger, J. D., *Catcher in the Rye*
(1951) 27
Saltman, Judith, and Sheila Egoff,
The New Republic of Childhood
(1990), 77